AF842390

A DYNAMIC APPROACH TO HANS KELSEN'S *GENERAL THEORY OF NORMS*

This timely and compelling book delves into the dynamic interpretation of Hans Kelsen's *General Theory of Norms* through the lens of 21st-century jurisprudential debates.

Engaging with key contemporary philosophical concepts such as fictionalism in the philosophy of science, explanation and understanding, and supervenience, this book sheds new light on Kelsen's original ideas.

By offering a contemporary interpretation of his later work, it re-examines classic concepts known from the 'Pure Theory of Law' like the basic norm, the separation of 'is' and 'ought,' validity and efficacy, imputation, and the concept of the legal norm. Integrating modern philosophy with Kelsen's lasting ideas, this book presents a novel theoretical landscape, inviting readers to explore fresh perspectives on Kelsen's contributions to legal theory and emphasising its enduring relevance.

Volume 16 in the series Law and Practical Reason

Law and Practical Reason

The intention of this series is that it should encompass monographs and collections of essays that address the fundamental issues in legal philosophy. The foci are conceptual and normative in character, not empirical. Studies addressing the idea of law as a species of practical reason are especially welcome. Recognising that there is no occasion sharply to distinguish analytic and systematic work in the field from historico-critical research, the editors also welcome studies in the history of legal philosophy. Contributions to the series, inevitably crossing disciplinary lines, will be of interest to students and professionals in moral, political, and legal philosophy.

General Editor
Prof George Pavlakos (Glasgow)

Advisory Board
Prof Robert Alexy (Kiel)
Prof Samantha Besson (Collége de France and Fribourg, CH)
Prof Emilios Christodoulidis (Glasgow)
Prof Sean Coyle (Birmingham)
Prof Mattias Kumm (New York and Berlin)
Prof Stanley Paulson (St Louis and Kiel)
Prof Arthur Ripstein (Toronto)
Prof Scott Shapiro (Yale Law School)
Prof Victor Tadros (Warwick)

Previous members of the Advisory Board
Neil MacCormick+
Joseph Raz+

Recent titles in the series

Volume 11: Law's Humility: Enlarging the Scope of Jurisprudential Disagreement
Triantafyllos Gkouvas

Volume 12: Rightful Relations with Distant Strangers: Kant, the EU, and the Wider World
Aravind Ganesh

Volume 13: The Making of Constitutional Democracy: From Creation to Application of Law
Paolo Sandro

Volume 14: New Essays on the Nature of Legal Reasoning
Edited by Mark McBride and James Penner

Volume 15: New Essays on the Fish-Dworkin Debate
Edited by Thomas Bustamante and Margaret Martin

Volume 16: A Dynamic Approach to Hans Kelsen's *General Theory of Norms*
Monika Zalewska

A Dynamic Approach to Hans Kelsen's *General Theory of Norms*

Monika Zalewska

•HART•
OXFORD • LONDON • NEW YORK • NEW DELHI • SYDNEY

HART PUBLISHING

Bloomsbury Publishing Plc

Kemp House, Chawley Park, Cumnor Hill, Oxford, OX2 9PH, UK

1385 Broadway, New York, NY 10018, USA

29 Earlsfort Terrace, Dublin 2, Ireland

HART PUBLISHING, the Hart/Stag logo, BLOOMSBURY and the Diana logo are trademarks of Bloomsbury Publishing Plc

First published in Great Britain 2024

Copyright © Monika Zalewska, 2024

Monika Zalewska has asserted her right under the Copyright, Designs and Patents Act 1988 to be identified as Author of this work.

All rights reserved. No part of this publication may be reproduced or transmitted in any form or by any means, electronic or mechanical, including photocopying, recording, or any information storage or retrieval system, without prior permission in writing from the publishers.

While every care has been taken to ensure the accuracy of this work, no responsibility for loss or damage occasioned to any person acting or refraining from action as a result of any statement in it can be accepted by the authors, editors or publishers.

All UK Government legislation and other public sector information used in the work is Crown Copyright ©. All House of Lords and House of Commons information used in the work is Parliamentary Copyright ©. This information is reused under the terms of the Open Government Licence v3.0 (http://www.nationalarchives.gov.uk/doc/open-government-licence/version/3) except where otherwise stated.

All Eur-lex material used in the work is © European Union, http://eur-lex.europa.eu/, 1998–2024.

A catalogue record for this book is available from the British Library.

A catalogue record for this book is available from the Library of Congress.

Library of Congress Control Number: 2024944188

ISBN: HB: 978-1-50994-276-3
ePDF: 978-1-50994-278-7
ePub: 978-1-50994-277-0

Typeset by Compuscript Ltd, Shannon

To find out more about our authors and books visit www.hartpublishing.co.uk. Here you will find extracts, author information, details of forthcoming events and the option to sign up for our newsletters.

*Acknowledgements**

Writing a book in the field of legal philosophy involves going on a fascinating intellectual journey which brings a lot of satisfaction. At the same time, it is a long, challenging and sometimes difficult process. Without people ready to help or provide encouragement this process would be a much greater challenge. I was lucky to meet on my path of writing this book remarkable mentors and scholars who were ready to help and lead me in the right direction. I would like to thank them, and I will do this in chronological order.

First, I would like to thank my mentor Marek Zirk-Sadowski for leading me through the initial process of conceptualising the theme of this book, and for being there for me, always ready to provide support when I needed it the most. It was his suggestion that I should look more closely at *General Theory of Norms*.

At that stage, Stanley L Paulson helped me to clarify that I should stick to Kelsen and during our long conversations in Warsaw gave me tremendous feedback on my work and helped me to achieve a better understanding of Hans Kelsen's pure theory of law. I would like to thank him for all the support I received when I was taking my first steps in Kelsen's world, and for his interest in my work and his time.

After I had developed the initial idea of what this book would be about, Clemens Jabloner invited me to the University of Vienna for a seminar to present my initial thesis that supervenience might be a link between Is and Ought. The support and openness to this brand-new idea and the opportunity for discussion with the tremendous Kelsenists from the University of Vienna gave me the courage to pursue and develop this idea further. I would also like to thank Professor Jabloner for all the support he has given me during these years, since I first showed up at the Hans Kelsen-Institut as a PhD student.

I would like to thank Carsten Heidemann, who believed in my project, supported me whenever I had doubts about the direction of my ideas, and encouraged me to keep developing them, devoting tremendous amounts of time to provide feedback of the highest quality, discussing points he believed required further clarification, and helping me with language. I am really grateful that there was someone who accompanied me in this way during the writing this book, and that I received such tremendous support.

* This project is funded by National Science Center Poland. Project number: 2021/41/B/HS5/01174.

I would like offer my thanks to Georges Mazur, who found time to read some chapters of my book and provide me with excellent feedback and advice concerning *General Theory of Norms*, offered advice concerning literature associated with this problem, and made suggestions concerning language.

During the final stage of writing this book, George Pavlakos gave me an opportunity to visit him at the University of Glasgow. He was a wonderful host during my stay at the Law School of the University of Glasgow and helped me to improve greatly the quality of the chapter concerning the explanatory gap. His suggestion that I should employ David Chalmers' strategy was a game-changer for the third part of this book.

I thank all the members of the Hans Kelsen-Institut in Vienna, especially Klaus Zeleny, for their constant support, delivering literature whenever I needed it, and their hospitality whenever I am in Vienna. Thank you for creating such a safe space and intellectual environment and for developing new ideas concerning Hans Kelsen's intellectual endeavour.

I thank Gonzalo Villa-Rosas for creating opportunities to discuss my ideas at workshops, and conferences, for all the encouragement, support and understanding, believing in my ideas, and being open to discuss them.

I also thank Agata Dąbrowska for her helping hand, support and feedback concerning the first two chapters.

During seminars and conferences, I received tremendous feedback while I was presenting my ideas. I would like to thank everyone who took part in discussions concerning my presentations on the topics of fictionalism and supervenience in *General Theory of Norms* and provided me with feedback which helped me to refine my thesis.

Finally, I would like to thank my parents, for their patience and understanding, love and support at each stage of my career. Thank you for supporting all of my choices and believing in me. This book is dedicated to you.

Table of Contents

Introduction

The Demise of the Pure Theory of Law?

HANS KELSEN ACHIEVED enormous success with his *Pure Theory of Law*, rooted in the Neo-Kantian paradigm.[1] This paradigm enabled Kelsen to ground his theory on a solid methodological basis; he was significantly influenced by the Neo-Kantian slogan, 'the method of cognition constitutes the object of cognition'. And indeed, the uniqueness of Kelsen's approach lies in his methodology. Kelsen does not mention the 'theory of pure law', but 'pure theory of law'. The 'purity' of the theory stems from the method, and the method aims to purify law from alien elements (such as metaphysics, ethical presuppositions and political prejudices) for the purposes of legal science. At the same time, his method is a consistent part of his pure theory of law, whereby the completed form of Kelsen's theory becomes defined. These assumptions brought an alternative name to the pure theory of law: Normativism.[2]

This methodology is determined by the paradigm characteristic for legal positivism, which serves Kelsen as a reference point – both positive and negative. While Kelsen accepted and adopted some parts of this paradigm, he rejected the others. His views were positivistic in terms of the separation of law and morality. Yet, he disagreed with legal positivists' so-called social sources thesis – that law is some kind of social fact.[3]

[1] By 'pure theory of law' I mean the theory tailored by Kelsen, which is based on the original methodology described above. When I use capital letters, as in *Pure Theory of Law*, I refer to the second edition of Kelsen's book, unless stated otherwise.

[2] Recently a comprehensive definition of Normativism was provided by Heidemann. Normativism consists of three theses: (1) a fundamental mode of Ought irreducible to the mode of Is exists; (2) there is objectivity of some kind associated with normativity; (3) normativity is 'constitutive of certain domains'. Heidemann names such domains as ontology, epistemology, language, morality and law. See: C Heidemann, *Hans Kelsen's Normativism*, Elements in Philosophy of Law (Cambridge University Press, 2022) 1.

[3] The social sources thesis, which characterises law as a form of social fact, has been a subject of ongoing examination, revealing its inherent vagueness. As Michael Green notes, the social thesis is ambiguous, because the relation between law and facts cannot be reducible 'the way a traffic jam is reducible to facts'. A very successful description of this problem was provided by Tomasz Gizbert Studnicki, who posed one of the main questions of legal positivists: 'what does it mean that legal facts are derived from social facts. Three solutions are possible: between legal and social facts a relation of reduction occurs, or relation of supervenience, or relation of grounding'. See T Gizbert-Studnicki, 'The Social Sources Thesis. Metaphysic and Metaphilosophy' in Banas, A Dyrda, and

Kelsen claimed that his project of building 'legal science' can be only perceived in normative terms, as Ought, and cannot be explained through facts. In other words, Kelsen claimed that a separation exists between Is and Ought. At some point, he even described using the metaphor of an 'unbridgeable abyss'.[4] According to him, only by separating legal science from alien elements – such as morality on the one hand, and sociology or psychology on the other – can one obtain objective and pure results. Otherwise, the process of cognising law might interfere with obtaining scientific outcomes. The purity is the key: in order to cognise law as it is, one must purify it from any alien elements. As the Neo-Kantians postulate, everything else is a consequence of this assumption; the normative method constitutes the subject of cognition.

Therefore, Kelsen's endeavour was supplemented by other successful constructs, such as the concept of a legal norm; the hierarchical structure of law called *Stufenbau*, which is grounded in the observation that norms are hierarchical in order, and links between them take in the form of the empowerment of a lower organ; and the basic norm, which is extensively discussed in the doctrine. The purity assumption determines the shape of these elements. In other words, Kelsen's most distinguished element of the pure theory of law which determines the originality of his thought is the normativity thesis asserting that law is to be separated from facts. This thesis leads to interesting consequences in terms of validity.

Since the validity of each legal norm is derived from the validity of a higher norm, the question about the validity of the first constitution emerges at some point. Kelsen cannot attribute the validity of the first constitution to either social facts or particular values, due to the assumption of the purity of his theory. Instead, he proposes an original solution: that the first constitution is valid because this was assumed by a lawyer. Kelsen called this hypothetical assumption the 'basic norm', one of legal theory's most recognised and discussed elements.

Kelsen's success did not prevent him from posing further questions concerning the law. His exile from Europe to the United States dragged him out of the comfort zone of the civil law system and continental philosophy, greatly influencing his pure theory of law. When confronted with the common law tradition and the analytic paradigm, Kelsen was eventually compelled to push his theory in a new direction. This, however, was not a radical turn but rather a matter of re-emphasis.[5] In time, parallel to the work of the second edition of *Pure Theory*

Tz Gizbert-Studnicki, *Metaphilosophy of Law* (Bloomsbury, 2016) 121–46; MS Green, 'The Semantic Thesis in Legal Positivism' in T Spaak and P Mindus (eds), *The Cambridge Companion to Legal Positivism*, Cambridge Companions to Law (Cambridge University Press, 2021) 2.

[4] In the reference to the Is–Ought separation Kelsen uses this metaphor at the initial stage of constructing his theory. See: H Kelsen, *Hauptprobleme Der Staatsrechtslehre* (Scienta, 1923).

[5] The genesis of Kelsen's turn is widely discussed by Stanley L Paulson, who claims that his emigration to United States was not the ultimate reason for Kelsen's reformulations and that the whole process started much earlier. See: SL Paulson, 'On the Origins of Hans Kelsen's Spatlehre' in

of Law, Kelsen started to engage in a brand-new project, the subject of which was not just law but rather norms in general. Additionally, this project was no longer so firmly rooted in Neo-Kantian philosophy.

For instance, according to Bulygin, the thesis supporting the Neo-Kantian paradigm in Kelsen's studies is the thesis of the normativity of legal science. Bulygin notes that this thesis is bound up with Kelsen's claim that legal science epistemologically creates its object, the legal norm. Kelsen substantially weakened this thesis in his late Neo-Kantian period. Instead of the act of cognition, which imposes order on alogical legal material, thus creating its object, the legal norm, Kelsen introduces a distinction between legal propositions and legal norms. While the nature of the legal proposition is descriptive, the legal norm is normative. For Bulygin, if propositions are descriptive, they are not normative. Hence, normativity is no longer associated with legal science.[6] It turns out that when viewed through a certain interpretation, the Neo-Kantian doctrine is defensible, at least up until 1960. Then, in his sceptical phase, Kelsen turns to the volitional theory of law, rejecting the Neo-Kantian approach, which has serious implications for the theory as a whole.[7]

The approach presented in this book deviates somewhat from this perspective. Specifically, it posits that while the Neo-Kantian approach has been rejected, particularly concerning its role in upholding normativity within *Pure Theory of Law*, the normativity itself has not been entirely eradicated. In *General Theory of Norms* (GTN) a paradigm change occurred, and now normative elements are sustained in the framework of adequately understood methodology of legal science. This methodology necessitates the separation of normative phenomena, exemplified by legal norms, from other social phenomena, as an essential step in comprehending law in its pure form. This distinctive framework can be elucidated in terms of a concept known as 'fictionalism'.

Nevertheless, Kelsen decided to experiment with the analytical paradigm in his last book, GTN, which is the main focus of interest in the present work.[8] The emphasis on linguistic matters came to substitute the Neo-Kantian approach to cognition. Instead of relative categories a priori being used as cognition devices, Kelsen drew on the conviction that linguistic analysis is based on semantic, syntactic (Frege, Carnap, early Wittgenstein) or pragmatic analysis, as represented by the late Wittgenstein, or John L Austin. In the second case, the findings are rather of a scientific-empirical than philosophical nature, as Heidemann notes, adding that Kelsen's 'linguistic turn' is far from being consistent or coherent, since it lacks clear semiotic terminology.[9]

D Diner and M Stolleis (eds), *Hans Kelsen and Carl Schmitt. A Juxtaposition* (Bleicher Verlag, 1999) 27–44.

[6] E Bulygin, 'An Antinomy in Kelsen's Pure Theory of Law' in *Normativity and Norms* (Oxford University Press, 1999) 297–315.

[7] SL Paulson, 'Toward a Periodization of the Pure Theory of Law' in L Gianformaggio Bastida (ed), *Hans Kelsen's Legal Theory: A Diachronic Point of View* (G Giappichelli Editore, 1990) 15.

[8] C Heidemann, *Die Norm Als Tatsache* (Nomos Verlagsgesellschaft, 1997) 163.

[9] ibid 163.

Kelsen's ideas in GTN are rather eclectic, a mixture of analytical, phenomenological and realistic approaches. Despite that, Kelsen – just like Frege, Wittgenstein, Russel and Carnap – creates his own semantics based on the Is–Ought separation. In this way, the philosophy of language becomes a part of Kelsen's theory of norms.[10] Other changes seem to just resurface from his past inquiries. For instance, Kelsen was familiar with Vaihinger's theory of fiction from almost the beginning of his Pure Theory enterprise.[11] Still, this theory gained significance in the final phase, where the basic norm was defined in terms of a Vaihingerian fiction. It seems that Kelsen switches paradigms depending on the topic: from positivistic to hermeneutical, from analytical to something that Ota Weinberger called 'norms-irrationalism'.[12]

The reason for such eclecticism – which some may consider suspicious – might lie in the fact that in the late 1950s, this was part of an experiment being conducted in legal philosophy, with only a few authors, such as Von Wright, taking on this challenge before Kelsen. This project, which almost 30 years later emerged as 'General Theory of Norms' was carefully prepared by Kelsen, although he did not manage to avoid some missteps.

For instance, first Kelsen gathered together the literature on the subject. This was done in quite a chaotic manner. He selected notable authors alongside less relevant figures from unrelated fields, lacking a rigorous effort to establish meaningful connections between their ideas.[13] This might have been caused by the polemical nature of Kelsen's remarks concerning certain schools of thought; nevertheless, there is a sense that thorough consideration was lacking. Another possible cause of the lack of coherence is that Kelsen did not finish the book, which was published posthumously. Despite the great work done by Walter and Ringhofer, the reconstruction of the book from an unfinished manuscript was bound to produce inconsistencies. Several repetitions can be found, and some issues are either underdeveloped or discussed in several parts of the book. This might give the impression that the book lacked careful consideration.

According to Michael Hartney, Kelsen's revision of his Pure Theory started when he published the second edition of *Pure Theory of Law*. At that time, Kelsen engaged in an exchange with Urlich Klug concerning the problem of applying logic to norms. This led Kelsen to expand his theory to all norms. On the other hand, we have Opałek's testimony based on his personal experience: he visited Kelsen in Berkeley around 1960 and reported that Kelsen was very

[10] ibid 164.

[11] H Kelsen, 'On the Theory of Juridic Fictions. With Special Consideration of Vaihinger's Philosophy of the As-If' in W Twining and M Del Mar (eds), *Legal Fictions in Theory and Practice*, trans Ch Kletzer (Springer Verlag, 2015).

[12] O Weinberger, *Normtheorie Als Grundlage Der Jurisprudenz Und Ethik* (Duncker Humbolt, 1981) 168.

[13] Heidemann (n 8) 159; K Opałek, 'Uberlegungen Zu Hans Kelsens "Allgemeine Theorie Der Normen"' (1980) 4 *Schriftenreihe Des Hans Kelsen Instituts* 7–10.

enthusiastic about his new project.[14] Therefore, it appears that by the time of the release of the second edition, the progress of the new project was considerably advanced. Perhaps the Urlich Klug exchange was the turning point, but the preparations to write GTN started before the 1960s. This timeline and Opałek's testimony are essential because they demonstrate that Kelsen's final revision of his theory was a well-prepared and thoroughly considered enterprise which took him years to finalise.

Overall, GTN is an impressive enterprise and a solid book. What one reader might perceive as flaws, others may view as offering the opportunity to push the pure theory of law further towards contemporary legal and philosophical thought. GTN – thanks to its eclectic nature, gaps and inconsistencies, and the impression of it being a 'work in progress' – is open to interpretation and is suitable for the dynamic approach. Kelsen sketched many new themes which can provide a guideline and framework from which his final pure theory of law can be interpreted.

In this sense, GTN is not the final form of Kelsen's pure theory of law. I believe there is not just one, but several, correct interpretation of GTN, and their validity depends on the strength of justification. In this book, I aim to propose one interpretation. It will employ contemporary philosophical tools absent from jurisprudence when Kelsen was writing his book. For this reason, I call this interpretation dynamic; due to introducing such elements, this interpretation is more than a reconstruction of Kelsen's views. One of its aims is to update Kelsen's thought to contemporary discussions rather than to provide a basic understanding of the pure theory of law – in terms of what Kelsen meant. It is even possible that Kelsen would not have agreed with some notions proposed in this book. Even if that was the case, this book is not a reconstruction of Kelsen's thought but rather a contribution to contemporary discussions in the spirit of pure theory of law. As such, this book focuses on a philosophical problem that requires solving – one represented in Kelsen's GTN. The central concern herein relates to the nature of the legal norm and its connection to factual circumstances. This work posits the perspective that the discourse surrounding this matter does not lend itself to unequivocal right or wrong answers; instead, various perspectives illuminate distinct facets of normative phenomena. While this assertion may appear self-evident, it appears to be insufficiently articulated in the jurisprudential debates that predominantly revolve around distinctions among specific legal theories and their inherent shortcomings.

One of the reasons I believe such dynamic interpretation is allowed is the conviction that there is something symbolic in the fact that Kelsen left his unfinished book for his students to complete. It can be perceived as Kelsen's testament that the pure theory of law is a project which should be updated repeatedly by subsequent generations. Hence, this theory is still alive, with the potential

[14] Opałek (n 13) 8; M Hartney, 'Introduction: The Final Form of the Pure Theory of Law' in H Kelsen, *General Theory of Norms*, trans M Hartney (Clarendon Press, 1991) ix.

to be actualised in the future. And so, the next versions have been written by the next generations of Kelsenists, such as Stanley Paulson, Eugenio Bulygin, Clemens Jabloner, Carsten Heidemann, Christoph Kletzer, and many others. Each of these authors proposed their own unique interpretation of Kelsen's pure theory of law in a more or less dynamic manner.[15] This book proposes an approach which adapts the dynamic interpretation deliberately and consciously. The approach stems from the character of the changes made by Kelsen in GTN.

Kelsen modified several elements of the final form of Pure Theory. The title itself signifies a substantial change. GTN is not merely a theory of the legal norm, but a theory concerning any norm.[16] As Heidemann notes, the categories created by Kelsen exclusively for legal science purposes, such as the basic norm, now have a more universal meaning.[17] However, GTN focuses mainly on legal norms and seems to be best adjusted to them, thus Kelsen's grand idea to extend his theory to all kinds of norms seems not to be particularly successful at this point. I will mostly focus on the legal aspects, and attempt to extract an updated version of the pure theory of law.

In this context, two of the most significant changes which resulted in the reformulation of Kelsen's Pure Theory are the definition of the norm and the rejection of the notion that norms are susceptible to logic.[18] They are bound up with each other and the rest of the elements of Pure Theory – such as the basic norm, the separation between Is and Ought, the hierarchical structure of law and imputation – required significant revisions. From the point of view of this book, the most significant is the revised definition of a norm.

There are several consequences of the updated definition of the norm. Firstly, such a definition, rooted to some extent in the Is sphere, moves Kelsen's Pure Theory closer towards positivistic grounds. Secondly, the volitional element leads Kelsen to conclude that logic does not apply to norms. Thirdly, the conception of the norm turns from hyletic to expressive.[19] Lastly, the revision of the definition of a norm led Kelsen to define the basic norm as a self-contradictory fiction. It diminished the role of the Is–Ought separation in favour of an empirical orientation.[20]

[15] In his book Heidemann (n 8) bases on similar distinction provided by Stegmüller, which is direct interpretation and rational reconstruction.

[16] Hartney (n 14) xi. As Hartney notes, although Kelsen claimed that he focused on norms in general, in fact this book is the 'expansion of the Pure Theory of Law' and as such belongs to his major books in legal theory. The book is written in a way which allows clear reference to be made to the legal system. More questionable is the adequacy of Kelsen's theory to other normative systems, such as morality. It begs the question of whether reading Kelsen's book as theory of moral norms might be a distinct endeavour. For this reason, and for the purposes of the clarity of the argumentation, I will focus solely on legal norms.

[17] Heidemann (n 8) 160.

[18] ibid 159.

[19] C Jabloner, 'Kein Imperativ Ohne Imperator. Anmerkungen Zu Einer Theorie Kelsens' (1988) 12 *Schriftenreihe des Hans Kelsen Instituts* 69–70.

[20] Heidemann (n 8) 159; SL Paulson, 'An Empowerment Theory of Legal Norms' (1988) 1 *Ratio Juris* 58.

The seemingly slight change in the definition of a norm became a game-changer, which according to many, questioned whether the final formulation of Kelsen's theory can still be regarded as belonging to pure theory of law, with all of the prominent elements mentioned above. Many claim that GTN means the end of 'pure theory of law as we know it', because the purity assumption can no longer be sustained due to these changes.[21]

There are several ways to approach this problem. One might read Kelsen's text in a direct, static way. In such a case, the inevitable conclusion is either that GTN encounters serious inconsistencies or that Kelsen abandoned the normativity thesis and the pure theory of law project, substituting it with another theory of norms. This solution is correct, and the reading in which Kelsen regards norms in the factual sphere and, to some extent, discards the normativity thesis might be an interesting endeavour.

However, this is not the approach I would like to take. I believe this would mean abandoning the most iconic element of Kelsen's theory, which distinguishes it from other theories from the positivistic and realistic camps. Such an approach would mean that the pure theory of law would join the group of theories which Kelsen opposed for most of his life, and this would probably make Kelsen's theory just one among many (and not the most successful among them). Kelsen's book seems to have much more to offer, and such an interpretation settles for less than can be gained. I believe there is value in Kelsen's distinctly normative approach, and I hope to demonstrate why this is the case in this book.

If this is true, delving into an interpretation that lends greater weight to Kelsen's arguments is imperative. For this reason, I will offer an interpretation in which the Is–Ought separation is sustained. This means that the interpretation proposed will be in the spirit of the pure theory of law and is based on the assumption that Kelsen's theory can be qualified as such as long as some kind of separation of Is and Ought is sustained.

To sustain the Is–Ought separation, two elements require clarification. First, the fictional character of the basic norm; and second, the strong link between Is and Ought which emerged from the updated definition of a norm. In the following chapters, these consequences of the Is–Ought separation and the fictional character of the basic norm are the foundations of the interpretation proposed in this book. Fictionalism will be a broad framework used for setting the stage to explain how the Is–Ought separation can be sustained, despite some connections between them, and how to understand these connections. As I mentioned before, I call such an approach dynamic.

Before I start this enterprise, the stage needs to be set, and the most significant changes will be described in GTN to gain clarity concerning the shape of the General Theory of Norms and the meaning of the categories I use. Due to

[21] SL Paulson, 'Metamorphosis in Hans Kelsen's Legal Philosophy' (2017) 80 *MLR* 860.

the limited scope of this book, I cannot present a complete list of the changes made by Kelsen in GTN or do justice to the secondary literature dedicated to these issues. I will select only the most relevant. In the following chapters, the presentation of these elements will follow the way that the doctrine has reconstructed their meaning, seeking to identify the meaning that Kelsen probably gave to these categories. This will be the task of the first two chapters of this book, which draw on static interpretation – interpretation focused on what Kelsen meant without adding new elements and contexts.

Chapter one explains how Kelsen modified the definition of a norm and its structure. It includes issues such as the definition of a norm, the modally indifferent substrate, imputation, and the problem of applying logic to norms. The latter problem is not directly related to the problem I am going to tackle, yet at the same time, it is extensively discussed in the doctrine. For this reason, I only formulate some general remarks and focus on the context of this problem. This context brings to light some categories and their meaning, and in particular, it describes Bulygin's brilliant solution to the problem of rejecting the application of logic to norms through the introduction of the expressive conception of a norm. This in turn introduces the pragmatic paradigm which displays some parallels with the hermeneutic approach, a matter of significance within the context of this book.

Chapter two describes the major problem discussed in this book, which results from the new definition of a norm. Namely, if read directly, GTN means the end of the paradigm characteristic for the pure theory of law, and at the same time, it might mean the end of the pure theory of law as such. This is the case because the definition of a norm has two consequences: firstly, it leads Kelsen to the notion that the basic norm is a self-contradictory fiction; secondly, it weakens the normativity thesis that Is is separated from Ought. In this chapter, following the arguments of the doctrine, I demonstrate how direct interpretation leads to the end of the pure theory of law.

At the same time, these first two chapters aim to provide a necessary outline for those readers who are not that familiar with Kelsen. For this reason, I limit discussions concerning GTN to the required minimum; I do not analyse them in detail, nor do I consider all possible arguments. Those familiar with Kelsen's thought, especially with its last phase, can easily skip these chapters. This is followed by dynamic interpretation stemming from this critical analysis of Kelsen's last book.

Chapters three to seven provide an alternative interpretation which aims to sustain the paradigm present in the pure theory of law and to bring its spirit back to GTN. I call such an approach 'dynamic' because it uses philosophical tools from domains outside the pure law theory. These tools were either recently updated, which is the case of fictionalism, or were not present in jurisprudential debates when Kelsen was writing his book, which is the case of supervenience.

To the best of my knowledge, fictionalism has not been systematically applied to the pure theory of law; nevertheless, some attempts have investigated related concepts. Maximilian Kiener applied the fictional account to pure theory of law, but in a different manner than I aim to attempt.[22] Otto Pfersmann, on the other hand, mentions supervenience in the context of the Vienna School of Law, but he does that in relation to moral realism rather than as a link between Is and Ought.[23] George Pavlakos's article on bridging the explanatory gap in the framework of pure theory of law became an important reference point for some arguments developed in this book.[24] Finally, over the course of recent years, Carsten Hedemann and I have attempted to apply the grounding relation to the basic norm, which resulted in the article 'Grundnorm y Fundamentación'.[25] Prior to this book I have also attempted to apply the supervenience category to several elements in pure theory of law in several publications. These are rather alternative ways in which supervenience might work in the framework of Kelsen's Normativism, as a solution to the specific problem (eg revolution, objectivity, legal power) and are not unified into one interpretation under a specific paradigm, which is the approach I take in this book. I mention them, when appropriate, in the footnotes.

The starting point for the dynamic approach is the problem of the fictional character of the basic norm. In chapter three, I argue that there is an interpretation which offers great potential to understanding the basic norm in terms of fiction. I start from the rehabilitation of Hans Vaihinger's 'Philosophy as if', which sets the stage for a more coherent and less destructive understanding of the basic norm as a fiction. Namely, if Hans Vaihinger's As-If philosophy is taken seriously, a more profound understanding of fiction emerges. Although fiction does not agree with reality and can even be self-contradictory, it is useful and should not be rejected. Next, I turn to contemporary debates about fictionalism and explain the main ideas of fictionalism in general and fictionalism in science, which is more beneficial for Kelsen. Finally, I turn to the much more interesting – from Kelsen's point of view – methodological fictionalism, which functions in the framework of the philosophy of science.

Chapter four explores the application of fictionalism to Kelsen's pure theory of law. In this chapter, I argue that the basic norm understood in terms of fiction

[22] M Kiener, 'Fictionalising Kelsen's Pure Theory of Law' in M Jestaedt, R Poscher, and J Kammerhofer (eds), *Die Reine Rechtslehre Auf Dem Prufstand*, Archiv Fur Rechts- Und Sozialphilosophie 163 (Franz Steiner Verlag, 2020) 99–124.

[23] O Pfersmann, 'Die Wiener Schule Und Der Moralische Realismus. Ein Problemskitze' in C Jabloner and F Stadler (eds), *Logischer Empirismus Und Reine Rechtslehre* (Springer, 2001) 191–207.

[24] G Pavlakos, 'A Non-Naturalist Account of Law's Place in Reality' in B Brożek, J Hage, and N Vincent (eds), *Law and Mind: A Survey of Law and the Cognitive Sciences*, Law and the Cognitive Sciences (Cambridge University Press, 2021) 473–89.

[25] C Heidemann and M Zalewska, 'Grundnorm y Fundamentación' in F Alberto et al, *Hans Kelsen Ante el Siglo XXI. Un Dialogo Critico* (Universidad Nacional Autónoma Mexico, 2023) 199–223.

is just the tip of the iceberg, because it is simply a consequence of a much larger fictional assumption, namely the purity of Kelsen's theory of law. Kelsen's methodological assumptions – the normativity and separation thesis – contain a fictional element. This does not mean that law is not distinct from facts or morality. On the contrary, the fiction of purity aims to highlight its distinct character. This chapter ends with a general conclusion concerning fictionalism, namely that the dynamic approach is rooted in the hermeneutical paradigm of understanding rather than positivistic.

While chapters three and four tackle the first puzzle of the basic norm, the second puzzle associated with the definition of a norm imputation and the relation between efficacy and validity is addressed in chapters five to seven.

In chapter five, I outline a general framework in which I attempt to solve the explanatory gap problem. This first occurred in the philosophy of mind and was then adopted in the jurisprudence field in relation to the question 'How do legal facts obtain?'. I argue that in the framework of dynamic interpretation proposed in this book such a gap cannot be filled, due to the fundamentality of Ought, as equally fundamental to Is. This framework enables me to adopt a strategy analogical to David Chalmers' argument from *Conscious Mind*, based on the assumption that the mind is of a fundamental character. Likewise, Ought is fundamental in the case of the pure theory of law. This approach requires the issue of possible links between the mind and the physical and Is and Ought, respectively, to be addressed.

Chalmers claims that such a link is natural supervenience, and so in chapter six I explore the general possibility of applying natural supervenience as a link between Is and Ought. In this chapter, I first explain how supervenience can be understood, then I present the arguments why supervenience has the potential to be the link which will leave the separation between Is and Ought intact and simultaneously provide a plausible link between them. Finally, step by step, I present how Chalmers' strategy can be adopted in the case of Kelsen's theory. I also introduce the category of borderline situations, that is, situations in which the link of supervenience occurs in the case of the pure theory of law. These are situations when the Is and Ought domains are in some way in touch. I distinguish the three main situations of this kind – associated with the application of law, law creation and validity. This chapter sets the stage for chapter seven, where I will explore concrete situations in which the Is domain is in touch with the Ought domain.

In chapter seven I apply supervenience to borderline situations by distinguishing three pairs in which supervenience might occur. Apart from the norm and empirical act of will, efficacy and validity, I will argue that one type of imputation concerning the judge's perspective can also be regarded as supervenience. Hence, in the case of law application, I explore the possibility that imputation is supervenience in the case of individual norms. In the case of law creation, I consider the possibility of applying supervenience to the relation between the norm and an act of will. Finally, in the validity domain, I explore the possibility of applying supervenience to the relations between validity, efficacy and the basic norm.

Chapter eight summarises all the findings stemming from the dynamic approach. Here I explain how the fictionalism paradigm is compatible with the notion that supervenience is the link between Is and Ought. I base my argument on the distinction between the epistemological approach, dominated by fictionalism, and the ontological approach, dominated by the problem of applying supervenience. Next, I evaluate the usefulness of the dynamic approach to GTN.

The assessment of the dynamic approach is based on the assumption that it can be justified if two conditions are fulfilled. Firstly, the consistency of Kelsen's theory is not diminished but somewhat enhanced; secondly, there is added value provided by these new elements. The attempt at restoring the spirit of the pure theory of law should be satisfied by the first condition. The added value condition will be satisfied if applying a new theory sheds new light on well-known categories. It might also happen that, as a result, new light is shed on the philosophical tools used when confronted with Kelsen's *Pure Theory of Law*.

Such an approach might raise questions concerning the relation between fictionalism and supervenience, which is associated with the explanatory gap problem. One domain does not necessitate another; however, I do not think such a strong link is necessary in my proposed framework. The main theme of this book is the reconstruction of the General Theory of Norms in the spirit of the pure theory of law. I indicated two main problems that cause doubts about whether GTN can be read in such a spirit: the fictional character of the basic norm; and the weakened separation between Is and Ought. These two problems find their solutions in two domains: fictionalism and the explanatory gap problem, which, in this case, finds its solution in supervenience. Therefore, it is enough that these two domains do not contradict each other or Kelsen's main assumptions, which constitute the pure theory of law; they do not necessarily need to constitute one unified domain. In addition, fictionalism does not contradict the notion of supervenience; it is actually compatible with it. Furthermore, there is an added value in introducing those two solutions because the fictional framework explains the introduction of a metaphysical element to GTN, namely supervenience. As is commonly known, Kelsen rejected the metaphysical approach, by opposing metaphysical dualism and its unscientific character. It is unclear if he would have opposed supervenience, which substantially differs from such vague categories as 'natural law'. I discuss this problem in chapter six. On the other hand, I argue that supervenience might reveal the thinking pattern about law envisioned as pure Ought in the fictional framework and law as we know it – blended in 'reality' with other social facts.

My conclusion is that the coherence gained from my dynamic approach, which applies philosophical tools such as fictionalism and supervenience, allows the claim that a more charitable interpretation of GTN exists than the one obtained by the static approach. When GTN is interpreted more dynamically, not only is the spirit of the pure theory of law sustained, but it also emerges in an updated version – one that is able to take part in contemporary discussions about the nature of law and introduce new and thought-provoking solutions.

1

The Definition of the Norm and its Structure

1.1. THE ANALYTICAL PARADIGM IN GTN

GENERAL THEORY OF *Norms* (GTN) can be perceived as Kelsen's attempt to introduce a brand-new quality in his pure theory of law. By introducing the analytical paradigm, Kelsen seemed to reformulate his theory in a way which would potentially grant even more scientific objectivity in modernised form. As a result, some have characterised the final stage of Kelsen's theory as analytical.[1] However, the manner in which Kelsen executed his ultimate endeavour did not attain complete success. Even if such an effort had been undertaken, the initial selection of literature during the early stages of the writing process did not consistently prioritise the most influential works of analytical philosophers. At times, the selection included authors who, from a contemporary perspective, are considered to have occupied the peripheries of analytical philosophy. Therefore, conducting a more in-depth examination of this issue is worthwhile to enhance our comprehension of the analytical paradigm within the General Theory of Norms. This inquiry is particularly relevant, as the forthcoming dynamic interpretation of the General Theory of Norms will largely adhere to this analytical perspective.

Ota Weinberger defines the scope of analytical philosophy by mentioning logical empiricism, Wittgenstein's theory of language, ordinary philosophy of language, hermeneutical philosophy and Habermas-Apel's discourse philosophy.[2] He notes that both versions of pure theory of law reveal some trends of analytical philosophy, even though in *Pure Theory of Law* Kelsen never explicitly mentioned these relations.[3]

On the other hand, GTN consists of a paradigm shift. The Neo-Kantian perspective recedes into the background, and the analytical paradigm emerges into the foreground.[4] Kazimierz Opałek, who had the opportunity to discuss the

[1] For instance, the description 'sprachanalytische' is used by Heidemann in C Heidemann, *Die Norm Als Tatsache* (Nomos Verlagsgesellschaft, 1997) 159.

[2] O Weinberger, 'Reine Rechtslehre Zwischen Kritizismus und Analitygscher Philosophie' (2000) 55 *Zeitschrift Fur Offentliches Recht* 367.

[3] ibid 374.

[4] Heidemann very aptly explains this transition in Heidemann (n 1) 161–65.

project of GTN with Kelsen himself in 1960–1961 at Berkeley, provides some historical reconstruction of this process and evaluation of its result.[5] As Opałek notes, Kelsen's idea of building a general theory of norms can be dated from the 1950s. Two trends influenced him in that endeavour. The first was the general tendency of construction sociology and psychology of law, which was applied to any type of norms, especially those that are instruments of social control but exist outside the law; this trend was evident in the United States.[6] The second was the tendency to describe norms in terms of analytical philosophy, from a linguistic and logical angle, especially in the field of metaethics and analytical ethics. Later this trend was extended to legal philosophy, which was aligned with Kelsen's formal-analytical interest, which had been present in his pure theory of law but was not developed until the end of the 1950s.[7] In GTN the priority is given to authors belonging to the field of analytical philosophy, which is one of the main sources of the analytical orientation of this book.

What is interesting is the proportion of literature in terms of its age. Opałek mentions that there are 94 works of 'old' literature (ie, works published before 1939) and 133 works published after this period. This means that a large amount of this literature had not previously been used by Kelsen.[8] The main question here is the relevance of the selected literature to the time when GTN was written and to the time when it was completed by Kelsen. As was mentioned before, Kelsen started his endeavour at the end of the 1950s, and died in 1973, but the book was published in 1979. It also begs the question of the relevance of GTN to today's knowledge, and for obvious reasons, this relevance cannot be that impressive, but this is one of my aims: to fill some gaps with contemporary analytical tools, hence here I will limit myself to Opałek's evaluation.

According to Opałek, Kelsen was up to date with the literature until 1965. After this date, Kelsen finished his literature research and was involved mainly in writing the GTN. The quality of the literature choice varies. Although there are some random items, which did not contribute much to the domains of legal philosophy or analytical philosophy, there are also noteworthy classics from these domains, from such authors as Chaïm Perelman, Richard M Hare, Georg Henrik von Wright, John L Austin, Charles L Stevenson, Peter F Strawson, Alf Ross, Norberto Bobbio and Ota Weinberger, to name a few. The problem is that although Kelsen was familiar with these authors, he was not necessarily familiar with all their ground-breaking works. For instance, Kelsen was familiar with

[5] K Opałek, *Uberlegungen Zu Hans Kelsens 'Allgemeine Theorie Der Normen'* (Schriftenreihe Des Hans Kelsen Instituts, 1980) 6.

[6] *cf* SL Paulson, 'On the Origins of Hans Kelsen's Spatlehre' in D Diner and M Stolleis (eds), *Hans Kelsen and Carl Schmitt. A Juxtaposition* (Bleicher Verlag, 1999) 27–28. Paulson very compellingly analyses the origins of the shift in Kelsen's theory from a conceptual angle, noting that this shift started much earlier when he introduced two types of empowerment: to issues norms, and to impose sanctions. These changes, initially introduced in the 1920s and finally carried out in the 1930s, are at odds with the 'strong normativity thesis', which decades later led to the reformulation of Kelsen's pure theory of law.

[7] Opałek (n 5) 7.

[8] ibid 12.

'The other minds' of Austin, but the performative theory was unknown to him. The other unfortunate omission is the 'Concept of Law' by HLA Hart, mainly because Hart dealt with some similar problems as GTN, in a manner that was similar to the analytical one, as Opałek notes.[9] The same can be said about von Wright's writings, which Kelsen was familiar with, though only in a limited way, and only with the early publications; as a result, Kelsen did not grasp the difference between deontic logic and the logic of norms.[10] Another problem was that Kelsen did not acquire a regular philosophical and logical education. Although he was able to move around these domains with competence, his knowledge of logic was restricted to the state of this discipline in the second half of the nineteenth century.[11]

Nevertheless, Kelsen's literature research in the 1950s and 1960s is impressive. Opałek argues that it was almost impossible to include all the new material that emerged in this period.[12] It is much easier to evaluate the selection of literature when the perspective of time is available, and it is clear which works turned out to be timeless and which are not. Overall, Kelsen's literature selection until 1965 cannot be called outdated or irrelevant.

More problematic is the second period, from 1965 until Kelsen's death in 1973. Opałek notes that although this period was rich in high-quality publications, most of them were not of ground-breaking character. Next, Opałek focuses on relevant publications which are missing from GTN. In this context, he mentions, from the logic of norms domain, J Kalinowski, O Weinberger, Carlos Eduardo Alchourrón, Eugenio Bulygin and GH von Wright, and from performative theory, John R Searle, and A Ross. Finally, the book *Directives and Norms* by Alf Ross is a significant absence in GTN, due to its ground-breaking character. All in all, the inclusion of these authors in GTN would have allowed for much more consistent development of the ideas which were present in GTN, significantly so as this inclusion would have contributed to the problem of the application of logic to norms and the theory of speech acts. For these reasons, it is correct to emphasise the analytical aspect of GTN and to interpret GTN in a dynamic way, in an analytical spirit, and this will be one of the main tasks of this book.

1.2. THE GAME-CHANGER: THE NORM AND THE ACT OF WILL

This section is entitled 'the game-changer' because the genesis of the pure theory of law that is 'decomposed' into the GTN lies in the seemingly slight but important modifications of several elements of pure theory of law. The origin of most

[9] ibid 13–14.
[10] ibid 13–14.
[11] Heidemann (n 1) 159.
[12] Opałek (n 5) 15.

of these changes lies in the slight change of the definition of a norm, which at the first glance seems to be almost identical to the previous conception. Namely, Kelsen, in creating a general theory of norms, uses one of many definitions he proposed earlier: 'the norm is a meaning of an act of will intended at another's behaviour'.[13] Although the definition of a norm in GTN does not seem to have changed much in comparison to previous phases, these nuances have a great impact on Kelsen's pure theory of law project. Namely, in GTN Kelsen explicitly assigned the act of will to the Is domain. As Kelsen states: 'the act of will (which is an Is) "has" the meaning of an Ought. This Ought is the norm'.[14] Earlier, in the second edition of *Pure Theory of Law*, he was vague with regard to what he understood as an 'intentional act'.[15] Hence, previously it was possible to reason that this act belonged to the Ought domain, and the Is-Ought separation, fundamental for purity, remained intact.

Several other modifications require descriptions here to develop some arguments in this book. Apart from the urgent need to explain the concept of will and an act of will, the clarification of how 'the meaning' is understood will help to prevent potential misunderstandings of the concepts of 'will', and an 'act of will', that may arise when developing arguments which present dynamic interpretation. The subsequent modification concerns another element of the definition of a norm, namely the 'behaviour' at which the will is directed. Here, Kelsen introduces a new category: the modally indifferent substrate.

The fourth change, stemming from the revised definition of a norm, concerns Kelsen's argument about the inapplicability of logic to norms. This adjustment provides insight into the pragmatic dimension of the concept of a norm. I treat the reading proposed by Bulygin, which advocates an expressive conception of the norm related to pragmatics, as an encouragement to explore GTN in a hermeneutical paradigm. At the same time, being aware of the differences between these two paradigms, I will elaborate on this problem later in this chapter.

The fifth change is associated with the category of imputation, one of the main categories of Kelsen's pure theory of law, which will appear in many chapters of this book, and as such requires basic clarification.

Consequently, the 'game-changer' becomes evident – one that revolves around the revised definition of the norm and its implications for the relationships between norms and acts of will, constituting the most profound impact. This transformation will be subject to separate discussion in chapter two, which primarily centres on the issue of the apparent 'decomposition' of the pure theory of law, rather than an exploration of the concepts within the GTN. Here it suffices to say that the reason why I called these alterations in the definition the 'game-changer' is that not only do they break the separation between Is and Ought, but they also question the meaningfulness of the concept of the basic

[13] H Kelsen, *General Theory of Norms* (Oxford, Clarendon Press, 1979) 2.
[14] ibid 26.
[15] Heidemann (n 1) 122.

norm, which as a result of this change in definition becomes a self-contradictory fiction. Static interpretation leads to the conclusion that when read directly, the pure theory of law cannot be 'pure' anymore; Ought is not separated from facts, and the basic norm as a fiction of a self-contradictory character seemingly has nothing to offer in terms of recognition of the legal system. The conclusion stemming from direct and static reading seems inevitable: whatever it was that Kelsen presented in GTN, he departed strongly from the pure theory of law as we know it.[16]

1.3. THE DEFINITION OF A 'NORM' AND THE MODALLY INDIFFERENT SUBSTRATE

The first puzzle in the definition of 'norm' concerns the terms 'will' and an 'act of will'.[17] Kelsen defines a norm as:

> When someone commands or prescribes, he wills that something *ought* to happen. The ought – the norm – is the meaning of a willing or act of will … an act whose meaning is that another person (or persons) is to behave in a certain way.[18]

What matters here is that, according to one of the most common interpretations in the secondary literature, the will is understood in empirical terms. For instance, Opałek, who was requested by the Hans Kelsen-Institute to evaluate GTN, notes that the final version of Kelsen's theory of norms has a foundation which lies in realism or even in psychology, primarily because of the theory of will it employs.[19] In this context, the normative concept is linked with an act of will, one that holds an empirical nature, similar to the empirical character of the will itself, as opposed to possessing metaphysical or idealistic attributes.[20] Heidemann suggests a similar solution. Kelsen follows Husserl and his model of an intentional act when he defines the norm and the meaning of an act of will directed at someone's behaviour, and from this follows the psychical character of the act of will, as an inner act.[21] As was stated before, the act of will belongs to the Is domain.[22]

This approach poses a challenge for the methodology of the pure theory of law, especially the thesis that Is and Ought are to be separated. This thesis

[16] See: SL Paulson, 'Metamorphosis in Hans Kelsen's Legal Philosophy' (2017) 80 *MLR* 860.

[17] An interesting view is presented by Carsten Heidemann, who notes the parallels between Kelsen's understanding of the meaning of the act of will and Husserl's phenomenology, but at the same time he remarks that Kelsen made use only of some elements of Husserl's ideas. See: Heidemann (n 1) 162–63.

[18] Kelsen (n 13) 2.

[19] Opałek (n 5) 22; C Jabloner, 'Kein Imperativ Ohne Imperator. Anmerkungen Zu Einer Theorie Kelsens' in T Olechowski and K Zeleny (eds), *Methodenreinheit und Erkenntinisvielfalt* (Manzlische Verlags – und Universitaetsbuchhandlung 2013) 6.

[20] Opałek (n 5) 22; Jabloner (n 19) 6.

[21] Heidemann (n 1) 174.

[22] Kelsen (n 13) 26.

entails prohibiting explanation of normative phenomena, such as the norm, through facts. However, the definition of a norm in GTN entails that in a static reading the norm is explained in exactly such a manner. This problem will be further discussed in chapter two.[23]

Another issue arising from this definition pertains to the fact that the concept of 'meaning' within it cannot always be identified with the term 'meaning' from the *Pure Theory of Law* (PTL). At that point 'meaning' was associated with the interpretation of a certain social practice as law.[24]

In the classic version of the pure theory of law, the meaning of the act of will when the man in the robe speaks and sentences someone to death is that a judge issues a sentence (objective Ought), while a secret organisation expressing the same act of will commits a crime (subjective Ought). In GTN, 'the meaning' is the mental content of the act. This means that instead of distinguishing between the fact and its interpretation, Kelsen now distinguishes between the mental act (of will) and its content, which is that someone ought to behave in certain way.[25] The existence of the norm is conditioned by reflecting precisely on the meaning, which occurred empirically and which is embodied in the Dubislav thesis '*Kein Imperativ ohne einen Imperator*'.[26] This approach strengthens the positivity of Kelsen's theory of norms.[27]

Hence, the starting point for Kelsen is the class of mental acts in which acts of thought and acts of will are to be distinguished. Both classes are associated with meaning – in the case of an act of thought this is a statement that something is the case, while acts of will result in the norm being directed toward another's behaviour. Mental acts are expressed through language in utterances and norms, hence 'mental activity is modelled on linguistic activity'.[28] This distinction is crucial, because it leads Kelsen to the conclusion forming one of the primary turns in his theory; namely, the rejection of the possibility that logic can apply to norms.

Such an approach to the definition of a norm is problematic. The main difficulty is that Kelsen does not offer a thorough explanation of how to understand the factual nature of the act of will. His philosophical–psychological

[23] However, Kelsen is not entirely consistent, and he also seems to ascribe the act of will to the Ought domain as a result of the distinction between thinking and willing. Kelsen distinguishes a new reality here: the psychical one, distinct from empirical reality (Heidemann (n 1) 174–75). This of course generates new problems; for instance, such a distinction probably falls under Ockham's razor. However, in this book I will not follow this direction and I will look closer to the concept of will as belonging to the Is domain. The dynamic interpretation which I would like to offer demonstrates that a break in Is-Ought dualism can be interpreted in a way that does not impair Kelsen's main methodological assumption, hence, my interest is to focus on the conception of an act of will in which it is understood in empirical terms as belonging to the Is domain.

[24] M Hartney, 'Introduction: The Final Form of the Pure Theory of Law' in Kelsen (n 13) xxxviii.

[25] ibid xxxviii.

[26] Weinberger (n 2) 382.

[27] Jabloner (n 19) 3.

[28] Hartney (n 24) xxxviii.

convictions, which could be potentially elaborated into philosophy of mind stem from ideas which were current at the beginning of the twentieth century, and hence are not very sophisticated. Kelsen mentions in this context the *Vorstellung*, which can be translated as the 'idea', 'concept' or 'image'.[29]

Furthermore, this turn, rather than being concerned with the imperative theory as a whole, is more concerned with the subjective Ought – that is, with Ought which is 'valid' only for the one who issues a corresponding act of will.[30] For instance, my conviction that John ought to go to the gym once a week is only a subjective Ought. John might not necessarily feel bound by my act of will. This is the core of the issue. Such an approach, departing from the definition of a norm from earlier versions of the pure theory of law, does not explain the initial puzzles of the pure theory of law.

Earlier, when the legal norm was the scheme of interpretation, it indicated how certain phenomena could be recognised as legal. According to Kelsen, thanks to the legal norm, which exists in the context of the hierarchical structure of law (*Stufenbau*), it is clear why one can distinguish the situation in which the judge issues a death sentence in his ruling from the case in which a secret organisation decides to assassinate someone. Thanks to legal norms, we have interpretation schemes which are helpful when distinguishing the former situation from the latter.[31] On the other hand, the problem with the updated definition of a norm is that if the GTN rested on the understanding of meaning as the mental content of the act, there is no way of determining whether a particular act of will results in a legal norm or just a norm of any kind.

If this is the case, why did Kelsen make this change? The answer is relatively simple. Kelsen needed such a change in his definition because he was constructing the theory of all norms, including those that are only subjective and binding for those who perform such an act of will. For instance, I might have the act of will 'my neighbour ought to not to park on my favourite parking spot'; this has a subjective meaning because it does not bind my neighbour in any way. Only if I owned my favourite parking spot according to law would this meaning be objective, and as such bound up with a legal norm concerning ownership. Contrary to PTL, which considered only legal norms, and hence regarded norms in their objective meaning, a norm thus defined does not need to stem from the individual empowered by law. The norms in their subjective meaning, for instance, a gunman's 'give me the money', also fall under this definition.

However, if GTN is supposed to be the theory of all norms, the mental state of the one who issues the norm is insufficient to explain the objective character of law. A second step must be considered, which addresses the question of how such a subjective act of will turns into an objective one. Fortunately, Kelsen did not reject this part of his theory. A few passages later, after providing his

[29] Jabloner (n 19) 6.
[30] ibid 76–84.
[31] H Kelsen, *Pure Theory of Law* (The Lawbook Exchange, Ltd., 1967) 2.

definition of a norm, he distinguishes between a subjective and objective act of will and a subjective and objective Ought by stating that:

> I can will 'Everyone is to marry upon reaching a certain age'. This is not a binding norm for there is no norm of a positive moral or legal order which empowers me to posit such a norm. The Ought in this case is only the *subjective* meaning of my act of will, not its *objective* meaning. Only when the Ought has an objective meaning, and so expresses a command, there exists a duty (i.e., a binding norm).[32]

Hence, it can be assumed that despite changes in the definition of a norm, the *legal* norm is still understood as a scheme of interpretation. This means that Kelsen has two concepts of the norm in mind, since he still distinguishes between the subjective and objective meaning of the norm, just like in PTL.[33] From this it follows that 'the meaning' (of an act of will) refers to both the *act* of will and to the will itself, which is the result of this act, depending on the context. Similarly, Jabloner notes that despite a relatively strong conviction concerning the psychological and internal nature of the act of will held by Kelsen, he does that from an external perspective.[34] In any case, both will as a psychological manifestation and an act of will belong to the Is domain, challenging the pure theory of law.

Despite the division between internal will and external imperative, what matters in GTN is the external manifestation of the will, which is the norm issued or commanded, and not the internal experience of the imperator. Hence, I will assume that in the case of law the 'meaning' concerns the *act* of will; this is in accordance with understanding the norm as a scheme of interpretation. Such a norm, let us say, a constitutional norm, allows us to interpret the act of some assembly as an act of parliament. In other words, the meaning of the act of will of parliament is the legal norm. This is recognised on behalf of the higher norm, which serves as a scheme of interpretation.

The second relevant change related to the problem of meaning, is associated with the modally indifferent substrate. The idea of a modally indifferent substrate – at first glance, odd but innovative – has grounds in some interesting intuitions. Namely, this idea draws on the observation that the content which can be potentially the content of a norm or a sentence is in the first step independent from the modes of Is and Ought.[35]

[32] Kelsen (n 13) 27. *cf* Opałek (n 5) 22. Opałek notes that since the act of will that stems from the real person is directed at the behaviour of another real person, 'the meaning' is to be understood as the meaning in empirical terms, as the meaning of the empirical act of will; such a 'meaning' is not associated with semantics (*Sprachliche Ausdruck*). As such, it has Neo-Kantian connotations, since this is some sort of 'Ought-meaning' (Soll-Sinn), which exists on a higher level than empirical reality. Such a fact needs to occur to initiate the process from the empirical domain (real; Is) into the non-empirical domain (ideal; Ought).

[33] Hartney (n 24) xxxix.

[34] Jabloner (n 19) 1–8.

[35] Kelsen (n 13) 58–63.

Depending on which mode will be applied to the modally indifferent substrate, one can obtain: 'John does not steal' or 'John ought not to steal'. From the distinction between acts of thought and acts of will, Kelsen draws the notion that the behaviour is not thought of as existing, otherwise it would be an act of thought. Such willed behaviour is firstly thought as a *modally indifferent substrate* and then on behalf of

> the act of will, whose meaning is a command or a norm it receives in the command or the norm the mode of Ought, just as in the statement which is the meaning of the act of thought it receives the mode of Is.[36]

In such a case, the interpretation (meaning) applied to a modally indifferent substrate distinguishes acts of will from acts of thought.

This category also gives rise to some difficulties. For instance, Opałek notes that from an ontological point of view, there is no room for indifferent modality in the dichotomy of Is and Ought. Either there are real objects (facts) or ideal objects (norms), and a modally indifferent substrate cannot exist. The fact that Is and Ought constitute such a clear dichotomy rules out the possibility of any intermediate ground between them.[37] Nevertheless, the modally indifferent substrate grants a new meaning to the category of imputation and is of help when untangling some puzzles. Its usefulness can justify its introduction.

1.4. THE REJECTION OF NORMS' LOGIC

The next change, the rejection of the assumption that norms are subject to logic is one of the most fundamental consequences of the revised definition of a norm. As such, this issue is also broadly discussed in the doctrine.[38] The application of logic to the problem of norms is not central to the matters presented in this book, but it greatly influenced the final shape of GTN. The rejection of the thesis that norms are subject to logic enables a better understanding of some categories Kelsen uses in GTN. Still, only some points are relevant to the elaboration of my arguments. As a result, the emphasis will be primarily narrowed to this specific domain rather than delving into an extensive evaluation and discussion of the correctness of this rejection.

[36] Kelsen (n 13) 167; see also: Heidemann (n 1) 166.

[37] Opałek (n 5) 27.

[38] One of the first and most important accounts of this matter was provided by Ota Weinberger. Weinberger was critical of Kelsen's claim that logic does not apply to norms, which includes the critique of Kelsen's conception of a legal norm and a statement about the norm. See: Weinberger, *Normtheorie Als Grundlage Der Jurisprudenz Und Ethik* (Duncker Humbolt, 1981); Weinberger (n 2); Eugenio Bulygin undertook the discussion with Wienberger's critical approach: E Bulygin, 'Norms and Logic. Hans Kelsen and Ota Weinberger on the Ontology of Norms' in C Bernal et al (eds), *Essays in Legal Philosophy* (Oxford University Press, 2015). Recently Stanley L Paulson presented a very comprehensive analysis of this problem: Paulson (n 16) 865–72.

Kelsen's knowledge of logic was based on the state of this field in the second half of the nineteenth century; it did not include the essential developments introduced by Frege, Whitehead and Russell. When the book was published in 1979 there was a 100-year gap in this field.[39] As such, Kelsen's thesis concerning the rejection of the assumption that norms are subject to logic is at best incomplete.[40] Nevertheless, the starting point for the rejection is Kelsen's thesis that statements about norms are acts of thought – in contrast to norms, which are acts of will.[41] This conception exists in the framework of the division of legal norms and legal propositions known from his earlier books.[42]

From the second edition of PTL onwards Kelsen sharply distinguished between the legal proposition and the legal norm. While legal norms constitute the normative relations between conditioning and conditioned circumstances (if X stole a car, X *ought to* be punished), the legal propositions *assert* that according to the certain legal order, certain conditions and consequences are given; the act of will is oriented at some other's behaviour and its meaning is a norm. Its meaning is the *assertion* that something either took place or did not.[43] To put it in another way, legal norms are created by a legal organ, while legal propositions are hypothetical judgements assuming that under a certain legal order, and in certain conditions, certain consequences ought to occur. In contrast to a legal norm, whose meaning is of an act of will, a legal proposition is a statement of legal science and as an act of thought has a logical value.[44]

At first glance, Kelsen incorporated this division into GTN with just a slight alteration. Instead of legal propositions, Kelsen tends to talk about 'statements about the norm'.[45] Since Kelsen is mostly referring to 'statements about the norm', it either means that he considers the broad class of 'statements about the norm' and one special case of the proposition of law, or they are synonyms; it is just that Kelsen cannot use the term 'legal proposition' for he is referring to moral norms as well. Since this book is restricted in its scope to the legal

[39] Heidemann (n 1) 159.

[40] There are projects which attempt to fill this gap; for instance, such attempts are made by Hajime Yoshino. Hajime Yoshino and his findings show the complexity of this issue, which deserves much broader analysis than can be made here. See: H Yoshino, 'Zu Anewndbarkeit Der Regeln Der Logic Auf Rechtsnormen' (1982) 7 *Die Reine Rechtslehre in wissenschaftlicher Diskussion* 142.

[41] In the context of thinking and willing modes, Kelsen notes that there is a difference between the 'logical function of the statement and psychological intention, which speaker connects with it'. This matters when the intention to persuade someone to do something lies behind the act of thought. For instance, the statement 'if you touch the red-hot stove plate, you'll burn yourself and it will be very painful' can be made in order to prevent someone hurting himself). As Kelsen argues, such an intention is prior to the act of thinking. Eventually the will is not expressed in the statement, because of the presupposition that as soon as one knows that touching a stove plate will result in pain, he will refrain from touching it. Such a statement provides true (or false) information, which helps to make the right decision, and as such is not a command (Kelsen (n 13) 167).

[42] Kelsen (n 13) 188.

[43] O Weinberger, 'Introduction: Hans Kelsen as Philosopher' in H Kelsen, *Essays in Legal and Moral Philosophy* (D Reidel Publishing Company, 1973) xxiv. Hartney (n 24) xxxviii.

[44] Kelsen (n 13) 27, 153.

[45] ibid 26.

dimension, I will use the term 'legal proposition' for the purposes of clarity. However, it is worth noting that this approach simplifies the problem and is used only for pragmatic purposes.

Legal norms are assigned by Kelsen to the category of acts of will, while legal propositions are understood as acts of thought. Since the logic does not concern acts of will and only acts of thought, therefore the assumption that norms are subject to logic must be rejected. What matters here is that Kelsen denied the possibility of the norm being subject to logic, but not the possibility of statements about the norm being subject to logic, for the latter belong to the class of acts of thought, and therefore true–false value can be assigned to them. In contrast, the norm as the meaning of the act of will does not fall under true–false evaluation. Instead, it can be valid or invalid.[46]

This analogy between true–false value and validity has been subject to criticism. For instance, Opałek notes that validity falls under the mode of the existence–nonexistence of the norm, while the true–false value of sentences does not: a sentence is not connected with the matter of its existence. A false sentence exists; it just has a false value.[47] This objection is developed by Hartney, who observes that Kelsen does not distinguish the norm as a kind of sentence from the norm as a 'contingent entity created and repeated by certain social events'.[48] The absence of this distinction affects Kelsen's argumentation concerning the norms' logic. As Hartney aptly reasons, Kelsen provides two arguments:[49]

Argument (1)

Logic presupposes truth value
Norms have no truth value
Hence, logic does not apply to norms

Argument (2)

Logic applies only to sentences, not to 'things'
Norms are 'things'
Hence, logic does not apply to norms

While the first argument concerns the norm understood as a sentence, the second one takes norms to be a 'kind of thing'. Hartney determines that as a result Kelsen presents two distinct conclusions, first, that 'logic does not apply to prescriptive sentences', and secondly, that 'the existence of one norm never entails anything about the existence of any other norm'.[50] Hence, Kelsen's arguments against the logic of norms can be divided into two analogical groups

[46] ibid 190.
[47] It is worth noting that for Opałek the distinction between an act of will and an act of thinking is even more prominent in GTN than the distinction between Is and Ought (Opałek (n 5) 31).
[48] Hartney (n 24) xliii.
[49] ibid.
[50] ibid.

The first group contains arguments against the idea that prescriptive sentences can be subject to logic; the second group contains arguments which stem from the assumption that the norms are entities which cannot be subject to logic. These arguments have an ontological character rather than a logical one.

When Kelsen maintains that norms are 'things' and no logical relations are possible between 'things', the arguments against the contradiction and inference of norms stem from such a vision of the norm.[51] Hence, under the general thesis that logic does not apply to norms Kelsen had two issues in mind. Firstly, the problem of the coexistence of two conflicting norms, and secondly, the problem of inferring an individual norm from a general one. Kelsen rejects the possibility of norms being subject to logic in these two cases and supports his claim with the authority of John Stuart Mill, Jean Piaget, Karl Popper and especially Rudolf Carnap.[52] Drawing on the views of the latter thinker, Kelsen concludes:

> [W]ith respect to the applicability of the two aforementioned logical principles to norms as objects of moral and legal science, there appears to exist between these sciences and their object the same relation as obtains between natural science and its object, natural reality: the two logical principles are applicable to the science (i.e. the cognition) but not to its object. Just as there are no logical contradictions in natural reality, and just as the existence of one fact of reality does not follow logically from the existence of another, so there are no logical contradictions between norms, and the validity of one norm does not follow logically from the validity of another.[53]

Despite similarities, Kelsen is aware that the parallel between these two types of science and its relations to its object are not total. The object of legal and moral science, which is a norm, is of a distinct character. It can only be given through sentences, which contain relations and concepts. These relations, although not necessarily the contradiction and inference between norms, are of a logical nature, and hence in their case the norms' logic applies to them.[54]

The principle of contradiction is the first case when logic does not apply to norms. The conflict between legal norms occurs when two norms regulating the same subject cannot be fulfilled simultaneously. In his Neo-Kantian period, Kelsen claimed that the principle of non-contradiction applies to such conflict and thus denies validity to one of the conflicting norms. In the second edition of *Pure Theory of Law* Kelsen claimed that the principle of contradiction applies directly to legal propositions, and hence indirectly to legal norms described by the former. Whereas legal propositions are subject to truth or falsity, legal norms, in contrast, are evaluated in terms of their validity

[51] Kelsen (n 13) 191. Hartney (n 24) xlii.
[52] Kelsen (n 13) 191–92.
[53] ibid 192.
[54] ibid 192–93.

or invalidity.[55] The principle of contradiction thus understood, which Kelsen associates with the basic norm, was supposed to ensure the unity of the legal system in the Neo-Kantian paradigm.[56]

In GTN, Kelsen slightly modified his view on the relations between legal propositions and legal norms, but this slight change led to a momentous consequence – the conviction that two conflicting norms can coexist in the same manner as 'two forces acting in different directions on the same point'.[57] In other words, Kelsen noted that the validity category is associated with the matter of existence or nonexistence, while true–false properties are not. From this he concludes that legal conflict is something *completely* different from a logical contradiction. The radicality of this thesis allows Kelsen to exclude any analogy between norm conflict and logical contradiction, which makes his thesis problematic, because he did not prove that a different kind of connection might exist between logical contradiction and norm conflict.[58] Nevertheless, a false statement still exists, while an invalid norm does not, and a false legal proposition has no impact on the validity of a legal norm.[59] This entails that in cases where two norms are part of the legal system, both norms retain their validity in the event of their conflict. This principle is a requisite, as only when both norms are deemed valid can they truly be in a state of conflict.[60] As a result, not only can two conflicting legal norms coexist, but two normative systems, such as law and morality, can be valid at the same time.

Celano argues that the question which is essential for Kelsen in this context is: 'why and in what sense are the two acts prescribed by conflicting norms incompatible? In other words: Why is that an individual who complies with one of the conflicting norms necessarily violates the other?'[61] The question posed thus reveals that the relation in the form of some sort of analogy between norm conflict and contradiction exists, because 'the norms conflict', and '*because* the corresponding obedience-statements are logically contradictory'.[62]

However, in GTN Kelsen claims that no logical contradiction between conflicting norms rules out the logical contradiction between corresponding statements about the validity of these norms. Hence, the norms are in conflict, but statements about the validity of these norms are not in contradiction. This solution sounds counterintuitive. Fortunately, Paulson compellingly solves this

[55] SL Paulson, 'Kelsen's Legal Theory: The Final Round' (1992) 12 *OJLS* 271, doi.org/10.1093/ojls/12.2.265.

[56] H Kelsen, *General Theory of Law and State*, trans A Wedberg (Cambridge, Harward University Press, 1945) 398–404; Paulson (ibid) 272.

[57] Kelsen (n 13) 125.

[58] B Celano, 'Norm Conflicts: Kelsen's View in the Late Period and a Rejoinder' in SL Paulson and B Litschewski Paulson (eds), trans B Litschewski Paulson and M Sherberg (Clarendon Press, 1998) 345, 348.

[59] Paulson (n 55) 272.

[60] Celano (n 58) 343; Paulson (n 55) 272.

[61] Celano (n 58) 351.

[62] ibid 352.

problem. Legal propositions understood in the classical version had the character of juridico-deontic propositions and 'stating what the norm commands' would be in contradictory relations, even if two norms remained valid.[63] Paulson suggests that it is not a coincidence that Kelsen abandons the term 'legal proposition' and substitutes it with 'statements about the validity of', which Paulson calls 'validity propositions'. The latter are dissimilar to deontic statements since they refer solely to validity. Such an interpretation resolves these puzzles because validity statements which describe whether the norm is valid or not are not in contradiction, since both conflicting norms are valid.[64]

Upon removing the principle of contradiction, two primary issues come to the forefront. First, the consistency of the legal system cannot be assessed, as Weinberger notes. In addition, Celano points out that the radical view of the relation between norm conflict and logical contradiction entails that Kelsen's theory cannot provide an understanding of the conflict between norms. If there is no analogy between them at all, how is Kelsen supposed to explain the nature of this conflict?[65] Second, the rule *lex posterior derigar legi priori* is 'absurd' since the concept of contradiction has been eliminated from Kelsen's theory.[66]

In the field of inference, Kelsen's argument is as follows: since the norm comes into existence by virtue of an act of will, the individual norm could be derived from the higher norm only if the act of will associated with the general norm implicitly contained the act of will concerning the lower norm. Nonetheless, this is subsequently followed by the stipulation that the author of the original norm must possess comprehensive knowledge of 'all the particulars concerning the derived norm'. However, it is evident that this condition is unattainable. The author of the general norm cannot know all the particular circumstances.[67]

The same argument does not apply to the relations between more and less general norms. For instance, from 'do not harm others' can be inferred as 'do not slander others'. Such norms are rather characteristic for the static system of morality, where norms are linked by their content. There is a much more complex situation with the hierarchical system of law, where the relations between norms are based on the empowerment contained in a higher norm to issue a lower norm. This, however, does not change the fact that if Kelsen is correct, it would not be possible to derive 'do not kill' from 'do no harm'.[68]

In this context, Weinberger presents a compelling argument why the rejection of norms' logic, especially in terms of inference, is 'absurd', as he describes it.[69] As he notes, if there is no possibility of inferring from general norms to

[63] Paulson (n 55) 273.
[64] ibid.
[65] Celano (n 58) 345.
[66] Weinberger (n 2) 386.
[67] Hartney (n 24) xlviii.
[68] ibid.
[69] Weinberger (n 2) 385.

individual ones, there is no reason for general norms to be created; moreover, the function of the condition in a general norm is unclear. In such a case, the circumstances described in a general norm are especially problematic and independent of human will, for instance, the passage of time. Kelsen tried to solve this dilemma by introducing legal propositions to which the logic of norms applies; however, as Weinberger argues, such a solution is of no help when the legal system SN consists of norm N, but does not consist of the norm N', which is a logical consequence of norm N. This means that the legal proposition 'in the legal system SN the norm N' is valid' is false, because of the lack of possibility of inference. This means that from the true proposition 'in legal system SN the norm N is valid' a false consequence is drawn.[70]

Weinberger's and Celano's arguments are compelling. However, the problem of the norm's logic in GTN can be fixed and supplemented by proper interpretation, as exemplified by Bulygin and Alchourrón's proposition of the expressive concept of the norm. They explain Kelsen's turn compellingly, asserting that this transition involves a transformation of his norm conception from a hyletic into an expressive one.[71] In their view, in the sceptical (analytical) phase, which is how some describe Kelsen's GTN,[72] the adoption of the expressive conception of the norm is imperative in order to comprehend Kelsen's intended meaning when he defines the norm as the meaning of the act of will directed at someone's behaviour.[73]

Bulygin and Alchourrón point out that two model conceptions of norms exist which can refer to the ontological status and the possibility of applying logic to norms: hyletic and expressive.[74] In the hyletic conception, norms are perceived as 'proposition-like entities'. In this sense, they are the meanings of so-called normative sentences, understood as linguistic expressions of norms. Although their existence is independent of language, they are dependent on operations made on descriptive propositions. On the other hand, the expressive conception of norms assumes that the sentence expressing the norm depends on the context.

Semantically identical sentences can be asserted, questioned, commanded and so on. Therefore, the ultimate form of the expression is dependent on pragmatic considerations.[75] In Kelsen's earlier studies, his account of the norm is reminiscent of the hyletic conception. The transition period began around

[70] Weinberger (n 2) 385–86. *cf* R Walter, 'Das Problem Des Normativen Syllogismus' in W Krawietz and J Wróblewski, *Sprach, Performanz Und Ontologie Des Rechts* (Duncker Humbolt, 1993) 347–55.

[71] CE Alchourrón and E Bulygin, 'The Expressive Conception of Norms' in SL Paulson, *Normativity and Norms* Alchourrón (Oxford University Press, 1999) 383–410.

[72] SL Paulson, 'Toward a Periodization of the Pure Theory of Law' in L Gianformaggio Bastida (ed), *Hans Kelsen' s Legal Theory: A Diachronic Point of View* (Torino, 1990) 15; SL Paulson, 'Arriving at a Defensible Periodization of Hans Kelsen's Legal Theory' (1999) 19 *OJLS* 351.

[73] Kelsen (n 13) 1.

[74] Alchourrón and Bulygin (n 71) 384–85.

[75] ibid 385.

the 1940s, during which time Kelsen gradually abandoned the hyletic conception in favour of the expressive norm. In the sceptical phase, there are no doubts that Kelsen's concept of the legal norm is expressive. Therefore, if the norm is the meaning of an act of will, it means that the moment of this act is crucial for cognition and will probably be recognised on a pragmatic level. The pragmatic level is not particularly specified here.

This change is also fundamental for the notion of the cognition of norms. Despite lacking Neo-Kantian tools of cognition, there is a new method by which legal norms in Kelsen's late studies can be understood, namely pragmatics. In this case an act of will could be perceived as a performative, which creates the norm, and in some cases, transforms the subjective meaning of a norm into an objective one.[76] This notion seems compatible with the approach taken in this book; however, I would like to go further.[77] Rather than adopting a pragmatic standpoint, I will embrace a framework akin to the pragmatic approach. Specifically, I posit that Kelsen's theory is not fundamentally concerned with scientific explanation per se, where the hyletic conception of norm appears more fitting, but rather revolves around a hermeneutical understanding characteristic of the social science. The hermeneutic approach can be derived not only from the expressive conception of the norm, but it has a much firmer foundation in Kelsen's clear inspiration by Max Weber, as well as the paradigm of fictionalism, which I aim to advocate in chapters three and four. As for parallels between the pragmatic and hermeneutic approaches, the following comparison was aptly made by Dascal:

> Like hermeneutics (and unlike semantics), pragmatics is concerned with the conditions pertaining to the actual use of language. Like hermeneutics, it purports to explain what is involved in our actual 'interpretation' and 'understanding' of discourse, above, beyond or in addition to the fact that the words and sentences we confront have certain given convectional meanings (accounted for by semantics).[78]

Despite stemming from different paradigms, the pragmatic and hermeneutic approaches share many similarities. These similarities are relevant for the approach I want to take and include such features as:

(1) being concerned with implicit or implied meaning, instead of linguistic expressions, which are regarded as incomplete and thus inadequate for facilitating a comprehensive understanding of the subject matter;
(2) having as one of their aims the articulation of the conditions which make understanding possible (although the manner in which these conditions are obtained, and their nature, is different for each discipline);

[76] Compelling analysis of the legal norm as a pragmatic category can be found in M Zirk-Sadowski, 'Norma Prawna jako kategoria pragmatyczna' in M Zirk-Sadowski, *Prawo w Kulturze. Eseje wybrane z teorii i folozofii prawa* (Wolters Kluwer, 2023) 35–50.

[77] I would like to thank one of the reviewers for this suggestion.

[78] M Dascal, 'Hermeneutic Interpretation and Pragmatic Interpretation' (1989) 22 *Philosophy and Rhetoric* 240.

(3) assigning an essential role to the process of interpretation in some way; and
(4) claiming universality, even in a limited version.[79]

I will take these similarities as encouragement to explore Kelsen's theory from the underinvestigated perspective of a hermeneutic paradigm; I will use this notion, understood broadly, and associate it with the category of understanding which will be described in chapters three and four.

1.5. IMPUTATION

Another change associated with the conception of the norm is imputation. In *Pure Theory of Law*, imputation played the prominent role.[80] Defined as a normative link between the condition and the consequence, imputation is analogical to causality; 'if X stole a car then X *ought to* be punished' is analogical to 'if X threw a stone at the window then the window *is* broken'. Imputation served as a Neo-Kantian relative category a priori, necessary to cognise the law.

When Kelsen constructed his theory according to the Neo-Kantian paradigm, the problem of the cognition of norms was central to his studies. Kelsen's idea was that norms are cognised in a manner similar to the way objects are cognised according to Neokantians, who propose that given alogical material is organised into an objective world by categories, especially the categories of causality and substance. In Kelsen's example of legal science, we also have alogical material given in the acts of will of the law-giver, which is cognised as legal norms by virtue of such relative a priori categories as Ought, the basic norm and imputation.[81] In the case of imputation, its connection with Neo-Kantian and Kantian influences is clear. While causality is a category typical for the empirical sciences, Kelsen's imputation is typical for the cognition of law. Causality is bound with necessity, while imputation has a normative character, and in this normativity lies its ability to make the cognition of norms possible. But imputation had a further function. It distinguishes law both from natural phenomena, ruled by causality, and from morality, thanks to its relating to a sanction imposed by the legal organ. Thus, it was a form of *differentia specifica* of legal norms, for no other normative system provides for such an institutionalised sanction.[82]

[79] ibid 240–54.

[80] Although Kelsen does not distinguish types of imputation in GTN, mentioning just 'imputation', I believe he means by this so-called 'peripheral imputation' associated with sanction. In his Neo-Kantian phase, alongside peripheral imputation, a central imputation existed as a link between organ and norm.

[81] Such a distinction is used by R Alexy, 'Hans Kelsen's Begriff Des Relativen Apriori' in R Alexy, L Meyer, and SL Paulson, *Neukantianismus Und Rechtphilosophie* (Nomos Verlagsgesellschaft, 2002). On the other hand, Carsten Heidemann claims that in Neoknatin phase legal Ought is imputation.

[82] Alexy (n 81).

According to the Neo-Kantian version of pure theory of law, imputation joins two states of affairs in a hypothetical judgement; their factual existence is not presupposed. Both the condition and the consequence were of a hypothetical character, hence there was no connection to the sphere of Is and they did not apply to any potential concrete states of affairs. The conditioning fact is bound up with the so-called secondary norm, which contains some regulations about human behaviour; eg 'you shall not steal'. Now it is time to explain the primary and secondary norm concept.

The distinction between the primary and secondary norm existed already in older versions of legal positivism, but Kelsen developed this concept and reversed the meaning of the categories in question. In the original version, the primary norm was the norm which prohibited X. For instance: 'One shall not steal'. The secondary norm was the norm which imposed the sanction 'who steals, should be punished'.

In contrast, Kelsen perceives the norm which imposes the sanction as the primary norm. From this it follows that secondary norms are not typical for law. They can also be found in morality (love thy neighbour as thyself) or any other normative system (you should say 'good morning' to your neighbour).

In GTN Kelsen even considers the secondary norm superfluous, which is consistent with Kletzer's observation that the pure theory of law envisions legal norms in terms of the authorisation of force.[83] For that, the primary norm (primary in Kelsen's understanding) is sufficient. The superfluous character of the secondary norm does not mean that Kelsen denied its existence, but rather that from the legal point of view, due to the existence of the primary norm, the secondary one brings nothing new to the equation.[84]

Hence, the primary norm, which contains imputation, distinguishes law from other normative systems. The primary norm has a structure of hypothetical judgement: 'if X, then the empowered organ ought to Y', where X is a violated secondary norm; for instance, the situation in which Smith stole a car, when the secondary norm forbids stealing cars. The conditioned human behaviour marked as Y is the behaviour of a legal organ which involves coercion. The connection between them (imputation) is of a normative character, and its grammatical expression in a sentence is 'ought'.

It is questionable whether in GTN such a robust conception of imputation exists as can be found in PTL. For sure, its function as a relative a priori was eliminated. The task of reconstructing imputation in GTN is not an easy one. Kelsen scatters information on this category throughout the whole book, including in the footnotes.

[83] Ch Kletzer, *The Idea of a Pure Theory of Law: An Interpretation and Defence* (Hart Publishing, 2018).

[84] ibid.

The definition of imputation does not seem to change significantly in GTN. It still concerns the connection between the condition and the sanction; however, the context has changed significantly. The section titled 'The Principle of Imputation' consists only of a few lines, where Kelsen defines imputation as the 'linking of a condition and a sanction brought about by a general moral or legal norm and described by ethics and legal science in moral and legal laws'.[85] Kelsen specifies the meaning of imputation by stating that 'every general norm which connects a certain consequence to a certain condition represents a relation between two states of affairs which can be described by the statement that under a certain condition a certain consequence is to occur'.[86]

Fortunately, these quotes give some hints as to how imputation can be understood in GTN. Firstly, imputation occurs in legal propositions, rather than legal norms, thus it is still an essential part of legal science. Secondly, in his sceptical phase, Kelsen discusses imputation not only in the context of legal norms, but also moral ones. This means that at this point, imputation, contrary to the Neo-Kantian phase, does not provide *differentia specifica* between law and morality.[87] This allows the argument that, although the role of imputation is limited, especially compared to previous phases, it still can serve as an indicator of the norm and be a necessary element in the process of cognising norms; this time, on a pragmatic level.

The doctrine broadly accepts this interpretation which seems to fit the framework I would like to propose. However, more puzzles concerning imputation in GTN need to be solved. A significant question arises regarding the elements to which imputation applies. At this point, I will only outline this problem and go into more detail in chapter seven.

Imputation has always been a problematic category, due to the question of what kind of elements imputation binds.[88] It is no exaggeration to state that Kelsen has always limited his description of imputation to the contention that it binds two states of affairs as condition and consequence, which is vague and hence unsatisfying. In the context of GTN this situation does not improve.

The first question is how to recognise the relevant state of affairs as a condition. Is it a fact that the law has been broken, and should this fact initiate a legal procedure? One could answer that only legal facts are relevant, but this

[85] Kelsen (n 13) 23.

[86] ibid.

[87] ibid 24.

[88] In the Neo-Kantian phase this problem is discussed eg by: J Renzikowski, 'Der Begriff Der "Zurechnung" in Der Reinen Rechtlehre Hans Kelsens' in R Alexy et al (eds), *Neukantianismus Und Rechtphilosophie* (Nomos Verlagsgesellschaft, 2002) 256–63; SL Paulson, 'Die Zurechnung Als Apriorische Kategorie in Der Rechtslehre Hans Kelsens' in M Kaufmann and J Renzikowski (eds), *Zurechnung Als Operationalisierung von Verantwortung* (Peter Lang, 2004); SL Paulson, 'The Neo-Kantian Dimension of Kelsen's Pure Theory of Law' (1992) 12 *OJLS* 311, 323–24; M Zalewska, 'Objectivity and Hans Kelsen's Concept of Imputation' 151 (2016) *ARSP/B*, Truth and Objectivity in law and Morals II, 153.

begs the question of what 'legal' means, since imputation is yet to be employed. In this context, the basic norm, understood as a fictional assumption made by a lawyer that law is valid, might help. With such an interpretation, the basic norm would be understood as a source of normativity allowing imputation and law to be recognised. However, this further raises the question of the nature of imputation and its function in the General Theory of Norms. If there is no good answer to this question, then the concept of imputation might be superfluous. Of help here could be Kletzer's observation that the pure theory of law perceives law in terms of authorisation to use force, instead of imposing demands regarding who ought to do what.[89] In this case, imputation would be at the core of the pure theory of law, constituting a scheme indicating when force can be applied.[90]

Secondly, elements of imputation require some further clarification. Kelsen describes the first state of affairs as a 'condition', the latter as a 'consequence'. They occur in legal propositions as a part of normatively interpreted reality.[91] For instance: if X stole a car, then X should be punished. The condition is the theft, while the consequence is the punishment for the theft. Here Kelsen attributes the norm with a hypothetical character, hence states of affairs are not understood as specific facts. This means that imputation is normative and 'happens' in the normative sphere, hence whether it binds just two facts from the Is sphere is a matter of debate.

A more plausible solution is that two states of affairs can be associated with a modally indifferent substrate, understood as a neutral component that becomes a sentence or a norm depending on the link, causality or imputation applied. The link, be it causality or imputation, determines by proper interpretation whether the state of affairs belongs to the realm of Is or Ought.[92] Hence, using a modally indifferent substrate appears to be a sound solution and indicates that imputation envisions something more than the norm structure as an interpretation scheme, when the use of force is authorised. As mentioned before, here the pragmatic function of imputation comes into the foreground. As I noted earlier in this chapter, in the framework of dynamic interpretation, instead of 'pragmatic function', I will use the category of understanding strongly associated with interpretation. In such a case, imputation is a mode of understanding, which allows certain propositions that authorise the use of force to be interpreted as legal.

The consequence in the legal sphere is understood by Kelsen as empowerment, according to Paulson, or authorisation, as Kletzer argues, of somebody

[89] Kletzer (n 83).

[90] See also: G Pavlakos, 'A Non-Naturalist Account of Law's Place in Reality' in B Brożek, J Hage and N Vincent (eds), *Law and Mind: A Survey of Law and the Cognitive Sciences* (Cambridge University Press, 2021) 473–89.

[91] I would like to thank Crasten Heidemann for this remark.

[92] Opałek (n 5) 26.

to exert coercion.[93] At first glance it seems that Kelsen successfully adjusted imputation to the moral context. For instance, it could be assumed that empowerment also exists in moral norms as the empowerment of the community to approve or disprove one's behaviour.

Interestingly, these examples differ from the classical understanding of imputation, which can be found in Pufendorf's, Wolff's and Kant's writings. In the classical version, imputation concerned responsibility and obligation. As such, it was based on the observation that, especially in law, responsibility cannot always be ascribed to the individual who caused the damage, for instance, if s/he is a child. In such a case, the responsibility is imputed to someone else deemed to be responsible, eg, their parent. Accordingly, imputation in law was more about what the organ is empowered to do than narrowly understood as being about the consequences or responsibility of some acts. In this way Kelsen eliminates obligation as an independent category from his *Lehre*.[94]

This change is substantial because it constitutes the main difference between the pure theory of law and the positivistic account. While the former binds the understanding of law with the issue of the authorisation of force, as Kletzer argues, the latter envisions law as the obligation constituting the demands model of law.[95] In GTN Kelsen takes one further step, and in the case of morality departs from the classical Pufendorfian understanding of consequence as responsibility. Instead, he transfers his legal understanding of imputation into the moral context.

Accordingly, Kelsen claims that morality is a 'sanction-prescribing normative order'[96] for it not only prescribes certain human behaviour, but also humans' reactions when people act in a contrary manner, namely, requiring the disapproval of immoral behaviour. Such disapproval can be carried out, for instance, in the form of criticism or utterances of contempt. The difference between law and morality lies in the absence of the necessary element of coercion, and in that the reactions concern not only the behaviour which breaks moral norms, but also that which is in accordance with them.[97]

Now that the stage is set, it is time to move to the more destructive part of the consequences for the pure theory of law project. To formulate the conclusion of this chapter, it can be stated that the definition of the norm introduced many changes to Kelsen's theory. It can be seen that some of them were well thought-out. Kelsen approached these changes with awareness and altered

[93] Kletzer (n 83).

[94] The problem of eliminating the obligation from Kelsen's theory was discussed by SL Paulson, *Hans Kelsen as Outlier The Defence of a Radical Norm Theory, Contemporary Perspectives on Legal Obligation* (Routledge, 2020) 60–63.

[95] Kletzer (n 83).

[96] Kelsen (n 13) 23.

[97] ibid.

further elements of his theory accordingly. However, some changes seem to be less intentional, at least at first glance. One example is the change in the definition of a norm, which combines the Is and Ought, constituting a clear link between these two domains, which seems to be against the methodology applied in the pure theory of law. The consequence of this change and its impact on the primary assumption of pure theory of law will be fully described in the next chapter.

2

The Normativity Thesis in General Theory of Norms

THE DEFINITION OF a norm is a game-changer. It affects most of the key elements of Kelsen's theory and, most importantly, puts the normativity thesis in question; when read statically, its introduction gives rise to a suspicion that Kelsen rejected the normativity thesis, or, in the best-case scenario, substantially weakened it to the extent that his purity project collapses.

Two factors contribute to this state of affairs. Firstly, the apparent link between Is and Ought, and, secondly, the understanding of the basic norm as a fiction. Moreover, the revised definition of a norm is not the first instance of Kelsen violating his own methodological rules and introducing a link between Is and Ought, thereby undermining the normativity thesis. Such inconsistency, in the form of the relations between validity and efficacy, which existed from the beginning, constituted one of the most puzzling issues of the pure theory of law.

Such a definition leaves no doubt that Kelsen did not have a radical separation between Is and Ought in mind. The connection between Is, represented by will, and Ought, represented by a norm, is strong enough to raise concerns here. Perhaps there is some further interpretation which would leave the Is–Ought dichotomy intact; unfortunately, Kelsen does not elaborate on how this link should be understood. One could argue, for instance, that Is–Ought separation is still sustained on a logical level. I do believe that this interpretation is coherent and can be justified, especially in the framework of GTN, however, it simultaneously contaminates the purity of Kelsen's theory. I will elaborate on this problem in chapters five to seven.

Hence, as a starting point, I assume that in the definition of a norm, a severe challenge to the normativity thesis arises. The weakening of the normativity thesis simultaneously entails a weakening of the foundations of the pure theory of law – a consequence which will be elaborated on in the next section. My aim in this book is to offer an interpretation which restores the separation of Is and Ought in a coherent way.

Furthermore, as a second consequence, the revised definition of a norm reformulates the understanding of the basic norm by assigning it a fictional character. In this context, Stanley Paulson claims that such a move means the end of the pure theory of law project as we know it.[1] This statement can be interpreted in its weaker or stronger form, and as the end of the pure theory of law in the latter case. I assume that Paulson meant rather the weaker meaning, and thus while the transformation of the pure theory of law is substantial, it still endures.

However, I believe that the strong version of this claim, namely that this is the end of the pure theory of law, is possible and justified. For such a justification it suffices that the weakened separation of Is and Ought is read as leading to the rejection of the normativity thesis. Without the normativity thesis there is no purity. Hence, the argument developed in this book will take into account this extreme scenario. My aim will be to propose an interpretation which without any doubt maintains the pure theory of law, perhaps read in a new paradigm, but which sustains its constitutive elements, especially the normative angle from which law is examined.

Therefore, two consequences of the revised definition of a norm need to be described: the weakened Is–Ought separation and the fictional character of the basic norm. If the consequences are accepted, they lead to the thesis that in GTN Kelsen departed from his pure theory of law project. I devote an entire chapter to these consequences because of their prominence.

2.1. THE NORMATIVITY THESIS, THE PURITY OF KELSEN'S THEORY, AND THE DEFINITION OF A NORM

There are two methodological assumptions in *Pure Theory of Law*, which are focused on ensuring the purity of legal science: the separation thesis, positivistic in its character, which constitutes the separation of law and morality; and the normativity thesis, which constitutes the Is (fact) and Ought (law) separation.[2] Kelsen was so insistent on this methodology due to his conviction that legal science is possible only if it is pure from alien elements.

Only by means of such purification can one cognise law as such and obtain a theory which is ideology-free. Otherwise, in Kelsen's view, one is only able to construct, for instance, a sociology of law, or postulate some requirements referring to the content of law, but in this case one is not able to describe law as it is, in its pure, scientific, ideology-free form. As Koyama Katsuoshi aptly notes:

> [I]t is logical to treat different disciplines separately. The description of law itself and the description of something other than law, especially human behaviour concerning

[1] SL Paulson, 'Metamorphosis in Hans Kelsen's Legal Philosophy' (2017) 80 *MLR* 860, 885.

[2] SL Paulson, 'The Neo-Kantian Dimension of Kelsen's Pure Theory of Law' (1992) 12 *OJLS* 311, 313–20.

> law are clearly different disciplines. It is rational to distinguish the former from the latter. If we want an accurate description of law itself, we must exclude anything other than law from the description.[3]

Kelsen's approach was supposed to achieve two main goals: to offer a scientific and objective approach to the cognition of law, and to construct a theory of law free from hidden ideological assumptions. The critical point of Kelsen's normativity thesis is that it consists of the prohibition of *explaining* normative dimension by facts. This prohibition is crucial for understanding why an updated definition of a norm generates a threat to the normativity thesis and thus to the purity of legal science. At this point it seems that the definition of a norm defines the norm in terms of an empirically understood act of will; hence it can be assumed that it provides an explanation as to what the norm is in terms of facts. This means the rejection of the normativity thesis, which is constitutive for the pure theory of law. In order to discover a more charitable interpretation it is worthwhile to look closer at the normativity thesis.

The Is–Ought separation led Kelsen in a new direction in legal theory and allowed him to create a unique theory of law that was coherent to a high degree. The originality of Kelsen's *Pure Theory of Law* lies exactly in the claim that, in its most radical version, there is an irreconcilable abyss between Is and Ought. The normative thesis thus understood is at the same time a critique of the positivistic approach. According to Kelsen, the legal positivists, who considered law as some sort of social fact, fell into the naturalistic fallacy. While Kelsen identified himself with the broadly defined positivistic camp, he also believed that legal positivism failed to carry out a scientific programme because it confused law with fact. He rejected the so-called social thesis ascribed to legal positivism and replaced it with the normativity thesis.[4] His brilliant idea threw down a grand challenge to the legal positivists, who nowadays still struggle with the issue of how legal facts can be derived from social facts.[5]

On the other hand, the separation between Is and Ought in Kelsen's *Pure Theory of Law* has always been problematic. The solution in which the world

[3] K Katsuoshi, *Introduction to the General Theory of Law*, 4th edn (independently published, 2023) 3.

[4] Paulson (n 2) 320–21.

[5] As Michael Green notes, the social thesis is ambiguous, because the relation between law and facts cannot be reducible 'the way a traffic jam is reducible to facts'. A very successful description of this problem was provided by Gizbert Studnicki, who posed one of the main questions of legal positivists: 'what does it mean that legal facts are derived from social facts. Three solutions are possible: between legal and social facts a relation of reduction occurs, or relation of supervenience, or relation of grounding'; in Gizbert-Studnicki, 'The Social Sources Thesis. Metaphysic and Metaphilosophy' in P Banas, A Dyrda and T Gizbert-Studnicki (eds), *Metaphilosophy of Law* (Bloomsbury, 2016) 121–46; MS Green, 'The Semantic Thesis in Legal Positivism' in T Spaak and P Mindus (eds), *The Cambridge Companion to Legal Positivism*, Cambridge Companions to Law (Cambridge University Press, 2021) 2.

of Ought is to be separated from the realm of Is created the problems of the degree of this separation, whether it has radical character or not. From the beginning of his career, Kelsen maintained that Is and Ought have to be separated if one wants to create legal science. At the same time, he mentioned bridging principles, such as a 'bridge' between validity and efficacy, which connected these two categories.[6]

Apparently, the most straightforward answer to the question of the character of the separation between Is and Ought in *Pure Theory of Law* was that the separation between Is and Ought is radical. Such an answer removes the inconvenience of defining and explaining the possible weak links between norms and facts. Kelsen also seemed to hint at this solution at some point, famously stating that an irreconcilable abyss lies between Is and Ought.[7] However, the main problem with the radical separation seems to be that if there was no bridge between Is and Ought, then the individual who exists in the realm of Is would not be able to think about Ought. Without any link between Is and Ought, the Ought would be unthinkable.

Furthermore, even analysing the internal strength of Kelsen's theory, one finds inconsistencies with the radical version of the separation thesis. Namely, Kelsen's 'troubles' began much earlier than in GTN, because from the beginning of his career he maintained that the efficacy which belongs to the realm of facts conditions the validity of a norm.[8] In spite of some passages suggesting that Kelsen leaned toward a radical separation, especially in his first book, he was somewhat aware that sustaining the radical character of Is and Ought causes inconsistencies, which can be potentially removed by assigning a less radical character to the Is–Ought separation. Otherwise, assuming that Kelsen considered the separation between Is and Ought in radical terms, his definition of a norm is indeed a threat to his pure theory of law project.

Hence, perhaps Kelsen never meant the separation between Is and Ought in radical terms. If that is the case, the weaker Is–Ought separation in GTN does not necessarily mean a dramatic shift in Kelsen's view. The problem seems to lie in the proper definition of the separation between Is and Ought and the identification of the surface where it is meaningful.

On the other hand, it is essential to define the link between Is and Ought which is weak, because when read in a static way, the link between Is and Ought in this definition is too strong. If the Is–Ought separation is supposed to be sustained in a satisfactory way, the Ought (the norm) cannot be *explained* in terms of Is (empirically understood will). Otherwise the only surface at which this separation is sustained would be logical, and this is not

[6] Kelsen, *Pure Theory of Law* (The Lawbook Exchange, Ltd, 1967) 211–14.

[7] H Kelsen, *Hauptprobleme Der Staatsrechtslehre* (Scienta, 1923).

[8] See: B Brożek, 'Law, Normativity, and Supervenience' in B Brożek, A Rotolo and J Stelmach (eds), *Supervenience and Normativity* (Springer International Publishing, 2017) 123–38.

enough to sustain the normativity thesis. In chapter five I will elaborate on this thesis in detail.

2.2. TOWARDS AN UNDERSTANDING OF THE NORMATIVITY THESIS IN *GENERAL THEORY OF NORMS*

The inquiry related to the issue of defining the relation between Is and Ought, which potentially might give a hint of how to tackle with this problem, can be summarised as follows: in what terms does the Is and Ought separation exist?

The Neo-Kantian phase was strongly associated with the normativity thesis. The Neo-Kantian slogan that the method of cognition constitutes its object led Kelsen to the conclusion that the only method possible for cognising norms is a normative method associated with the normative thesis, which rules out the explanation of law through facts. At the same time, Ought was considered as a category employed in cognition, which is primary, and thus undefinable (relative a priori). Since the Neo-Kantian aspect almost vanished from pure theory of law, the Is–Ought separation was reformulated.[9]

In *General Theory of Norms* (GTN) Kelsen seems to weaken this separation further by defining the norm as the meaning of the act of will and, as a result, introducing the fictional character of the basic norm. Now, following Moore and Sidwick, Is and Ought are described as categories, modes or forms of thinking and concepts (*'Denk' – oder 'Vorstellung' – Formen*).[10] Kelsen explains them by stating that one cannot derive Ought from Is.

> An Ought cannot be reduced to an Is or an Is to an Ought; and so an Is cannot be inferred from an Ought, or an Ought from an Is. Ought and Is are two wholly different meanings, or – since the plural of meaning is not idiomatic – two wholly different meanings-contents.[11]

This passage provides some clarity. Firstly, it is evident that, despite revisions in the definition of a norm, Kelsen did not intend to abandon his signature normativity thesis; secondly, not only did he reject the logical possibility of deriving Ought from Is, but he also excluded the possibility of reducing Ought to Is. This passage rather confirms that Kelsen perceived Is and Ought as fundamental. In this case, the question that needs to be addressed is how to reconcile the normativity thesis with the elements in GTN which, at first glance, contradict it. In order to find a solution to this puzzle, the meaning of the Is–Ought separation requires closer investigation.

Secondly, there are several possibilities for how to understand the Is and Ought modes. One option is that the Is–Ought separation refers to the meaning of linguistic expressions; in other words, they function as 'modes for different

[9] More about rejection of the Neo-Kantian paradigm can be found in: Paulson (n 1).
[10] C Heidemann, *Die Norm Als Tatsache* (Nomos Verlagsgesellschaft, 1997) 165.
[11] H Kelsen, *General Theory of Norms* (Clarendon Press, 1979) 58.

types of utterances'.[12] In such a case, Is corresponds with sentences, but Ought with norms. This way Kelsen distinguishes the meaning from the content. While the meaning of the sentence is that something is the case, the meaning of the norm is that someone ought to act in a certain way. On the other hand, the content of a norm or sentence is understood by Kelsen as a modally indifferent substrate and includes all other details pertaining to what is or ought to be the case.[13]

In this framework it is unclear whether Kelsen uses these modes as semantic forms, or as different types of language use and are thus pragmatic, as Heidemann notes.[14] In any case, both approaches refer in the end to modes of thinking. The 'linguistic' approach focuses on the language in which mental processes are expressed, while the pragmatic approach, which is associated with the expressive conception of a norm, is also related to the approach oriented to cognitive processes and understanding, elements of which are present in GTN.[15] This third approach, associated with the mode of understanding which I propose to introduce, can be called hermeneutic, and in the following chapters this is where my emphasis will be placed.

Furthermore, some more hints concerning the relations between Is and Ought can be found in the passages of GTN where Kelsen analyses the aforementioned normative and teleological approaches. The normative and teleological approaches are connected to each other, but at the same time they are distinct modes of thinking. As Kelsen notes:

> An end is an effect, which is wanted. Only the person positing the norm by an act of will – and not the norm itself – can aim for something or pursue an end, for only a person can want something; a norm does not "want" anything.[16]

Here Kelsen very aptly drew the map of the relations between normative and teleological necessity, and the place of the norm in the normative sphere, as well as in the broader context of a teleological framework. This is also a map which envisions the relations between Is and Ought.

It is evident that sometimes in a teleological framework of pursuing a certain end, one issues a norm through a norm-positing act. This norm decrees that certain behaviour is obligatory. The person who posits an act, his will, and the norm-positing act, all belong to the Is domain. As such, they have an end. This end again situated in the 'Is' domain, is identified by Kelsen as a specific form of

[12] Heidemann (n 10) 166.

[13] ibid.

[14] ibid.

[15] On the other hand, in Heidemann's view the separation between Is and Ought is understood in ontological-realistic terms, as in the late Neo-Kantian phase of PTL2. In this way Kelsen is able to preserve the thesis concerning the existence of the ideal sphere, where the norms are, signified by Ought, contrary to Is, which is ascribed to causality and the empirical sphere. Heidemann (n 10) 166.

[16] Kelsen (n 11) 11.

behaviour.[17] Only the meaning of his act of will belongs to the Ought sphere. The norm itself 'is not concerned with any means to which the obligatory behaviour is an end, or with any end to which the obligatory behaviour is a means'.[18]

This signifies that norms exist within the framework of the 'Is' domain and its associated causal relationships. Yet, they retain a distinct status from these elements by virtue of their placement within the normative realm. Even though they are created in the means-end framework, they are unconcerned with it. In other words, when considering the creation or derogation of laws, one could ask if factual moments are needed to explain norms, mainly since norm creation is described in the dynamic structure of law itself. Within the framework employed by Kelsen, it appears that prior to the actual establishment of a norm, sociological or psychological aspects prevail rather than normative ones. This transitional phase is, to a certain degree, of limited relevance to the field of legal science.

However, at the same time, Kelsen, by establishing bridging principles such as the validity and efficacy relation, or norm and will, seems to be compelled to address these issues, at least in part. They exist as borderline situations, belonging as a whole to neither of the spheres. In this sense, it could be said that Kelsen did not deny that facts influence the law, but he aimed to build legal science only on normative terms. Kelsen was honest and did not avoid addressing the difficulties that this approach brings.

These hints shed some light on Is–Ought relations, but are not enough to fully explain them. Hence, a new challenge emerges, namely of how to define these thought processes, and of how facts influence law in the framework of GTN. So far, it has been established that direct interpretation implies some sort of 'Ought' reality in linguistic terms in its semantic or pragmatic context. Such an approach is possible in the framework of GTN. However, an alternative interpretation could be provided within a hermeneutic approach in which GTN is read in the spirit of identifying mental processes which take place when jurists think about law. Later, in chapters three and four, I will argue that this new hermeneutic framework can potentially substitute the Neo-Kantian paradigm existing in the earlier versions of *Pure Theory of Law*. Now it is time to analyse the problem of the relations between validity and efficacy and their impact on the normativity thesis. Some arguments concerning this issue might set the stage for the dynamic approach offered in this book.

2.3. VALIDITY OF LAW AND ITS EFFICACY

The problem of the validity of law is bound up with social practices understood in terms of efficacy, which gives the impression that the Is–Ought separation is

[17] ibid.
[18] ibid.

illusory in this case.[19] Validity is associated with the existence of a norm, but its connection with efficacy comes to light when Kelsen states, that '"to be valid" in its specific – objective – meaning signifies ought-to-be-observed'.[20] Elsewhere he adds: 'and if not observed, then applied'.[21] Having established the main categories, Kelsen distinguishes validity from efficacy:

> Since on one hand the *effectiveness* of a norm consists in the fact that it is actually observed by and large, and since on the other hand the *validity* of a norm consists in the fact that it *ought* to be observed, then applied, therefore the validity of a norm must be distinguished from its effectiveness as an Ought from Is … Now even though validity and effectiveness are completely different, there nonetheless exists an essential relation between the two. Effectiveness is a condition for validity to the extent that a single norm and a whole normative order lose their validity – cease to be valid – if they lose their effectiveness or the possibility of effectiveness. In case of general norms this means: if they cease to be observed by and large, and when not observed, to be applied … An individual norm loses its validity if it remains non-observed until it can no longer be observed or applied.[22]

Several points can be noted in this passage. Firstly, efficacy is defined in terms of the observance of a norm, while validity is associated with the fact that the norm ought to be observed. It follows that, secondly, efficacy belongs to the Is sphere, but validity to the Ought domain. Finally, they stand in relation to each other: efficacy conditions validity. In other words, Kelsen claimed that the norm loses its validity when it loses its efficacy or the possibility of efficacy. Crucially, the connection between validity and efficacy is most apparent at the level of the legal system, rather than at the level of a norm. Hence, this does not mean that the norm must be efficacious to be valid. Kelsen notes that the norm becomes valid before it is efficacious and that it can become efficacious after it becomes valid. What matters here is the possibility of efficacy.[23] The efficacy of a general norm concerns a primary norm, hence when a competent court makes a subsumption and posits an individual norm.

The doctrine noted several problems with this approach, including the main one: the weakening of Kelsen's normativity thesis. Eugenio Bulygin aptly analyses the major inconsistency of the radical approach concerning the Is–Ought separation.[24] He referred to the ontological interpretation of the Is–Ought separation which would refer to the two worlds (Is and Ought) thesis, while the semantic one is reminiscent of Hume's Guillotine.[25]

[19] For compelling analysis of the relations between validity and efficacy see: R Guastini, 'Kelsen on Validity (Once More)' (2016) 29 *Ratio Juris* 402, 402–09.
[20] Kelsen (n 11) 171.
[21] ibid 3.
[22] ibid 139.
[23] ibid 140.
[24] Bulygin, 'An Antinomy in Kelsen's Pure Theory of Law' in SL Paulson, *Normativity and Norms* (Oxford University Press, 1999) 300.
[25] ibid 300–02.

Bulygin's critique is focused on three aspects of law which cannot be considered if the thesis of the two worlds (Is and Ought) were true. Firstly, the action of issuing the norm by a lawmaker; secondly, the act of cancelling a norm, or derogation; and thirdly, the efficacy of the legal system. tied to the inquiry of norm existence. The issuance of a norm stands as a necessary condition for its existence, whereas its cancellation or derogation marks its termination. The efficacy of the legal system conditions the existence of the norm when it belongs to this system. For Bulygin, this implies a connection between the world of Is and Ought, which is even stronger in the last phase.[26] Bulygin's argument is sound. While the issuing and derogation of a norm can be covered by examining the relations between the norm and an act of will, validity and efficacy are distinct cases. What is common for these cases is that they signify borderline situations between Is and Ought.

Various valid approaches can be employed to address the issue highlighted by Bulygin. One such approach, as demonstrated by Brożek, is to contend that Kelsen's pure theory of law is intrinsically inconsistent and to present arguments against the normativity thesis, particularly when understood in its radical form.[27] This approach favours a static interpretation of Kelsen's Normativism, which is possible especially in GTN. It does not add new categories, but just follows the text.

Brożek, assuming the radical character of Is–Ought separation, notes that it results in the construction of validity independent from any facts. This normative meaning of validity is possible due to the basic norm, which in Brożek's argument is understood as fiction. However, Kelsen adds to this equation the category of efficacy. For Kelsen, the validity of the norm is dependent on whether the whole legal system is efficacious.[28]

Brożek argues that efficacy is a condition of and not a reason for validity, hence 'a norm is not valid *because* it is efficacious; it is valid *if* the order to which belongs is, on the whole efficacious'. Therefore, 'it is impossible that the norms of the legal order are valid and the order, as a whole is not efficacious'.[29] On the other hand, according to Kelsen there can be norms which are efficacious but not valid, as in the case when the norm has absolute efficacy (the sun shall rise each day). Brożek points out that validity is conditioned both by efficacy and the basic norm, and that due to the law of transitive implication, the basic norm implicates efficacy.[30] At the same time, he remarks that Kelsen does not claim that the legal order is efficacious whenever a thought basic norm is valid.

[26] Bulygin, 'Norms and Logic. Hans Kelsen and Ota Weinberger on the Ontology of Norms' in C Bernal et al (eds), *Essays in Legal Philosophy* (Oxford University Press, 2015) 303; Bartosz Brożek came to the same conclusion in 'Law, Normativity, and Supervenience' (n 8) 123–38.

[27] Brożek (n 8) 265.

[28] ibid 260.

[29] ibid.

[30] ibid 261.

It shows that Kelsenian intuitions cannot be formalised in the standard modal logic'.[31]

Even though Kelsen never directly claimed this, it might be worth exploring an interpretation in which some kind of relation between the basic norm and efficacy occurs. Kelsen points out that the basic norm is a reconstruction of how lawyers unconsciously think when interpreting some facts as having a normative character.[32] Therefore, it can be assumed that if the lawyers interpret some social facts in a normative, legal way, it means that at the same time they recognise some normative order as efficacious.

Similarly, Bulygin asks, 'When and in what circumstances is the basic norm presupposed? The answer is not difficult to find: The basic norm is always presupposed where an efficacious set of norms is at hand'.[33] Bulygin goes further, however. He concludes that this implies that validity depends upon the assumption of a basic norm and, at the same time, on efficacy. Both Brożek and Bulygin present compelling arguments against maintaining the strict division between 'Is' and 'Ought,' while pairing efficacy with validity and the basic norm. When read directly, the pure theory of law is in danger.

This interpretation can be challenged by the findings put forth by Robert Walter, who raised two fundamental questions: firstly, what is the relation between efficacy and validity which stems from basic norm; and secondly, what is the meaning of the efficacy of the basic norm?[34] According to Walter, the first question belongs to the area of the pure theory of law, while the second is just the rule of the economy of thinking. As such, it indicates the boundaries of the pure theory of law.[35] From the early stages of his work, Kelsen consistently asserted that efficacy does not pertain to the domain of law but, instead, is a meta-rule inherent in the realm of legal methodology as 'a rule of the economy of thinking'. It aims to provide a correspondence between the legal system and legal practice.[36]

This solution can sustain the Is–Ought separation; however, it does not seem plausible. Treating efficacy as a rule of the economy of thinking, moving this category from the sphere of facts into the meta-level, seems counter-intuitive. Efficacy belongs to the factual sphere, and even though from the normative perspective, it could be treated as some sort of rule, it does not change the factual character of efficacy and its connection as fact with validity, mainly since Kelsen himself associates efficacy with facts. According to him, efficacy is understood as consisting 'in the fact that it is actually observed, and when not observed

[31] ibid.

[32] Kelsen (n 6) 204–05.

[33] E Bulygin, 'Remarks on Kelsen's "Validity and Efficacy of the Law"' in C Bernal et al (eds), *Essays in Legal Philosophy* (Oxford University Press, 2015) 73.

[34] R Walter, 'Wirksamkeit Und Geltung' (1961) 3/4 *Österrieches Zeitschrift Für Öffentliches Recht* 532.

[35] ibid 532–41.

[36] H Kelsen, *Das Problem Der Souveränität Und Die Theorie Des Völkerrechts* (Mohr Siebeck, nd) 98–99; Walter (n 34).

then applied'.[37] If efficacy is a fact, it cannot be a rule simultaneously. The most charitable interpretation leads to the notion that Kelsen meant two aspects of efficacy: factual and as a rule.

Hence, efficacy as a rule of the economy of thinking does not invalidate Bulygin's and Brożek's argument and leaves at least two inquiries open. Firstly, the inquiry defined by Bulygin concerning the broken separation between Is and Ought; secondly, the inquiry concerning the type of relation between Is and Ought. The proper answer to the latter inquiry can potentially provide the answer to the former. The resolution of these enigmas may be found in the proper formulation of the interplay between efficacy and validity, as well as between the will and a norm. Such an approach should uphold the demarcation between 'Is' and 'Ought' without entirely disregarding certain interdependencies between them. I will discuss this possibility in chapters six and seven, where I analyse the possibility of supervenience being the kind of link which occurs in such borderline situations. I will argue that supervenience sustains the normativity thesis without losing the coherence of the final version of the pure theory of law.

2.4. THE BASIC NORM AND ITS FUNCTIONS

Even though there is a potential to solve the puzzles surrounding borderline situations, one element might cause that attempt to collapse: namely, the attribution of a fictional character to the basic norm by Kelsen. It seems that if the basic norm, which grants validity to the legal system, is indeed a self-contradictory fiction, the whole concept of validity and the pure theory of law in the normative sphere cannot be sustained in any way. In this section, I will explain in detail why this is the case.

The concept of the basic norm is derived from methodological assumptions made by Kelsen, particularly the separation and normativity theses, to which Paulson attributes the foundation of the pure theory of law. While the separation thesis, characteristic of legal positivism, postulates a separation between law and morality, the normativity thesis postulates a separation between Is and Ought.[38] The latter also distinguishes the pure theory of law from legal positivism, which claims that law is some sort of a social fact, and should be examined in the Is realm. Both theses serve as a foundation for the scientific purity of Kelsen's legal theory. Nonetheless, adopting such an approach comes with its own set of challenges. Kelsen encounters difficulties in addressing a fundamental query regarding validity: why is law valid?

Natural law doctrines provide a relatively simple answer: law is valid because it conforms with natural law, which can be inferred from the will of

[37] Kelsen (n 11) 3.
[38] Paulson (n 2).

God or reason, among other things. Such an answer is possible because natural law doctrines do not separate law from morality. In contrast, legal positivists perceive law as a social fact and hold that law is valid because circumstances at some point in history lead to the foundation of the first constitution.

Kelsen, who claimed a separation exists between law and both morality and facts, could not provide such a straightforward answer to the question of validity. To address this issue, Kelsen, following Adolf J Merkl, introduces the concept of hierarchical structure, dubbed *Stufenbau*. According to this line of reasoning, the validity of each legal norm is derived from its compliance with a higher norm within the hierarchy, as well as from its issuance by a competent legal body following a relevant procedure, with the constitution serving as the ultimate link in this chain. Nonetheless, one could contend that the validity of the constitution is grounded in its conformity with the preceding constitution. Yet, pursuing this line of inquiry inevitably raises questions regarding the validity of the initial constitution.

When addressing this issue, Kelsen introduced the basic norm, which he understood as a hypothetical assumption that must be presupposed by a jurist only if a law is valid. In one of many accounts of the basic norm, Kelsen explains that it illustrates how jurists think.[39] Thanks to the basic norm, which belongs to the Ought realm and lacks content, except some empowerment for constitution-makers,[40] Kelsen is able to sustain both separations of law: from morality as well as from facts.

The basic norm serves various functions, with its most significant role being its utility as a category essential to cognise law.[41] Kelsen notes: 'it must moreover be possible to ascertain from this basic norm which part of the material is valid "law"', and also the objective meaning of the legal material which actually may conflict with its own subjective meaning,[42] and concludes that 'the basic norm merely states the conditions under which the empirical material can be more closely defined as positive law by juridical science'.[43] In this regard, the basic norm represents scientific objectivity, as a Neo-Kantian category a priori. In his quest to describe the conditions for legal science, Kelsen employs a Neo-Kantian paradigm; he builds a transcendental argument demonstrating the necessity of the basic norm for legal science. The argument reconstructed by Paulson is as follows:[44]

1. Legal science exists (as a fact).
2. Legal science is possible only if the basic norm is presupposed.

Therefore: the basic norm must be presupposed.

[39] Kelsen, *General Theory of Law and State*, trans A Wedberg (Harward University Press, 1945) 395.
[40] Kelsen (n 11) 257.
[41] Kelsen (n 39) 405.
[42] ibid.
[43] ibid.
[44] Paulson (n 2).

As Paulson notes, the starting point for Kelsen is the existence of legal science, which he regarded as an undeniable fact. One could argue whether legal science is a science *par excellence*; however, for Kelsen it was obvious that such a project is possible: what remained to be clarified was the necessary conditions of legal science. Kelsen argued that legal science is possible precisely due to the relative category a priori, analogical to Kantian categories, in other words, the basic norm.

In GTN Kelsen no longer refers to the basic norm as a relative category a priori and seems more focused on the validity aspect rather than cognition itself. However, a closer look reveals the aspect of the cognition of law still exists in GTN due to the second function of the basic norm, which is the transformation of the subjective meaning of a norm into an objective one. In *Pure Theory of Law*, Kelsen distinguishes the subjective from the objective meaning of the act. I have mentioned this division several times in chapter one, but now it is time to explain it in more detail in the context of the basic norm.

Kelsen begins by differentiating natural science from social science.[45] Unlike natural objects, social acts can be interpreted in many ways. For example, assume a secret organisation condemns someone to death for betrayal and kills him; in this case, the subjective meaning of this act is the death penalty, but the objective meaning of the act is assassination. The legal phenomenon belongs to the social sciences and consists of two elements: the act, understood as human conduct perceived by the senses; and the meaning of this act conferred by law. In social reality some acts are interpreted as legal acts, one ascribes objective meaning to them.

In clarifying the distinction between objective and subjective meanings, Kelsen initiates his argument with the widely recognised issue of the 'gunman situation'. Kelsen describes a highwayman who orders people to hand over their money and argues that such a command is not a prescription or norm. To become such, there must be the empowering act of a positive or moral order.[46] The existence or the absence of such an empowering act determines whether the act of commanding has a subjective or objective meaning. The subjective meaning of the act of commanding means that 'it is the meaning the act of commanding has from the point of view of commander and not from the point of view of the addressee or any third party'.[47] If such a command is not observed, then behaviour that does not conform with the command will not be judged immoral or illegal.

The objective meaning of a command (or the objective meaning of Ought) concerns empowered commands, and these are understood as binding norms. Such a norm is binding on an addressee. Therefore, not every ought as the meaning of an act of will is a binding norm. Only an objective one is associated

[45] Kelsen (n 6) 2.
[46] Kelsen (n 11) 27.
[47] ibid.

with bindingness. Hence, according to Kelsen, the order of a highwayman can be distinguished from a binding norm according to the objective–subjective criterium.[48]

Within this framework, Heidemann contends that, in contrast to earlier versions of the pure theory of law, in GTN the subjective 'Ought' has a more prominent role than the objective 'Ought'. This is the case due to the definition of a norm as the meaning of the act of will.[49] It can be suggested that this approach stems from the fact that Kelsen wanted to create a theory of all norms, not only legal ones. Kelsen notes that the legal meaning must be interpreted based on a particular human act and is understood as the objective meaning of the act. Hence, if legal norms are considered, I will assume that the objective meaning is the one which prevails, for legal norms can be regarded only as valid, and only valid legal norms have an objective meaning.

The question arises of what causes the subjective meaning of the act to acquire objective meaning. Kelsen observes that without additional presuppositions, this mode of reasoning would result in an infinite regress concerning the justification for the validity of a particular norm, as each norm necessitates a rationale for its own validity. Hence, it becomes imperative to introduce a break in this regress. For Kelsen, such an interruption transpires in the form of a basic norm. The basic norm, standing at the top of the hierarchy of norms, allows them to be cognised and simultaneously grants them objectivity. As Kelsen notes:

> This Basic Norm empowers the individual or individuals who posited the historically first constitution to posit the norms which represent the historically first constitution. If the historically first constitution was posited by the resolution of an assembly, then it is individuals forming this assembly who are empowered by the Basic Norm; if the historically first constitution arose by way of custom, then it is this custom, or to be more exact, it is the individuals whose behaviour forms the custom creating the historically first constitution, who are empowered by the Basic Norm. That is the Basic Norm of the legal order resting ultimately on the historically first constitution.[50]

Hence, the reason why the subjective meaning of the legislator's act also has an objective meaning is that it was empowered by the norm of the constitution, understood as the meaning of the act of will of the author of the constitution. Such reasoning leads to the issue of the objective meaning of the norms of the first constitution. According to Kelsen, their objective meaning originates from the underlying assumption of each jurist, who assumes that one must act in accordance with the norms laid out in the first constitution. This assumption is the basic norm.

On the other hand, the basic norm enables norms to be cognised as legal. For instance, the validity of a testament is affirmed because it was executed following

[48] ibid.
[49] Heidemann (n 10) 167.
[50] Kelsen (n 11) 255.

a specific procedure outlined in a legal norm outlined in accordance with the constitution. The constitution is valid because of a hypothetical assumption, namely the basic norm. Kelsen expresses this thought as follows:

> The assumption of the basic norm which establishes supreme authority for the purpose of law-making is the ultimate presupposition which enables us to consider as 'law' only those materials which have been fashioned by a certain method. ... If it is correct and if this imputation of an objective meaning is possible (without which there can be no legal science), then it must be the basic norm itself which gives the significance of law to material produced by a certain procedure.[51]

To sum up, in GTN Kelsen focuses primarily on this function of the basic norm and how it grants objective meaning to the act of will, thus validity. The norm has an objective meaning only if it is empowered by another norm 'presupposed to be valid'.[52] This division stems from the objective and subjective Ought. While the objective Ought is bound up with validity, the subjective Ought concerns one's intention and thought.[53] Not every subjective Ought turns into an objective and valid one.

The third function of the basic norm is to make the legal order meaningful (*sinnvoll*). Kelsen understands 'meaningful' in a narrow sense.[54] As the legal order cannot be contradictory, although particular legal norms can be, rules such as *lex superior derogat legi inferiori*, *lex posterior derogat legi priori* and *lex specialis derogat legi generali* must be presupposed. All are built into the basic norm. This function definitely vanishes in GTN after the rejection of the rule of contradiction applied to norms. After this discussion of the function of the basic norm, I will now move to the significance of the basic norm in GTN.

2.5. THE FICTIONAL CHARACTER OF A BASIC NORM IN ITS STATIC INTERPRETATION

In chapter 59 of GTN, Kelsen draws attention to the basic norm, reformulating its meaning and indicating that the concept of the basic norm is a proper fiction. According to Kelsen, such a fiction not only contradicts reality but is also self-contradictory. While it empowers the ultimate authority, it also needs to stem from a higher fictional authority on behalf of the definition of norms, understood as the meaning of the act of will.[55]

This seemingly slight change from hypothesis to fiction has vast implications. The basic norm seems to suffer following the reformulation of the theory:

[51] Kelsen (n 39) 405.
[52] Kelsen (n 11) 254.
[53] Heidemann (n 10) 167.
[54] Kelsen (n 39) 401–04.
[55] Kelsen (n 11) 256.

if it is fictional, then in the best-case scenario it is insignificant. In the worst-case scenario, it puts the pure theory of law project under question. The doctrine quickly raised the question of what led Kelsen to such a conclusion about the fictional character of the basic norm, which at first glance seems to be a matter of speculation.

However, a thought-provoking and convincing theory has been presented by Neil Duxbury.[56] He argues that Kelsen's rejection of the basic norm occurred as a consequence of the reformulation of the definition of a norm. Starting in 1960, Kelsen favoured the definition of the norm as the meaning of an act of will. At first, the basic norm was excluded from this definition and had an axiomatic character.[57]

Yet, in one of his late texts, 'Function of the Constitution', Kelsen departs from this reading and regards the basic norm as the meaning of a fictitious act of will. This definition of the basic norm leads to the problem of *regresum ad infinitum*, and contradicts the idea of the basic norm. In other words, such a basic norm must represent the will of a specific authority empowered with competence by a higher norm.[58] Such a higher authority contradicts the idea of the basic norm, since the higher authority must be empowered by a higher norm in order to perform an objective act of will. Yet the higher norm needs to stem from a higher authority, and so on. Hence, Kelsen also had to admit the fictional character of the basic norm in GTN due to the revised definition of a norm.

Since the basic norm played a fundamental role in guaranteeing the project of legal science, the question arises of whether this function can be maintained in GTN. As we already know, in GTN the concept of the basic norm is perceived as a self-contradictory fiction, resulting from a fictitious act of will. Kelsen stresses very clearly that reality does not agree with this fiction. Is such a fiction able to confer scientific objectivity?

Kelsen maintains that the function of the basic norm is to interpret the meaning of the act of will in an objective sense as the norm, which is valid, by claiming – following Vaihinger – that fictions can be helpful when no other cognitive option is available.[59] However, Kelsen does not elaborate on this thought, leaving the reader with a sense that the pure theory of law project ultimately collapsed.

Hence, if read statically, Kelsen's conclusion about the fictional character of a basic norm is damaging to his pure theory of law project. From this character of the basic norm it can be potentially inferred that imputation is also fictional, for these two elements are strictly bound together. The basic norm can be perceived as some sort of gatekeeper for normativity.

[56] N Duxbury, 'The Basic Norm: An Unsolved Murder Mystery' (2007) 17 *LSE Law, Society and Economy Working Papers* 2; N Duxbury, 'Kelsen's Endgame' (2008) 67 *CLJ* 51, 51–61.

[57] Duxbury, 'The Basic Norm' (n 56) 2–3; Duxbury, 'Kelsen's Endgame' (n 56) 55–58.

[58] R Alexy, 'Hans Kelsen's Begriff Des Relativen Apriori' in R Alexy, L Meyer and SL Paulson (eds), *Neukantianismus Und Rechtphilosophie* (Nomos Verlagsgesellschaft, 2002).

[59] Kelsen (n 11) 256.

Separation from facts is only possible if there is a norm which 'closes' the legal system. Otherwise, the first constitution is opened to the realm of Is as the genesis of its validity. Remaining in the realm of Ought would only be possible at the price of opening Kelsen to some natural law doctrine. Since Kelsen rather tended to weaken the Is–Ought separation on behalf of his definition of a norm, which is the meaning of an act of empirically understood will, it can be assumed that normativity suffers as a result of the fictional character of the basic norm.

Normativity still might be derived from imputation, as was possible in earlier versions of *Pure Theory of Law*, however, imputation in GTN seems to have little power to constitute normativity. Again, with the definition of the norm as the meaning of an act of will, and without a solid gatekeeper, a role which the basic norm fulfilled, this foundation of normativity is not sound at all. In the best-case scenario, the pure theory of law project in GTN is incoherent. Or, as Paulson aptly puts it:

> In the classical period, his claim that the law is normative represents his underlying thesis in the Pure Theory of Law, with countless counter-arguments and objections addressed to many psychologically and naturalistically inclined theorists of his day. Now in, in the late period, he treats normativity as a fiction. He proceeds *as if* the law were normative.[60]

Paulson suggests that the result of the fictional character of the basic norm is the fictional character of the normative character of law, which seems contrary to the essence of the pure theory of law and probably contrary to the mainstream of jurisprudence. 'With this, the Pure Theory of Law as we know it from the classical period no longer exists.' Paulson concludes.[61]

To some extent, the following chapter will explore this notion, but in a constructive way, which will not deny a normative character to law, because if read in a static way validity can also be considered as fictional. This would reduce the existence of the legal system to fiction.

If Kelsen meant such a change in the understanding of the basic norm, this would be a hazardous turn indeed for the pure theory of law. In such a framework, normativity and law could be envisioned as an illusion. Yet, it does not seem that Kelsen had such an intention when introducing the fictional character of the basic norm. For this reason, looking for a more dynamic interpretation to solve the puzzles surrounding the basic norm in GTN will be worthwhile. In the following chapters, I will argue that such a vision of the relations between Is and Ought is consistent if interpreted as compatible with the contemporary doctrine of fictionalism in the philosophy of science domain (methodological fictionalism). The doctrine of fictionalism is not alien to Kelsen and GTN. He introduced it himself in the reformulation of the basic norm. This reformulation, which at first glance is catastrophic for pure theory of law, with a closer

[60] Paulson (n 1) 885.
[61] ibid.

look and modern twist might be a key to saving the normativity thesis and purity in Kelsen's doctrine.

2.6. THE END OF PURE THEORY OF LAW?

Briefly summing up, the radical separation between Is and Ought is seemingly a simple and a strong solution. However, it raises the problem of how the normative domain can be accessed and cognised, if the separation was of this kind. If the normativity thesis in its radical version is taken seriously, the human being, who exists in the world of facts, would have no access to Ought. However, Kelsen intended to preclude any factual explanation when constructing legal science.[62] Such a preclusion thus formulated means that some other links exist between Is and Ought; they just cannot have explanatory power. This is good news for the pure theory of law in GTN, because it means that the weakened separation of Is and Ought introduced in GTN does not automatically mean abandoning the normativity thesis.

However, there are more problems to solve. The definition of a norm 'breaks the wall' between Is and Ought in quite a spectacular way. In addition, it does not seem that Kelsen managed to solve puzzles associated with validity and efficacy, namely, that efficacy somehow conditions the validity of a legal system. As Brożek concludes, 'it is difficult to imagine a purely "separationist" view of legal rules',[63] but this conclusion opens the possibility of investigating whether the Is–Ought separation is and has to be of such a radical character.

Finally, in assigning a fictional character to the basic norm, Kelsen seems to make the closing step of eliminating the constitutive elements of the pure theory of law from his theory. At first glance, the fictional character of the basic norm, which stems from the definition of a norm, might also mean the end of pure theory of law. However, Kelsen's oblique references to Vaihinger might not be that random on closer investigation. They might include a solution as to how fictionality can be understood in order to sustain the purity of Kelsen's project.

Although, in GTN Kelsen radically departed from his pure theory project and substituted it with something else, such a substitution is incoherent. It does not qualify as a sound theory when interpreted statically. In any case, to make sense of GTN and perceive it as a consistent project, further interpretation of its elements is required, whether in the spirit of the pure theory of law or not.

On closer investigation, with a more dynamic approach, it can be observed that perhaps Kelsen never gave up his pure theory of law project. He tried to extend it and update it, but he did not reject it. The fact that he died before finishing his book does not help its quality. We do not know what form the final

[62] Paulson (n 1) 80.
[63] Brożek (n 8) 263.

version would have taken. We can only assume that there might be some gaps to fill, and try to identify them. In this chapter, this was my aim. I tried to identify two such gaps which constitute a dramatic shift in Kelsen's theory. I identified two such elements: the problem of the separation between Is and Ought; and the fictional character of the basic norm. The task of the following chapters will be to fill these gaps with appropriate interpretation.

Hence, two key problems emerge: (1) what does it mean to say that the basic norm is self-contradictory fiction? And (2) what kind of link exists between Is and Ought? The former question will be discussed in chapters three–four, the latter in chapters five–seven. In these chapters I will demonstrate the key elements of this interpretation, and how they prevent pure theory of law from collapsing. I will offer an interpretation which can sustain the purity of his theory. I will discuss both problems, proposing the solution to the first one in fictionalism, and the second one in supervenience.

3

Fictionalism: The New Framework for the General Theory of Norms

As INDICATED IN chapter two, Kelsen's novel conception of the basic norm appears to dismantle his entire endeavour to establish legal science as an actual science. Considering the basic norm as fiction seemingly bestows a fictional quality upon the validity of the legal system.[1] However, when interpreted in a more dynamic manner, it may become evident that Kelsen's conception possesses greater profundity and a more robust foundation than initially appears.

The primary inquiry of this chapter concerns the issue of what fictionalism can contribute to the General Theory of Norms. Interestingly, Kelsen saw the potential in Vaihinger's fictionalism. He had been acquainted with Vaihinger's ideas since the early stages of his career as a legal scholar. Despite the considerable criticism aimed at Vaihinger, Kelsen recognised the value in his thinking at a time when it had almost faded into obscurity. This sets the stage for interpreting the General Theory of Norms from a fresh perspective – that of contemporary fictionalism.

3.1. VAIHINGER'S PHILOSOPHY OF 'AS-IF'

The idea that the legal system is founded on self-contradictory fiction seems to be unfortunate. At first glance, the difficulties associated with the conception of the basic norm as a fiction seem to have far-reaching consequences, and to be destructive for Kelsen's theory as a whole. If a proposition is self-contradictory, anything – including true or false conclusions – can be derived from it.[2] So, it seems impossible to use a self-contradictory fiction – even if it might be a useful heuristic tool – to ground legal science, which should be objective and consistent.

However, even if such a view did not misinterpret what Kelsen meant by proper fiction, it is not helpful for a coherent reading of Kelsen's last book.[3]

[1] T Spaak, 'Kelsen's Metaethics' (2002) 35 *Ratio Juris* 158, 170.

[2] Although according to paraconsistent logic such a thesis is false, I will assume that Kelsen did not use such non-standard logic in order to explain the self-contradictoriness of the basic norm. It seems more straightforward and useful for the sake of argument to assume that he understood self-contradictoriness in Vaihingerian terms.

[3] The process of rejecting the basic norm as a hypothesis is described very convincingly by Stanley L Paulson. Paulson recalls a famous passage from 1962 in which Kelsen openly expressed his

This can instead be accomplished by taking seriously Kelsen's vague reference to Vaihinger.[4] Such an attempt was made by Hakan Gustafsson in 'Fiction of Law'. His interpretation of the basic norm focuses on Hans Vaihinger's 'Philosophy of As-If' as a backdrop for Kelsen's fictionalism, and he concludes: '[I]n spite of – or even thanks to – the self-contradictory presupposed basic norm, legal science is able to, according to Kelsen, reach its cognitive goal *only* by means of a fiction.'[5] Hence, it is worthwhile to follow Kelsen's account of the basic norm along with the Vaihingerian account of fictionalism.

Vaihinger, today somewhat forgotten, was an important figure in the second half of the ninenteenth century, and was connected to two prominent journals. First, as a Neo-Kantian, he founded *Kantstudien* and later initiated *Annalen der Philosophie*, which was in due course taken over by the Vienna Circle and renamed *Erkenntnis*.[6] His philosophy is concentrated on the role which fictions play in scientific inquiry as well as in human thought and action. He demonstrated that various fictions are present in almost every field of human endeavour and that, as such, they are a fundamental human faculty.

Vaihinger's philosophy of 'As-If' was based on the observation that knowledge is the reduction of the unknown to the known; however, this process may need to stop at some point still in the unknown, and at this final point, fictions might appear to be useful.[7] For science, it is essential to develop only such ideas which have objective correlates and eliminate those with a subjective component.[8] However, the process of gathering objective and non-contradictory constructs is difficult and slow, and requires appropriate methodology to be applied. Such questions as the origin of the universe, or the problem of the relation between mind and body, are impossible to solve, hence many thought processes are based on fictional assumptions. In such case, there is no necessary connection between importance and rightness, because reliable conclusions can be derived from apparent fictions.[9] This leads Vaihinger to the conclusion that fictions can be essential for thinking in a scientific sense – when they are used as thought devices. In this framework, the task of fiction is to 'provide us with an

doubts concerning the basic norm in the context of the definition of a norm as a meaning of an act of will (SL Paulson, 'Metamorphosis in Hans Kelsen's Legal Philosophy' (2017) 80 *MLR* 860, 883); indeed, at that point Kelsen sounds pessimistic about the character of the basic norm. However, such pessimism is absent in GTN. Instead Kelsen, following Vaihinger, vaguely and in a neutral manner mentions that such fictions can be useful. It is not my intention to suggest what Kelsen had in mind at that time, but I believe this remark can be elaborated into an interpretation which could restore to some extent the significance of the basic norm in GTN.

[4] H Kelsen, 'Zur Theorie Der Juristischen Fiktionen. Mit besonderer Berücksichtigung von Vaihingers Philosophie Des Als Ob' (1919) 1 *Annalen Der Philosophie* 630.

[5] H Gustafsson, 'Fiction of Law' (2010) 41 *Rechtstheorie* 319, 329.

[6] KA Appiah, *As If: Idealization and Ideals* (Massachusetts, Harvard University Press, 2017) 2.

[7] H Vaihinger, *Philosophy of As If: A System of the Theoretical, Practical and Religious Fictions of Mankind*, trans CK Ogden, 2nd edn (Routledge & Kegan Paul, 1984) 61–62.

[8] ibid 13.

[9] Gustafsson (n 5) 21.

instrument for finding our way about more easily in this world'.[10] Specifically, epistemological fictions are perceived as 'vehicles of thoughts'.[11]

The brilliance of Vaihinger's theory also lies in the observation that 'the object of the world of ideas as a whole is not the portrayal of reality – this would be an utterly impossible task – but rather to provide an instrument for understanding certain phenomena in an easier way.[12] The conceptualised world is a product of the real one, and as such, cannot be identical to it, ie it serves as its 'copy'. It has the qualities of a symbol which allows one to orientate oneself in the real world more efficiently. Such a symbol very often has the characteristic of self-contradictory fiction (real fiction).[13]

Vaihinger investigates fictions in different branches of science. He mentions, for instance, the concepts of infinity in mathematics, egoism in economics, eternity in religion, and finally, an original contract, a general will, and a legal person in law.[14] This allows Vaihinger to distinguish two types of fiction: real or proper fiction which contradicts reality and is self-contradictory – for instance, the atom[15] – and half-fiction, or semi-fiction, which merely contradicts reality or deviates from it.

Real fictions contradict reality, are self-contradictory, and already have these features when they are introduced. If they enable a better understanding of the world, their *ratio* exists.[16] Despite being self-contradictory, fictions cannot be dismissed on the basis of their self-contradictoriness. Their utility decides on their applicability.[17] Semi-fictions satisfy only the first condition by contradicting reality. For instance, Adam Smith's assumption that all human action is driven by rational egoism is semi-fiction because Smith knew that this assumption was false, but it allowed him to construct his economic theory.[18]

[10] Vaihinger (n 7) 13.

[11] Gustafsson (n 5) 21; For instance, Kant uses 'heuristic fictions' such as the freedom of the soul in his *Kritik der reinen Vernunft*, or the presupposition of freedom in *Metaphysik der Sitten*.(Vaihinger (n 7) 42–45).

[12] Vaihinger (n 7) 13.

[13] ibid 65–66.

[14] Gustafsson (n 5) 22–23.

[15] A Fine, 'Fictionalism' (1993) 18 *Midwest Studies in Philosophy* 10, doi.org/10.1111/j.1475-4975.1993.tb00254.x.

[16] Hence, Vaihinger, in contrast to pragmatists, is aware of the gap existing between the utility of a concept and the truth, and explores the role of untruth in thinking about reality. In contradistinction to pragmatism, Vaihinger claims that the utility of fictions is by no means a proof of their objective truth. At the same time, Vaihinger rejects the idea that his philosophy should be regarded as scepticism, since he considers scepticism to be a philosophy which raises doubts and questions fundamental principles. The 'As-If' philosophy does not represent this direction of thought, and while scepticism is rather based on some cognitive pessimism, Vaihinger's notions are optimistic: our knowledge is full of fictions, but this is good news; these vehicles of thought enable us to understand reality better. Vaihinger argues that, based on such an approach, 'relativism' would be a more appropriate description. Vaihinger (n 7) 67.

[17] ibid 63.

[18] Appiah (n 6) 6.

Semi-fictions are similar but distinguishable from hypotheses. The latter are verifiable and selected according to the probability criterion.[19] Hence, what changes are the criteria of evaluation. Hypotheses are valid until proven otherwise, which subjects them to Popper's criteria of falsification.[20] On the other hand, genuine fictions are of a different kind. They are justified if they fulfil a utility criterion.[21] There is no possibility of mistaking them for hypotheses, due to their self-contradictory character. As such, they cannot be verified by observation; rather, they are subject to justification than verification.

Fiction must not be confused with 'the usefulness of *speaking* untruths' as Appiah notes.[22] Fine notes in this context that some important features in a human being's life can be fictional, yet the fact that they are fictional does not make them unimportant.[23] Appiah adds: 'Very often we can reasonably proceed as if what we know to be false is true *because it is useful for some purpose to do so*'.[24] Fine describes this approach as 'critical tolerance' and notes that this caused Vaihinger to use the term 'fiction' in a far from rigorous manner, as a concept of proposition.[25]

The employment of justified fictions is not damaging to science as long as some rules are observed. Firstly, the use of fictions requires an awareness of their nature. They should not be confused with hypotheses, or dogma. A fiction is not an immediate consequence of reality, nor does it belong to 'reality' – whatever, if anything, is considered 'reality' in the context of a particular fiction. The awareness of their fictional nature is crucial here. 'As soon as the mechanism by means of which these [fictional] concepts perform such efficacious service is disclosed, the illusion of their truth disappears, for this only persists as long as the mechanism is concealed' – Vaihinger notes.[26] Otherwise, if fictions are used without awareness of their nature, their self-contradictoriness might also be misleading and lead to fruitless word riddles or illusionary problems; these should be avoided.[27] Such situations may arise when fictions are misused: when they are mistaken for reality and treated as dogma.

Secondly, fictions have a temporary character – they function as long as they serves their purpose: 'The logical function similarly destroys its fragile framework as soon as it has attained its goal – the establishment of unchangeable relations and connections'.[28]

[19] Interestingly, Vaihinger argues that when a hypothesis proves to be false, one does not need to give up on it, but one should rather treat it as a fiction from that point on. Appiah (n 6) 9.

[20] Gustafsson (n 5) 23.

[21] Fine (n 15) 7; A Bokulich, 'Explanatory Fictions' in M Suárez (ed), *Fictions in Science: Philosophical Essays on Modeling and Idealization* (Routledge, 2010) 93.

[22] Appiah (n 6) 3.

[23] Fine (n 15) 16.

[24] Appiah (n 6) 2.

[25] Fine (n 15) 16.

[26] Vaihinger (n 7) 63.

[27] ibid 111. However, currently, the view that fictions have a temporary character is rather rejected. Fictions are perceived as a permanent feature of science (see: Bokulich (n 21) 92).

[28] Vaihinger (n 7) 63.

Finally, fictions should be restricted to their original context. While they are not a part of reality, they only have value when they are 'in relation to particular phenomena in a certain context'. Fictions 'regarded apart from their purpose … are valueless'.[29] As a result, Vaihinger also introduces a second division: virtuous (eg atoms, thing-in-itself) and vicious fictions (eg dormitive power). While the first are scientific, the latter are not.[30] The first kind receives the most attention. They are justified by the assumption that although we are not able to understand all aspects of the world when analysing its phenomena, we can understand it through experience and intuition. Hence, due to their 'As-If' semantic expression, fictions have the potential to possess great practical importance. They assist thinking and indirectly help attain the goal of reaching a correct conclusion.

3.2. THE BASIC NORM AS A PROPER FICTION IN THE VAIHINGERIAN SENSE

The presence of Vaihinger's thought in *General Theory of Norms* (GTN)[31] did not appear from nowhere. Kelsen was familiar with Vaihinger's theory from almost the beginning of his career. In 1919, he wrote the article 'Zur Theorie Der Juristischen Fiktionen. Mit besonderer Berücksichtigung von Vaihingers Philosophie Des Als Ob',[32] in which he criticises Vaihinger's analysis of legal fictions. In this article, Kelsen notes that Vaihinger regards legal fictions as formally identical to scientific and, in general, epistemological fictions. Kelsen points out the ambiguity of the term 'legal fiction' used by Vaihinger. Only a few of the legal fictions mentioned by Vaihinger are indeed proper fictions.

As Kelsen notes, Vaihinger's concept of fiction is characterised by the means–end relation. The end can be defined as cognition of reality, and the means are fabrication, contradiction, sleight of hand, detour and passage of thought. As such, Vaihinger's fictions have an epistemological rather than a logical character.[33] This remark is interesting in the context of the interpretation of the basic norm in GTN. It opens the possibility that epistemology, so strongly accented in the previous phases, is now hidden behind the fictional character of the basic norm. As such, it loses its function of being constitutive for cognition and takes on a heuristic character. In other words, it enables the understanding of law as such and the cognitive mechanisms underlying legal practice.[34]

According to Kelsen, the mechanism behind Vaihinger's notion of fiction is defined by the fiction's consciously opposing or contradicting reality in order to further cognition. Legal fictions, however, do not always serve cognition, and

[29] ibid 112.
[30] Fine (n 15) 5.
[31] H Kelsen, *General Theory of Norms* (Clarendon Press, 1979).
[32] Kelsen (n 4).
[33] ibid 631–32.
[34] I would like to thank Carsten Heidemann for his question concerning the constitutive and heuristic character of the basic norm.

they might postulate the existence of some state of affairs which is in contradiction to reality without being explicit about it. This character of legal fictions contradicts the meaning ascribed to fictions by Vaihinger. He would have regarded such fictions not only as useless, but as harmful errors.

Kelsen notes that Vaihinger was aware that legal science is directed at an Ought. Legal institutions can exist in reality, but then they are the subject of sociology, not of legal science. Kelsen argues that if fictions merely serve the cognition of empirical reality, Vaihinger formed the concept too narrowly and made it incompatible with such fields of science as ethics or legal science. Therefore, Kelsen postulates that one must not speak of 'actual reality' as the object of cognition, but of the 'object of cognition', in more general terms. In such a case, the fictions of legal theory, such as 'legal subject' or 'subjective right', could be justified, when juristic cognition takes a detour 'in knowing its object' (law, ie, the legal order) and contradicts this object in order to better grasp it.[35] At this point, though, as Gustafsson notes, Kelsen was still at the beginning of the process of developing the basic norm. Hence, the property of being a fiction can only be ascribed to the basic norm 60 years later in GTN.

The connection between Kelsen's GTN and Vaihinger's philosophy of 'As-If' lies in the concept of the fictional basic norm. By attributing a fictional character to this category, Kelsen opened the door for further exploration of fictionalism in GTN and interpretations in such a spirit. Interpretation of GTN in terms of fictionalism, and its selection over other theories from the field of philosophy of science, is justified if the concept of the fictional basic norm makes sense in Vaihingerian terms.[36] Hence, before I move further into contemporary fictionalism, and its application to GTN, an explanation as to how the fictional basic norm fits with Vaihinger's concept of fictionalism, as initially used by Kelsen, is useful. I will do this by first drawing a distinction between the hypothetical and fictional basic norm, then I will analyse the key features of fiction and compare it with the conception of the basic norm in GTN.

The distinction between proper fiction and hypothesis can serve to elucidate the contrast between the basic norm conceived as a hypothesis and the basic norm interpreted through the lens of fiction. With the former, the legal system is perceived as valid unless disproven, while with the latter, the validity of the legal system is envisioned as persisting despite the inherent self-contradictions of the basic norm. Moreover, it appears that such a basic norm may endure if its utility can be demonstrated, despite conflicting with factual evidence pertaining to the validity of a specific legal system. Hence, the division between hypothesis and fiction introduced by Vaihinger helps to discern how the hypothetical basic norm posits the legal system's validity as a working assumption until proven

[35] Kelsen (n 4) 638–45.

[36] A compelling example is a successful interpretation of Kelsen's pure theory of law in the light of critical rationalism: T Fitzsche, *Hans Kelsen Und Kritische Rationalismus* (Schriftenreiche Des Hans Kelsen-Instituts, 2002).

otherwise, whereas the fictional basic norm embraces the legal system's validity even in the face of inherent inconsistencies.

As mentioned above, Vaihinger lists four features characteristic of fictions: firstly, fictions need to serve the purpose for which they are created; secondly, they need to contradict reality or be self-contradictory; thirdly, their fictional character needs to be explicitly stated; and finally, they need to be eliminated during the later stages of inquiry.[37] The concept of the basic norm formulated by Kelsen in GTN can be interpreted in such a way that it has at least three essential features of fictions. It is used to enable legal knowledge and its methodology. The usefulness of the basic norm, in Kelsen's view, is associated with understanding validity and the norm as an objective meaning. The basic norm contradicts reality and is self-contradictory, as Kelsen states explicitly:

> For the assumption of a Basic Norm – for instance, the Basic Norm of a religious moral order 'everyone is to obey God's commands' or the Basic Norm of a legal order 'Everyone is to behave as the historically first constitution specifies' – not only contradicts reality, since there exists no such norm as the meaning of an actual act of will, but also self-contradictory, since it represents the empowering of an ultimate moral or legal authority and so emanates from an authority – admittedly, a fictitious authority – even higher than this one.[38]

Gustafsson explains this by dividing Kelsen's reasoning into two steps. The first step assumes that the concept of the basic norm contradicts reality because it does not correspond to an actual act of will. It is impossible for the concept of the basic norm to be exemplified in the realm of facts, and jurists are aware of this. In a second step, Kelsen claims that the concept of the basic norm contradicts itself due to the final authority mentioned above not being final. Hence, Gustafsson concludes, 'the basic norm is consequently invented'.[39] Only by means of this fiction can one proceed as if 'the material of law was irreducibly normative', so that 'the legal system can be treated as valid as if there really existed a basic norm'.[40]

Thirdly, there is no doubt that Kelsen explicitly stated the fictional status of the basic norm; he admits it himself in the following words: 'As such, it [the basic norm – MZ] is a genuine or 'proper' fiction (in the sense of Vaihinger's philosophy of As-If) whose characteristic is that it is not only contrary to reality, but also self-contradictory'.[41] Kelsen subsequently adds:

> According to Vaihinger, a fiction is a cognitive device used when one is unable to attain one's cognitive goal with the material at hand (1935: 13). The cognitive goal of the Basic Norm is to ground the validity of the norms forming a positive moral or legal order, that is, to interpret the subjective meaning of the norm positing acts as

[37] Vaihinger (n 7) 97–100.
[38] Kelsen (n 31) 256.
[39] Gustafsson (n 5) 29.
[40] ibid 30.
[41] Kelsen (n 31) 256.

> their objective meaning (ie as valid norms) and to interpret as relevant acts as norm-positing acts. This goal can be attained by means of a fiction. It should be noted that the Basic Norm is not a hypothesis in the sense of Vaihinger's philosophy of As-If – as I myself have sometimes characterized it – but a fiction. A fiction differs from a hypothesis in that it is accompanied – or ought to be accompanied – by the awareness that the reality does not agree with it.[42]

Finally, the problem faced when comparing Kelsen's concept of the basic norm and Vaihinger's theory of proper fiction is that, according to Vaihinger, fiction should vanish as soon as it fulfils the purpose for which it was created,[43] which is not the case for the basic norm. However, it is unclear in which sense the basic norm should vanish when its purpose is served. Should it vanish from the legal system as soon as the first constitution is established? Such an interpretation would be in conflict with the meaning given to the basic norm by Kelsen when *tracing back* the entire hierarchy of norms, from the bottom to the top, in order to detect this fictional assumption. Despite being fictional, this assumption is present every time the problem of validity comes into question.

One possible solution is to indicate that fictions in the humanities and social sciences differ, and hence behave differently, and that no such need occurs in the case of the basic norm. Furthermore, nowadays Vaihinger's thesis that fictions ought to be discarded when their purpose has been served is not strictly followed. Instead, different approaches dominate, according to which fictions have their *ratio* as long as it is substantially useful.[44] Despite this, I believe the basic norm fulfils this condition as well, if read correctly, as a prohibition on extended and unjustified usage of fictions. Fictions only serve their purpose and only function in a specific context. Beyond that they are useless. This is a crucial point for comprehending how the fictional basic norm is useful in the GTN project.

Now it is time to address the key point of the inquiry: how is it possible that its fictional character does not damage the pure theory of law? The value and dangers of fictions, as well as how to deal with them, can be subsequently explained by the pragmatic theory of truth. The pragmatic theory of truth puts stress on the utility and coherence of a concept within a system. For instance, the statement that a corporation is a legal person is true within legal language, although it is false within natural language due to inconsistency in denotation. Contrary to everyday language, the term 'person' in law includes corporation in its extension.[45]

[42] ibid.

[43] G Samuel, M Del Mar and W Twining, 'Is Law a Fiction?' in M Del Mar and W Twining (eds), *Legal Fictions in Theory and Practice* (Springer International Publishing, 2015) 38.

[44] Bokulich (n 21) 92; On the other hand, Yablo tends to believe that 'any make believe elements that do make their way in will eventually drop out'. S Yablo, 'Does Ontology Rest on a Mistake?' (1998) 72 *Aristotelian Society Supplementary Volume* 229, 245.

[45] D Lind, 'The Pragmatic Value of Legal Fiction' in M Del Mar and W Twining (eds), *Legal Fictions in Theory and Practice* (Heidelberg, New York, Dordrecht, London, Springer International Publishing, 2015) 91–93.

Kelsen's methodological distinction between Is and Ought works well here, since it indicates that an Ought statement is meaningful, while as an Is statement its value is false, because of inconsistency of denotation. Hence, such fictions contradict reality but are internally consistent. Such inconsistencies are valuable if they are helpful within the legal system and at the same time they do not impair 'the general stock of beliefs outside law', hence they are harmless.[46] To sum up, in the case of proper fictions, the *ratio* of their existence (pragmatic value) falls under two criteria: 1) they are beneficial within the system in which they function; and 2) they are harmless to external systems of belief.

However, in the case of proper fictions which are self-contradictory, at first glance, the pragmatic theory of truth seems to be of no help. The basic norm could have been supported by the pragmatic theory of truth before Kelsen's turn from hypothesis to fiction. Fictionalism, in contrast to pragmatism, entails awareness of the gap between utility and truth. However, the criteria provided in the framework of the pragmatic concept of truth might be helpful here. If we return to the two criteria mentioned above, it can be stated that the concept of the basic norm as a proper fiction fulfils both of them.

Firstly, the basic norm is beneficial in the world of Ought, as an explanation of how lawyers think when dealing with the puzzle of the validity of the legal system and the first constitution.

Secondly, the basic norm is harmless for the world of Is, since it does not interfere with the general stock of belief outside law. Thus, the question is whether the absence of contradictory character is a vital condition, given the fact of its usefulness. In other words, if the pragmatic concept of truth is considered, one must weigh whether the explanatory power of the basic norm, which makes the notion of validity consistent, is worth the price of the self-contradictory character of the basic norm.

At this point, it is worth returning to Vaihinger, who presented valid examples of when it was worth paying the price of self-contradiction – to gain in return a proper explanation or understanding of the phenomena. This claim begs another question, namely whether the self-contradictory fiction contradicts the system per se. What Lind means is: 'But to the extent it [a fiction] wrecks intersystemic havoc – generates confusion or incoherence, frustrates ability to function – or does not work some genuine utility within law, it is not useful [...] and is a problematic fiction'.[47] Hence, the answer to the question of whether the basic norm is harmful or not does not depend on its hypothetical or fictional character, but rather on the general concept of the basic norm. This construction is perhaps the most debated of all the elements of Kelsen's pure theory of law; however, this discussion is fruitful, since it allows us to take one more step towards solving the enigma of law. Its further evaluation can be carried out after an examination of contemporary fictionalism.

[46] ibid 94.
[47] Lind, 101.

Hence, the most general answer to this inquiry is that, in the framework provided by Vaihinger, the basic norm was not rejected in GTN. It still exists, and one can expect that it has analogical functions to the classic basic norm understood in terms of hypothesis. What changed is the cognitive mechanism by virtue of which the basic norm works. Instead of the Neo-Kantian framework, fictionalism is introduced.

Hence the basic norm enables the normative and legal character of the norm to be grasped. This assumption needs to be made in order to distinguish law from other social facts as well as from morality. This process involves two perspectives, which I will call, following Rudolf Carnap, external and internal.[48]

As Yablo notes, the internal perspective exists in some sort of framework and, according to Carnap, utterances are meaningful in some sort of linguistic framework. Queries concerning the existence of X make sense if they are done within the framework which Carnap refers to as the internal existence question. Hence, there are some applicable rules which authorise one to say that there are certain Xs.[49] There is also another perspective, outside the framework, namely the external one, which is often taken by philosophers.

I will adjust Carnap's internal/external division to fit into the pure theory of law framework. It seems that the notion of the basic norm is internal and implicit from the perspective of a lawyer, who *uses* the basic norm, while it becomes explicit from the external perspective of someone who tries to *describe* on a meta level how lawyers think, and provide an understating of how lawyers think. This means that the task of the legal philosopher is to describe what practitioners do, by identifying implicit factors and making them explicit, and the basic norm is such a case.

How does it fit into the fictional framework? For Yablo, the internal/external division is crucial to introduce some sort of fictionalism based on metaphor statements. For the purposes of this chapter I will not go into the details of Yablo's compelling conception and will just use the general notion of fictionalism which stems from Yablo's concept of a make-believe game typical for modern fictionalism, which will be discussed below.[50] Hence, from within the internal perspective one operates in a make-believe framework. The external perspective unveils the fictional character of some assumptions. For instance, when telling the story of Robinson Crusoe, one is engaged in it, and one tends to say, that yes, it is true that Robinson Crusoe lived on a deserted island. However, from all external perspectives, we all know that this is false. Getting back to Kelsen, GTN provides an understanding of the hidden fictional assumptions which make some social practice *legal* – that is, normative, and different from morality.[51]

[48] For a comprehensive explanation of Carnap-Quine's debate on the internal/external division, and its relation to fictionalism, see Yablo (n 44) 230–39.

[49] ibid 233–34.

[50] ibid 242–44.

[51] I would like to thank Carsten Heidemann for his remarks concerning the implicit and explicit aspects of basic norm.

At first glance, the claim that what transforms social facts into law is a fictional assumption sounds suspicious. It sounds as if in reality there was no law, as if law was some sort of fictional contrast based on fiction. However, keeping in mind the nature of fiction in Vaihinger's terms, we can avoid such a destructive conclusion. The fiction cannot constitute the entire theory, be fundamental to it, or be extended to the concepts surrounding it. These concepts are primary, given. The fact of legal science is also given, and the fact of law's existence is another given. Fictions serve as mere 'servants' that facilitate our comprehension of how these concepts function. They would prove futile if they were related to any other spurious notions. Fiction finds its purpose solely within the framework of truth. As Vaihinger observed, fictions derive meaning only within a context, and embod a certain resemblance of reality, that unfolds in actuality.

In this case the basic norm 'closes' the sphere of Ought and as such enables this sphere to be cognised as pure; that is, as normative in its essence. Normativity is not a fiction; it is real – but in order to understand it, we need a fiction. The same regards the separation between law and morality. For this reason, I claim that the basic norm is not a central fictional concept in GTN, but rather a symptom of a much more powerful fiction, namely the fiction of purity. Hence, within the fictional framework, the basic norm is perceived not as the foundation of law but as a symptom of this larger fictional framework. Consequently, it serves as a cognitive device enabling lawyers and legal scholars to comprehend law in its pure form, devoid of any alien elements

If indeed the fictional basic norm emerges as a mere consequence of a broader fictional framework, the concerns about the veracity of Kelsen's concept of validity and the foundation of his theory as a whole lack substantial merit. Kelsen's theoretical framework is predicated on methodological presumptions of purity that underpin the integrity of his theory and incorporate certain fictitious or fictive elements, much like many other theories. Before I justify this claim, modern fictionalism first needs to be presented. Thus, in the following section, I shall present an overview of contemporary perspectives on fictionalism, followed by a subsequent exploration of potential interpretations of Kelsen's General Theory of Norms within this particular framework.

3.3. ONTOLOGICAL FICTIONALISM

Vaihinger wrote *The Philosophy of As If* in 1924. At the same time, the logical positivists were developing their radically different philosophical approach – from their point of view Vaihinger's theory of fiction was unintelligible. Not only did it not conform to the strict criteria of logical positivism, but Vaihinger was also vague in the most significant parts of his book. He held that the concept of fiction denoted an extremely broad category of objects, did not provide clear guidelines on how to proceed with fictions and was not always clear concerning the meaning of the fiction, as he extended it with suggestions that thought does not agree with reality, but was still useful due to its sufficient closeness to the truth.[52] Ultimately, his theory gave fictionalism a bad name for decades, until its rebirth in the 1980s.

However, Kelsen did not have the opportunity to witness the rebirth of fictionalism in the 1980s. Hence, it might be worthwhile to outline the basic ideas of modern fictionalism in order to find out whether there are some potential elements which could elaborate Kelsen's account of the fictional character of the basic norm and the implications of such a stance. This section aims to describe fictionalism in general terms. Later on, some problems will be discussed in more detail in the context of Kelsen's doctrine.

In the most general terms, fictionalism, when applied to the field of discourse, is 'the view that claims made within that discourse are not best seen as aiming at literal truth but are better regarded as a sort of "fiction"'.[53] This thesis is described as 'linguistic' and contrasted with the 'ontological' thesis, according to which the entities in question either do not exist or have a fictional status. These theses can run together, because the linguistic thesis is often derived from ontological concerns, but one can commit to one of the theses without committing to another.[54]

In the case of the basic norm, these two theses seem compatible and linguistic fictionalism stems from ontological concerns. From the 'General Theory of Norms' point of view, one of the most essential distinctions seems to be the one between ontological and methodological fictionalism. Ontological fictionalism identifies strategies for when dealing with a fiction of some sort. Such fictionalism attempts to explain why specific claims concerning entities, whose existence can be questioned (such as number) are valid.

On the other hand, methodological fictionalism, which is more related to Vaihinger's approach, describes strategies which involve fictions in science, and addresses the question of how fictions may be useful in a scientific framework, which directs attention to methodological issues and philosophy of science. The attention here is mainly devoted to models, idealisations and abstractions. Although the methodological version clearly inspired Kelsen, it might turn out that ontological fictionalism also exists in Kelsen's theory. And if this is not the case, such a hypothesis is still worth examining.

The problem with ontological fictionalism in philosophy can be derived from the problem of existence, especially when problematic cases are considered. Traditionally there are two approaches to the problem of existence and modes of inquiry into what reality is like: realism and idealism. Realism postulates the

[52] F Kroon, J McKeown-Green and S Brock, *A Critical Introduction to Fictionalism* (Bloomsbury Publishing, 2018) 101–20.

[53] M Eklund, 'Fictionalism' in EN Zalta (ed), *The Stanford Encyclopedia of Philosophy*, Winter 2019 (Metaphysics Research Lab, Stanford University, 2019).

[54] ibid.

existence of a reality independent from our mental life. Idealism raises some concerns for the realist account, indicating that some objects are mind-dependent and might undermine the reality of an existing object. For instance, redness is associated with the dispositions of our eyes, hence it is possible that some kind of object might come into existence by virtue of how we regard it. This leads to the problem of whether there is anything beyond our mind's construction. Furthermore, the inquiry concerning existence is especially problematic when the discussion concerns abstract objects, like the redness mentioned above; or fictional characters, for instance Robinson Crusoe; or objects of science not accessible to our senses, which occur, for instance, in quantum mechanics or string theory.

One way to tackle this problem is to avoid direct inquiries concerning existence, and here fictionalism offers some strategies, of which two are the most important: prefixing and prefacing.[55] These strategies stem from the conviction that some false claims can be acceptable for a particular purpose. Such acceptance is sometimes described as tentative. By avoiding the problem of existence, fictionalism allows concepts to be saved, and prevents debates about them, which otherwise might be problematic from an existential point of view. As such, fictionalism offers strategies for truth relegation.

Prefixing occurs to make the problem of existence less problematic in a certain domain. This approach is useful in the field of scientific inquiry. For instance, in the case of string theory their existence is less problematic if statements are prefixed with 'according to string theory, one-dimension strings exist'. Prefixing is also useful when dealing with literary works, if one claims for instance, that Robison Crusoe lived on a deserted island for several years. Obviously, such a person has never existed, hence true statements should not apply here. However, with prefixing: 'in one novel, *Robinson Crusoe*, there was Robinson Crusoe, who lived on a deserted island', such a statement can be considered true without giving rise to any controversy.[56]

The other way of dealing with objects that are problematic in terms of their existence is prefacing. In contrast to prefixing, prefacing does not assert anything, but starts with a phrase such as 'let's pretend that …', which Yablo calls: a 'make-believe or pretend game' and defines as 'the paradigm activities in which we "assent" to sentences with little or no regard to their truth-values'. As such they are 'true internal statements (that is, a statement endorsed by the rules), whose external truth value is as may be, the point being that that truth value is from an internal standpoint quite irrelevant'.[57] Hence, such conduct allows us to accept certain propositions without believing in them, and what is acceptable is decided by certain norms characteristic for a specific area. Furthermore,

[55] Kroon, McKeown-Green and Brock (n 52) 55–56.
[56] ibid 56–60.
[57] Yablo (n 44) 243–44.

some norms apply specifically to literature, while others apply to science. In this interpretation, one pretends that there was someone like Robinson Crusoe.[58] Another way prefacing can be carried out is referred to by Vaihinger as the 'As-If' procedure, and can also be named the 'for the sake of argument' strategy. The main challenge of this type of fictionalism is the explanation of what the preface is and what kind of standard of evaluation is used. One of the main attitudes in the scope of prefacing is pretence, or 'make believe' conduct.[59]

Prefixing and prefacing are descriptive and hermeneutic, since they are interpretive practices that identify a discourse's actual nature.[60] Such fictionalism uncovers the structural processes and norms hidden beneath the surface in its attempt to describe the way of thinking about problematic objects.[61] It is also a prescriptive (revolutionary) approach, if one believes that although we should not commit to the existence of a particular object, we should construe the relevant practice. While admitting that some claims are false, prescriptive fictionalism argues simultaneously that it is worthwhile to consider them. For instance, it can be argued that although moral claims are error-ridden and morality does not fall under true–false evaluation, morality should be sustained as a fiction, due to its beneficial impact (utility).

Three prominent fields in which fictionalism thrives are: mathematical fictionalism, which deals with the problem of numbers perceived as non-existent entities; modal fictionalism, which deals with the problem of possible worlds; and metaethical fictionalism, which deals with the problem of propositions concerning morality. A distinct category of fictionalism is fictionalism in science (methodological fictionalism), where Vaihinger's theory of 'As-If' has the strongest provenience, although currently it is treated as too broadly conceptualised. The latter fictionalism will be in the central scope of the inquiry concerning Kelsen; however, the problem of existence, for instance of the basic norm, also clearly requires consideration.

Hence, fictionalism is a powerful strategy which enables us to engage in certain valuable discourses which contain problematic categories, mainly from an existential point of view. Fictionalism does not offer a solution to the problem of existence; instead, it avoids it for the sake of a discourse. This way the discourse can continue to operate, instead of being stuck on issues that are less relevant to the discourse, which might potentially disturb it by dragging the discussion to another philosophical domain. There are, however, arguments against the fictional strategy.[62] I will mention only the objection which might be relevant for Kelsen.

[58] Kroon, McKeown-Green and Brock (n 52) 57.

[59] The make-believe game in the Yablo–Walton version is linked to metaphorical statements. See: KL Walton, *Mimesis as Make-Believe: On the Foundations of the Representational Arts* (Harvard University Press, 1990); S Yablo and A Gallois, 'Does Ontology Rest on a Mistake?' (1998) 72 *Proceedings of the Aristotelian Society, Supplementary Volumes* 229; Yablo (n 44).

[60] Eklund (n 53).

[61] Kroon, McKeown-Green and Brock (n 52) 61.

[62] All the objections are mentioned by Eklund (n 53).

It is objected that there is not much difference between the attitude advocated by fictionalism and belief. This objection has its rejoinder: As-If p behaviour is not always followed by a belief that p. Whether or not this is the case depends only on whether one believes p.[63] Yablo argues in the same manner when tackling Carnap's rejection of abstract entities as fictions, by considering them as some sort of a 'myth' or 'superstition'. As Yablo points out, with a close analysis of Carnap's terminology, myth is understood by him as 'a false (or dubious) internal statement'. At the same time, for Yablo a fiction (or myth) is 'a true internal statement' which may also be externally true.[64] In the case of the basic norm, one may observe that its assumption does not necessarily entail a belief in the actual existence of the basic norm. The purpose of this construct is solely to aid in comprehending the normative essence of law, which is already established, in contrast to the fundamental nature of the basic norm itself. Hence, what is given and undisputable, at least in the framework of Kelsen's theory, is the normative nature of law. The task of the basic norm lies in enabling us to understand the normative nature of law in terms of validity and cognition.

Overall, it seems that fictionalism undeniably enables an understanding of strategies taken in a particular discourse where a lack of literalness of some kind is involved, and it gathers all these strategies under one label. From Kelsen's point of view, the most significant version is a close cousin of ontological fictionalism – the methodological one that tackles the issue of fictions in science.

Hence, one more component is still missing before I determine the extent to which fictionalism can be applied to Kelsen's theory: methodological fictionalism, the closest type to Vaihinger's 'As-If'. While, given the functions which the basic norm fulfils, the problem of fictionalism connected with ontology might explain the status of the basic norm, which seems to fall under the strategy of prefacing, the account of fictions in science could offer a broader perspective on Kelsen's legal science project, especially the part of Vaihinger's theory which is connected with the problem of models. This asserts that we construct models of the world which enable us to gain a better understanding of certain phenomena. Hence, in the following section the theory of models in the framework of methodological fictionalism will be explored.

3.4. METHODOLOGICAL FICTIONALISM

Methodological fictionalism is associated with philosophy of science. It is described as a close cousin of the fictionalism described above. However, due to the specific domain in which fictions are identified, namely science, the framework in which this type of fictionalism exists is slightly different, although it

[63] G Rosen, 'Metaphysics as a Fiction' in B Armour-Garb and F Kroon (eds), *Fictionalism in Philosophy*, (Oxford University Press, 2020) 28–47.

[64] Yablo (n 44) 244.

employs the analogical categories of realism and anti-realism. Namely, two approaches to accepting scientific theories exist – realism and anti-realism. As Bas van Fraassen notes, according to realism 'Science aims to give us, in its theories, a literally true story of what the world is like; and acceptance of a scientific theory involves the belief that is it true'.[65] Hence, two elements determine realism thus understood: the truth ascribed to the theory; and the language requirement referring to literalness.

The alternatives to realism, which are grasped in the category of anti-realism, mainly question the claim that theories, in order to be scientific, must be 'literally true'. From this point of view, it suffices that the proposer '*displays it* [theory – MZ], and claims certain virtues for it'. Van Fraassen mentions the virtues of empirical adequacy, comprehensiveness and acceptability for various purposes.[66] As a result, two kinds of anti-realism emerge: one that does not require the literalness criterion to sustain the truth criterion, and one that sustains the literalness criterion without the truth criterion. It seems that methodological fictionalism must be at least an anti-realism of the latter kind.

It follows that the distinction between realism and anti-realism is based on the degree of acceptance of the theories. Realists accept theories on the basis of the truth criterion. The approach of anti-realists is different: it is more tolerant, due to its acceptance criteria for a scientific theory. As Van Fraassen aptly argues:

> I claim that the success of current scientific theories is no miracle. It is not even surprising to the scientific (Darwinist) mind. For any scientific theory is born into a life of fierce competition, a jungle red in tooth and claw. Only the successful theories survive – the ones which *in fact* latched on to actual regularities in nature.[67]

Hence, anti-realism tends to grant acceptance to theories which would be rejected in a realistic framework. Vaihinger's 'As-If' theory can be perceived as one of the first milestones towards a broader acceptance of such theories in science. As such, it deserves rehabilitation, since Vaihinger's philosophy of 'As-If' was not well regarded in the field of philosophy.[68]

Perhaps this is the reason why only the deconstructive component of the fictional basic norm was noted in the doctrine. This point is worth noting because the term 'fiction' has a negative and positive aspect. The negative aspect seems to be in the foreground, associated with the common intuition that if something is fictional, it is not valid. From this premise stems the false conclusion that something should be rejected if it is false. Such a conclusion is false because it does not consider the positive aspect of fiction.

[65] BC van Fraassen, *The Scientific Image* (Clarendon Press, 1980) 8.
[66] ibid 10.
[67] ibid 40.
[68] It is noteworthy that there were significant exceptions among scholars who took the concept of fictionalism seriously. For example, Izydora Dąmbska in 1962 observed that models, when comprehended as patterns, can indeed possess fictional attributes. *cf* I Dąmbska, *Dwa studia z teorii naukowego poznania* (Towarzystwo Naukowe w Toruniu, 1962) 22.

Indeed, fictions do not agree with reality, but some epistemic value is assigned to them, which prevents the rejection of fictional concepts. Only when the positive aspect of fictions is grasped can fictionalism be adequately understood. In the end, this is not a deconstructive project; on the contrary, it restores fictions to their proper place. Stating that something is fictional is good news for the concept in question because it means that no one can determine its epistemic value without awareness of its fictional parts, and this prevents the researcher from carrying out fruitless deliberations. From now on, thanks to the tools offered by fictionalism, the researcher is able to focus on the answers that fiction provides. It is in this spirit that Vaihinger's philosophy of 'As-If' should be interpreted, yet for many years this was not done.

Arthur Fine shed some light on the reasons why Vaihinger's theory was rejected in the field of philosophy and why it should be rehabilitated.[69] The main problem with Vaihinger's fictionalism, which is of particular relevance for the approach represented in this book, is that he extended the meaning of fiction too far. This approach could lead to the consequence that if the inquiry is not answered by recalling general principles, we are free to answer it as we please. Adopting such a nihilist stance was not Vaihinger's intention, since his fictionalism was resolutely opposed to nihilism.[70]

Furthermore, Vaihinger makes several mistakes of a rather technical nature. He draws too many inexhaustive and incomplete distinctions, takes the accounts of other scholars at face value, his individualistic concept of cognition turns out to be universal compared to what he allows in his theory, and his choice of fictions is sometimes questionable.[71] However, all these flaws do not mean that his ideas were not worth discussing, which is what logical positivism suggested, limiting its comments on Vaihinger primarily to mockery. It was not until the 1980s that fictionalism was reborn, with this school of thought somewhat hesitantly admitting its debt to Vaihinger, even though it is relatively easy to find common ground between fictionalism and Vaihinger's original theory. 'As-if' resembles the prefacing strategy, for instance.

Fine argues that the well-known critique of Vaihinger from the past should not bind present attitudes. Vaihinger offers a new approach to understanding science, which is critical and tolerant at the same time.[72] Vaihinger's legacy entails the need to adopt a more cautious approach to the universal projects of the philosophy of science and reduces the focus on language and meaning.

[69] Suárez notes that Fine's essay should not be read as a historical reconstruction, but rather as a commentary on a historical figure. The reconstruction of Fine's argument in this chapter will be conducted in this spirit (in Suárez (n 21) 4). Although one of the first defences of Vaihinger's fictionalism was probably presented by van Fraassen when he advocated for his anti-realist positions in his polemic with Hilary Putnam, it is Fine's article which is considered as a milestone in the rehabilitation of Vaihinger's fictionalism. For these polemics see: Fraassen (n 65) 34–37.

[70] Fine (n 15) 12–13.

[71] ibid 13.

[72] Fine (n 15) 15.

Instead, it shifts the emphasis to a non-theory-dominated orientation, in a pragmatic spirit. The pragmatic aspect means focusing on scientific practice concerning scientific theory.[73] Vaihinger revealed that we think constructively and that we adopt an imaginative approach to social and intellectual problems, often by employing metaphors and analogy. This leads to the vast role of imagination and play, which encompass most human activity realms in Vaihinger's project.[74]

The introduction of fiction to scientific theory seems to be counter-intuitive. After all, should science not reflect reality as closely as possible? In fact, this is not necessarily the case. As Fine concludes, scientists are engaged in treating something 'As-If' during most hours of their working day.[75] Science is full of idealisations, representations and approximations. They all have a fictional component and require imagination to create such conceptual and visual elements as 'genetic code', 'software', 'systems', 'chaos' and 'biological clock'. Catherine Elgin notes following a similar observation made by Vaihinger:

> Science is not, cannot be, and ought not be, a mirror of nature. Rather, science embodies an understanding of nature. Since understanding is not mirroring, failures of mirroring are not necessarily failures of understanding.[76]
>
> If science's aim is not to mirror reality but rather to understand specific phenomena, then this paves the way for the justification of fictions in science. In the meantime, new strategies, which are fictions in the Vaihingerian sense, are constantly being developed, such as computer simulations, game and decision theory, or modelling natural phenomena.[77]

Vaihinger did not provide an instant formula for such interpretations, and probably, there is no such thing. But thanks to his thought, our approach to models and other fictions in science can be more aware.[78] In the end, Vaihinger's observations on fictions seemed valuable, yet they were dismissed unjustly. Even though Vaihinger extended the meaning of fictions too far, there is no doubt that his theory can apply at least to some part of scientific inquiry.[79]

Fine's re-evaluation of Vaihinger's ideas introduced fresh avenues of exploration within the discourse surrounding the philosophy of science. Fine's article outlined a framework for adopting fictionalism in this context. His observation that Vaihinger's philosophy of 'As-If' raises awareness of the nature of such scientific practices as model buildings or simulations, gave an impulse to other scholars to develop this thought. The main inquiry concerning such fictions is focused on how they can contribute to scientific understanding.[80]

[73] ibid 15.
[74] ibid 15–16.
[75] ibid 16.
[76] C Elgin, 'Exemplification, Idealization, and Scientific Understanding' in Suarez (n 21) 77.
[77] Fine (n 15) 15.
[78] ibid 16.
[79] Kroon, McKeown-Green and Brock (n 52) 115.
[80] J Rouse, 'Laboratory Fictions' in Suárez (n 21) 37.

Suarez provides some answers as to how fictions can be used in science efficiently or – in Vaihingerian terms – expediently. As Suarez aptly puts it, the aim of fiction is to

> substitute the real process (with all its complications, disturbing factors, and exogenous causes) with a simpler, streamlined and coarser-grained fictional account (one where all the factors and causes are fully and carefully identified), which is more expedient in the practice of reasoning and inference making. We then go on to investigate the properties of the substitute rather than the real process.[81]

The successful outcome of this process requires the fulfilment of several conditions. Firstly, fiction enables expedient inferences to be made; secondly, at least some of the conclusions stemming from such inferences can be empirically verified. This second condition is characteristic of scientific inquiries.[82] In the social sciences or humanities, empirical verification might be problematic, but not impossible, if understood in some broad sense. In Kelsen's case this verification would be based on a specific legal or scientific practice in question. Finally, Suarez warns that during the process, many scientists lose the awareness of the fictional assumptions made.

There are at least two ways in which fictions in science can be identified.[83] Firstly, by appealing to the falsehood of a description, or inaccuracy in the case of models. Secondly, by focusing on the function of certain claims. This is the so-called functional account of fiction. In the latter case, whether the description has a truth value is irrelevant; the cognitive function is sustained regardless. Hence, in order to identify a fiction in science, one can employ two strategies. Either one finds a falsehood or inaccuracy, or by employing a fiction, one relinquishes concerns about truth value and truth conditions, and nevertheless, one acquires some understanding of certain phenomena. In Vaihinger's account, these two strategies went hand in hand. Also, in fictionalism, as described in the section above, the criteria of factuality and utility (along with quasi-fictionalism) were considered together to be essential features of fictionalism.[84]

In the case of falsehood (or inaccuracy) there is one substantial distinction between narrow and wide fictionalism.[85] Namely, an assumption (representation) may be *fictional*, when no such entity in reality exists, or *fictive*, when although such an entity exists, it is described inaccurately. While there is agreement in the doctrine that fictional representations are fictions, fictive representations are

[81] M Suárez, 'Scientific Fictions as Rules of Inference' in Suárez (n 21) 169.
[82] ibid 169.
[83] Suárez (n 21) 12.
[84] See: Kroon, McKeown-Green and Brock (n 52) 71–101. It seems that when referring to science, methodological fictionalism has a more liberal definition of fiction. The reason for this might stem from the strict criteria of science: by narrowing what can be considered to fall under the scientific method, it leaves more room for methods which at the first glance might not appear scientific, but their utility for science is nonetheless undeniable. This is the case with fictions.
[85] Suárez (n 21) 12–13.

more controversial. Some authors, such as Fine, Barberousse, Ludwig, Suarez and Ankeny, consider them fictions. In contrast, others, such as Morrisson, Winsberg, Teller and Giere, reject this idea and claim that these are cases of idealisation or abstraction. On the other hand, idealisation and abstraction, as well as most modelling practices, are considered by wide fictionalism as a type of a fiction.[86] These differences reflect the scientific realism of narrow fictionalism and the instrumentalism in epistemology of science in wide fictionalism.[87] For the purposes of this book, my starting point will be the position of wide fictionalism, but this standpoint will be critically assessed.

As Vaihinger noted, a falsehood is always acceptable in a specific context – here Teller uses the phrase 'for present interests'.[88] It means that a certain fiction can be justified with respect to a certain theory or a scientific activity for which it turns out to be useful. When a fiction is regarded in a broader context than those outlined above, it might turn out that such a fiction does not enable understanding. On the contrary, it provides misconceptions. As Teller notes: 'In every case a statement that counts as true enough, or as accurate enough, will be incomplete until we specify both the respects of interest and then a standard of deviation that must be met'.[89]

So far, these claims are made in a Vaihingerian spirit. However, not all elements of Vaihinger's theory were sustained in the contemporary account. According to some scholars, fictions in science, contrary to Vaihinger's conviction, do not express contradictions; they are not internally contradictory. Instead, their content might contradict something external: some standard theories in the field of physics, biology, psychology, or even metaphysics. What matters is that these standard theories must be understood and partially accepted when setting the stage for fictional account. In other words, as Barberousse and Ludwig aptly put it:

> A fiction is always grounded an at least some accepted conceptions about physics, biology, the behaviors of human beings etc, but may deviate from pure (historical) facts, and even, in some cases, from the very laws governing physics, biology, or human beings.[90]

Barberousse and Ludwig seem even to dismiss self-contradictory fictions, claiming that such fictions would not be able to provide useful information or understanding.[91] Although this sounds reasonable at first glance, Vaihinger's observations show otherwise: even self-contradictory fictions can enable understanding of the matter in question. On the other hand, it could be argued that they are not as informative as semi-fictions – but is this the case? These types of

[86] ibid 13–14.
[87] ibid 13.
[88] P Teller, 'Fictions, Fictionalization, and Truth in Science' in Suárez (n 21) 237.
[89] ibid.
[90] A Barberousse and P Ludwig, 'Models as Fictions' in Suárez (n 21) 59.
[91] ibid 59.

fictions 'do not agree with reality' (and 'reality' is defined here as 'pure (historical) facts'), or the 'laws governing physics, biology or human beings', which seems to be the crucial component for informativeness. However, self-contradictoriness might tell us something significant about reality by highlighting its absence. Thought experiments are a case in point – for example Schrodinger's cat, which is dead and alive at the same time.

This challenge posed by Barberousse and Ludwig is essential for the self-contradictory character of the basic norm. Even though it was the case that self-contradictory fictions enable understanding and are informative, it is still to be determined whether this is the case when analysing the basic norm. Barberousse and Ludwig hint at a solution which refers to the concept's meaning – in the case of a fiction this is changed from the standard one. Namely, such a fiction needs to be interpreted so that self-contradictoriness is removed. In the case of the basic norm, it would probably mean a departure from defining it in the same manner as any other typical norm, thus as the meaning of the act of will. Otherwise, self-contradictoriness occurs, as was argued in chapter two.

There are doubts, however, as to whether following this reasoning would be beneficial for Kelsen's theory, especially if one tries to interpret it in a fictional spirit. Hence, there are reasons for not accepting Barberousse and Ludwig's claim: not only can counter-examples be provided, but also such an assumption is incompatible with interpreting the basic norm as a fiction. For these reasons, and since in contemporary debates, the requirement of self-contradictoriness is not necessary for the definition of fiction, I will assume that a fiction occurs when the construct in question is contradictory externally (does not agree with reality) or both externally and internally (is self-contradictory). Fictionalism, thus understood, is relevant to Kelsen's account. Even though some elements constitutive of fictionalism changed, its function did not. The self-contradictoriness of the basic norm does not rule out the possibility of dealing with a fictional construct.

There are two main ways in which fictions occur in science. Firstly, scientists might include fictional assumptions in 'representations of real systems', or they might refer to 'fictitious entities or processes'.[92] It seems that in Kelsen's case, both situations occur. In chapter four I will argue that the purity of the theory of law contains a fictional component and can be regarded as a representation of a real system (*a model*). The hierarchical structure of law can be understood in terms of *a model* with a fictional component, which envisions the hierarchical structure of law in terms of a stairway or pyramid, while counter-examples can be provided. For instance, international law can hardly be envisioned as a stairway.[93]

[92] Suárez (n 81) 171.

[93] M Potacs, 'EU-Recht Und Staatlichen Recht Im Lichte Der Stufenbaulehre' in C Jabloner, Th Olechowski and J Kulik (eds), *Hans Kelsen in Der Tschechischenund Internationalen Rechtslehre*, Schriftenreiche Des Hans Kelsen Instituts 39 (Manz'sche Verlag und Universitaetsbuchhandlung, 2018) 191–201.

In the pure theory of law, fictional entities can also occur as processes. The basic norm or imputation is the main example of such an entity, illustrating the thought process of jurists. For instance, a possible point of discussion is whether imputation as analogical to causality is not a fictional entity. If causality is read in Hume's spirit, as some fiction, then analogically imputation – as a part of an interpretation schema which enables specific facts (a man in a robe talks) to be interpreted as legal (a judge issues a ruling – appears as a fiction which enables us to understand the nature of positive law. In the framework known from Hume's argument concerning causality, imputation would not be an a priori category innate in the human mind. It is rather a relation between facts, which humans employ in order to understand law.

For, as Kletzer convincingly argues, the pure theory of law is defined in terms of the authorisation to use force.[94] As such, imputation is a central part of the aristocratic *model* of law, as Kletzer calls it.[95] In this case, reality consists of facts which, with the help of specific cognitive tools, are interpreted in a way that grants them new meaning. In the case of law, the basic norm grants the attributes of normativity and validity, while imputation requires that law be understood as an authorisation to use force. In order to further understand the underlying mechanism of these fictions, it will be worthwhile to present the main scientific category in which fictional components might occur. In this context, the main category is that of a *model*.

3.5. SCIENTIFIC MODELS

The main problem associated with the fictions used in science is focused on models. Teller, for instance, notes that 'It is now widely recognized that most, if not all, of the representations of the real world that science provides come in the form of models'.[96] The variety of models is overwhelming, and this causes difficulty in constructing a universal theory of models which would be true for all of them.[97] For this reason, this section will attempt to grasp the standard features of the model as a fictional or fictive entity, focusing on what would be relevant for social science, especially in Kelsen's case.

Teller notes that a model is 'an object, concrete or abstract, that bears some relevant similarity to what we want to represent'.[98] Similarity does not constitute representation; it appears in a statement about the relation between the

[94] Ch Kletzer, *The Idea of a Pure Theory of Law: An Interpretation and Defence* (Hart Publishing, 2018).

[95] ibid 34.

[96] Teller (n 88) 238.

[97] Barberousse and Ludwig (n 90) 56.

[98] Teller (n 88) 238.

object and a representational target. In other words, we treat these similarities as representational.[99]

A notable distinction of models is introduced by Izydora Dąmbska. She observes that models can be perceived as either patterns or mappings. Some models function as mappings of specific objects. For instance, the Eiffel Tower model serves as a mapping of the Eiffel Tower itself. On the other hand, models often take on the form of patterns. For instance, figures like St Francis, who exemplify specific moral behaviour, exhibit distinct behavioural patterns, which, according to Dąmbska, can be considered models. Such objects exemplify some intrinsic value which is worthwhile to follow.[100] In contrast to the first type, which relates to mapping, in their case, being a model is contingent upon a relative criterion based on some value judgement. As such, in most cases, it incorporates a normative component.

Both functions – mapping and serving as a pattern for something – can be concurrently fulfilled.[101] Kelsen's endeavour is a good example of this. Constructing legal science primarily involves mapping activities and their objective character. However, the normative component becomes apparent when Kelsen asserts that legal science can only be constructed in one specific manner, namely, by purifying the law of alien elements. A similar situation occurs when in *Pure Theory of Law* Kelsen requires the law to be in the hierarchical structure of Stufenbau, Consequently, it has the potential to disqualify systems where only the will of the lawmaker is paramount, as opposed to systems characterised by a normative structure with the constitution occupying the highest position. Therefore, Kelsen initially formulates a particular model of law and subsequently asserts that this represents the superior model of law.

Fictionalism explores and adjusts the example of a map for its own use, probably inspired by the famous example of an Eurasian railroad network map presented by Carnap.[102] I will provide here my own simplified example. Imagine a map of Vienna. This map contains details allowing one to orient oneself in the city, find Hofburg and determine how to get to Stadtpark. One knows from this map where Donaukanal is and that the Danube River is divided by Donau Insel. The map gives us a good idea about Vienna; however, it does not convey the city's complexity, atmosphere and beauty. It allows us to orientate ourselves in the city, but even when studied in the smallest detail, the map is insufficient to say, 'I know Vienna really well'. Such a map can be regarded as a model of a much more complex reality. The model should be distinguished from direct representation, which contains no fictive or fictional components. They can be evaluated as true or false, and ought to provide faithful information on what

[99] ibid.
[100] Dąmbska (n 68) 22.
[101] ibid.
[102] R Carnap, *Der Logische Aufbau Der Welt* (Ohlenrothsche Buchdruckerei Erfurt, 1928) 17.

they represent, for instance, a report from an accident.[103] Fictions, however, do not fulfil such a condition.[104]

Although scientific models are diverse, they share several properties. Firstly, like most fictions, they are representations, and secondly, they possess intentional content. Being a representation means standing for something else. For instance, pictures or linguistic descriptions represent their subjects; a diagram represents data. As Elgin explains, 'Pictures, equations, graphs, and maps represent their subjects by denoting them. They are representations of the things they denote'. Hence, representation provides epistemic access to features of certain objects which are otherwise not apparent.[105]

For the purposes of this analysis, I will focus on linguistic representation. In these cases, the intentional content possessed by models is understood broadly as the language and words which express a particular concept, along with the context in which they are used, especially facts which determine the conventions for such language use. Despite not being accurate about reality, fictions convey intentional content.[106]

In models, two aspects are to be distinguished. Firstly, they have usable content, which has the power to obtain new scientific knowledge, and secondly, they have an aspect of falseness and do not represent the object truthfully.[107] These aspects constitute their fictionality and, at the same time, provide a framework which enables the evaluation of a model. Namely, each model should be examined regarding its utility and fictional component. The relation of these two aspects to each other should answer whether a particular model is successfully associated with the adequacy issue.

Elgin notes that whether the model fits its target is a matter of degree. It can fit well, its accuracy can be limited, or it might not fit at all. Optimally, a model should fit well to its target, but it might suffice if it is just true enough. In the latter case, the model might depart, with its features, from its target because it was supposed to be an approximation or because its relegation of truth concerns irrelevant factors, but, in any case, the representation is true enough for a specific purpose.[108] In any case, the function of the model is to highlight some aspect of the phenomenon in question; by doing this, it contributes to understanding such a phenomenon (target). This means there might be more than one model of the

[103] The question is how to distinguish, in practice, fictions from direct representations, for the line between them seems to be thin. Firstly, it is already established that 'a representation that involves inaccuracies' is a fiction. But the question remains – what type of inaccuracies would qualify as fictions? Does the omission of a date in a report on the accident mean that this representation is a fiction? The answer is no, it just would not be the most successful direct representation made, because their purpose is to provide the most faithful information that is possible (Barberousse and Ludwig (n 90) 57). As was mentioned before, I assume the wide meaning of 'fictions'.

[104] ibid.

[105] Elgin (n 76) 77, 80.

[106] Barberousse and Ludwig (n 90) 60.

[107] ibid 56.

[108] Elgin (n 76) 84.

same target. All of them would be correct, just manifesting different features of the target. As Elgin notes:

> The models afford different perspectives on the same reality. And it is no surprise that different perspectives reveal different aspects of that reality. There is no perfect model for the same reason that there is no perfect perspective. Every perspective, in revealing some things, inevitably obscures others.[109]

The fact that models reflect only a particular aspect of reality leaves a field open for interpretation. For this reason, models enable understanding[110] rather than being in the mode of scientific explanation. I will explain the difference between these two modes in the final section of this chapter.

Models have an epistemic function and are believed to rely less on imagination than typical fictions due to scientific requirements. As Morrison notes, a model assumes the existence of a relationship between the real world and the world described by the model. As she puts it, the model makes 'some realistic claim about the world'.[111] The means used to achieve this are metaphors (eg Stufenbau, the basic norm), analogies (imputation), and – according to some – idealisations and abstractions. The map is a *fictive* representation of a real entity, (so are a model of an atom, or the normative concept of law). Still, there are also representations of fictional entities[112] (for instance, Maxwell's model of the ether, or in some cases Kelsen's imputation as a model of interpretation when the usage of force is authorised).

In such cases, as Barberousse and Ludwig note, 'models represent *fictional* situations, namely, situations that are not, and cannot (for all we know) be, instantiated in our world'.[113] Hence, there are models which contain a fictional component, often presented in the form of metaphor or analogy, and those which do not contain a fictional component but are fictive representations in the form of abstractions or idealizations, which will be described in section 4.5. The latter is a fiction in the broad sense mentioned in the previous section.

In most cases, the inaccuracy of a model stems from the strategy of idealisation or abstraction. Idealisation is a 'process where one starts with a concrete object and then mentally rearranges some of its (inconvenient) properties'.[114] Such a clear and conscious departure from real situations means omitting irrelevant problems. On the other hand, abstractions 'subtract features in order to focus on a single set of properties or laws as if they were considered in isolation'.[115]

[109] ibid 87.
[110] ibid 89.
[111] M Morrison, 'Fictions, Representations, and Reality' in Suárez (n 21) 113.
[112] Suárez (n 81) 159.
[113] Barberousse and Ludwig (n 90) 56.
[114] Morrison (n 111) 127.
[115] ibid 128.

Suarez notes that idealisations correspond with the concept of Vaihinger's semi-fictions – they are empirically false, but not self-contradictory.[116]

In the case of social science and Kelsen's theory, the imaginative aspect is extended and reflected in the metaphors used. What matters here is a particular type of representation: representation as in which x represents y as z.[117] Elgin explains that 'The model is representation – a denoting symbol that has an ostensible subject and portrays its ostensible subject in such a way that certain features are exemplified. It represents its target as exhibiting those features'.[118] Caricature is a typical example of representation, for instance, a bulldog represents Churchill as certain type of politician, or, in Kelsen's case, the metaphor of a stairway (Stufenbau) represents the structure of law as hierarchical.

Next, Elgin adds

> in being z-representation, x exemplifies certain properties and imputes those properties or related ones to y. The properties exemplified in the z-representation serve as a bridge that connects x to y. This enables x to provide an orientation to its target that affords epistemic access to the properties in question … Then the fiction of the model is to make those features manifest and display their significance. We may see the target system in a new and fruitful way by focusing on the features that the model draws attention to.[119]

Some perceive the relation between the fictional and the real as the relation between abstract and concrete (or less abstract). In this case, an abstract fictional entity enables us to understand a more concrete target.[120]

In Kelsen's case, such a bridge would be 'built' on the property of the hierarchical structure through a stairway metaphor. Such a metaphor, which serves as a model of the hierarchical structure of law, is a counterpart of some tangible objects which are models in an empirical science. Imagine the model of an atom made from plastic. The model of the hierarchical structure of law or another abstract, non-observable entity requires a different means than plastic to envision this structure, and metaphor seems to be one of them.

Such metaphors should be distinguished from Lakoff and Johnson's conceptual metaphors. While the former are created consciously and with precision by the scientist in order to *provide* an understanding of a particular abstract phenomenon or one of its aspects, conceptual metaphors exist independently and *determine* the understanding of a target domain (some abstract entity).[121] It is possible to construct a model based on a counter-intuitive metaphor. At the same time, it is hard to imagine a counter-intuitive conceptual metaphor, because a conceptual metaphor corresponds with basic intuitions – this is how one is able to trace it back.

[116] Suárez (n 81) 158.
[117] Elgin (n 76) 77.
[118] ibid 84.
[119] ibid.
[120] Morrison (n 111) 113.
[121] G Lakoff and M Johnson, *Metaphors We Live By*, 2nd edn (University of Chicago Press, 2003).

Models thus understood are regarded by some as fictions, but this issue is far from being settled in the doctrine. Hence, it is worthwhile to consider the discussion concerning the fictional character of models and in the context of the pure theory of law. Such an analysis will enable us to draw the line for fictionalism, and prevent us from falling into the trap not avoided by Vaihinger, who, as we have seen, saw fictions everywhere.

The strategy of scholars who claim that all models are fictions is simple. They consider fictions in the broad sense, including in this category idealisation and abstraction. The fact that idealisation and abstraction are associated with inadequacy in reflecting reality suffices to count idealisation and abstraction as fictions.

The argumentation of another camp is more complex. Giere, for instance, denies models the attribute of fiction. He rejects the approach in which one assumes common essential and intrinsic properties for models and works of fiction, arguing that the variety of both kinds rules out distinguishing properties. For this reason, Giere turns his argument from the theoretical to the normative sphere, posing the question of whether scientific models *should* be regarded as fictions.[122] It can be derived from Giere's argumentation that one can find models which are fictions due to their having some common essential intrinsic properties, although there are reasons for not treating models as such. One might make a rejoinder here that in some other cases there might be reasons to treat models as fictions. This approach has interesting implications for treating something as a fiction or not, depending on the utility of approach chosen. This is an honest answer to the problem and is commonly used when using a phrase such as 'for the sake of argument'.

In this cautious framework, the strategy offered by Giere is interesting and is based on the claim that ontologically, the statuses of models and fictions are alike, but in terms of functionality, they are different. As he notes: 'It is their different functions in practice that makes it inappropriate to regard scientific models as works of fiction'.[123] For Giere, the claim that models and fictions have the same ontological status means that both categories are products of human imagination facilitated by language.[124] However, Giere argues, that the imaginary objects of fiction and imaginary objects as models do not function in the same way. The problem with his argumentation is that he compares scientific models with works of fiction as they are known from literature. For instance, Giere explains:

> One indication of this difference is that although works of fiction are typically a product of a collective effort. Scientists share preliminary descriptions of their

[122] R Giere, 'Why Scientific Models Should Not Be Regarded as Works of Fiction' in Suárez (n 21) 248. On the other hand, in the same manner Giere argues that all fictions should be regarded as models, which means that he believes that fictions should be treated as some special kind of model.
[123] ibid 254.
[124] ibid 249.

> models with colleagues near and far, and this sharing often leads to smaller or larger changes in the description. The descriptions, then, are from the beginning intended to be public objects. Of course, authors of fiction may share their manuscripts with family and colleagues, but this is not part of the ethos of producing fiction.[125]

It seems that Giere identifies fiction with the most common meaning of this word – as a literary work of fiction – and excludes any other examples of fictions from the domain of science. If this is the case and he claims that scientific models function differently than works of fiction in literature, then this thesis is not particularly controversial, but it does not solve the problem of why scientific models are not fictions despite not being accurate in reflecting reality. His argument could potentially solve this issue if, instead of the example of works of fiction, Giere provided an example from the domain of science and explained how in this domain the fictional and fictive differ functionally. Giere's argument seems to confuse the concept of fiction in literature with the concept of fiction in science. As a result he disregards the fact that fictional elements in science – fictions in science, in the narrow sense – are functionally different from the works of fiction he writes about.

Giere seems to object, on a semantic level, to the fact that this specific conduct in science which deviates from reality is dubbed 'fictional'. He might be right to some extent; this term might indeed be confusing, but even if he is correct, this does not confirm that scientific models are not fictions in the meaning used in the philosophy of science, which is determined by deviation from reality and utility for scientific purposes. Such an approach disregards the fact that this word provides a good description of some scientific practices and has strong explanatory power for solving the problem of why something false or inaccurate can contribute to the development of a particular scientific field. 'Fiction' is understood here in the special context of philosophy of science and in this context is justified.

There is one more problem with Giere's argument. Not only does he argue against using the word 'fiction'; he explains why scientific models should not be treated as fictions. In the first case, one admits that such a phenomenon as inaccuracy or falsehood, which is useful in scientific models actually exists, and further debates concern the issue of whether and how to change the name of this phenomenon. Giere's claim seems to be different. His argument can be interpreted as attempting to demonstrate why such phenomena should be disregarded even if they existed. In the best-case scenario, Giere demonstrated the former but not the latter.

Giere's subsequent strategy focuses on three cases. Firstly, he claims that idealisations and abstractions are not fictions; secondly, fictional elements within a model do not make the model as a whole fictional; and thirdly, there are

[125] ibid 251.

fictional models (such as the model of the ether), but their function is heuristic rather than representational.[126]

These arguments are interesting but they lack profound justification. Why are idealisations not fictions, even though they are inaccurate? Or perhaps it is a matter of degree? Why does a fictional component existing within a model not determine the fictionality of the whole model? Or perhaps it is a matter of a case? These are valid inquiries, which might build a case against models regarded as fictions, but unfortunately, the bare thesis is left without justification.

Finally, Giere seems to be correct with his objection that 'if idealization and the resulting lack of perfect fit imply that models should be regarded as fictions, most of what everyone thinks and says should be regarded as fictional'. But what if this is the case, and what everyone thinks and says is actually to some extent fictional? For instance, perhaps, implications can be regarded as kinds of fictions without which communication would not be possible? Hence, so far, the question of whether idealisations and abstractions – scientifically adequate representations of real systems – are the phenomena referred to in philosophy of science as 'fictions' remains unanswered.

Further clarity is provided by Teller, who discusses the problem of inadequacy. His strategy is to indicate that the concept of truth encompasses cases which he dubs 'true enough' and draws a line between fictions and veridical representations. He notes that most statements uttered are more 'true enough' than true. For instance, if one says that the circumference of the Earth is 40,000 kilometres, such a statement, being strictly speaking false, is true enough for the present purposes.

Teller argues that in many cases, the only way to speak meaningfully is to accept true enough statements, for total accuracy might not be obtained. For instance, the earth's circumference is constantly shifting.[127] For this reason, Teller claims that 'we need substantially to rethink how we think about truth'.[128] What matters for a statement to be accepted as true (enough), is a specification of interests and a standard of deviation. Hence, the statement is true enough in the relative sense.[129]

Teller describes representations which fulfil these conditions as veridical, and he does not regard them as fictions, because, as he claims, 'Complete precision and accuracy are not required to count as nonfictional'.[130] On the other hand, as he notes, there are representations which can be regarded as fictional; for instance, an extended object is described as a point particle. Hence, it is a matter of degree whether a true enough representation is fictional and when it

[126] ibid 253.
[127] Teller (n 88) 236–37.
[128] ibid 236.
[129] ibid 237.
[130] ibid.

is not. Teller's reasoning seems to be compelling, but it might be argued that fictions explain why the statements which are merely true enough are considered true.

There is another claim that Teller aims to defend thanks to his distinction between fictional and veridical. Namely, a fiction embedded in a more extensive representation does not make the more significant representation fictional. This argument was also raised by Giere, but Teller elaborates and justifies this claim. Teller distinguishes two meanings of idealisation, leading to a misunderstanding about fiction.[131] Various strategies for building models exist, and a prominent category among them is idealising strategies, which are part of a model. Such idealisations Teller calls component idealisations.[132] Accordingly, they are component fictions which 'radically misrepresent but that nonetheless, facilitate the accurate representational function of other aspects of the model'.[133] These models are often based on idealising simplifications, which distort 'only things that, for the context in question, are relatively unimportant, but that otherwise preserve accuracy, at least sufficient for present purposes'.[134] For instance, Newton's law applies to point particle idealisation, which represents an irregularly shaped body.

On the other hand, there is a tendency to describe models as idealisations because such models contain a component idealisation. In such cases, containing idealisation takes place.[135] Analogically to component idealisations, there is a misleading tendency to consider these containing idealisations, which tend to be models, as fictions. Teller argues that models are not just useful fictions that contradict facts – they are veridical. Teller sums up: 'successful models are not themselves fictional because they use fictional elements'.[136] Obviously, he adds, models which are fictions, such as thought experiments, exist.

What Teller seems to oppose is the qualification of all models as fictions. Most of them are not. This brings us back to the division between fictionalism *sensu stricto* and *sensu largo*. Teller rejects fictionalism *sensu largo*, which considers idealisations and abstractions as fictions. He opposes considering such models as fictions, for they are veridical, and if veridical, therefore not fictional. However, as was mentioned before, moving the category of veridical into the extended concept of truth does not explain how the inclusion of non-existent elements turned out to be in tune with the concept of truth. However, fictionalism which distinguishes fictions from mistakes does explain this. Hence it seems that being veridical and being a fiction might be two different modes of a model. While veridical can be considered a property, fiction

[131] ibid 240.
[132] ibid.
[133] ibid 243.
[134] ibid.
[135] ibid 240.
[136] ibid 244.

might be considered a strategy or a process that turns something that does not agree with reality into something that contains the property of being veridical. Nevertheless, there is another difficulty with this approach. Namely, a part of some larger whole might determine the nature of the whole, but not necessarily.

Addressing the primary concern regarding the fictional character of the basic norm – namely that it leads to law having a fictional character – it can be argued that even though the pure theory of law contains the fiction of the self-contradictory basic norm, it is not itself considered as a fiction. Neither is law or its validity in the framework of the pure theory of law. Hence, even if ontological idealizations such as the pure theory of law share the ontological qualities of fiction (both are imaginary constructs facilitated by language), they differ functionally.[137] Hence, the pure theory of law is not fictional, because it is veridical, but the strategies which lead to veridicality are based on fictions. Both fictional and fictive elements are introduced to the pure theory of law. As a whole, they might offer a successful model of law.

There is another reason why one should follow Teller's lead and not treat a model which contains a fictive component as a fiction. Extensive usage of the fiction category could deprive fictionalism of its explanatory power. Vaihinger is accused of seeing fictions everywhere and this is considered a weakness of his theory and the weakness of subsequent fictionalism.

For this pragmatic reason, I am somewhat in the camp which finds it necessary to impose some limitations on fictions and models, and I see such a necessity here, in the case of the pure theory of law,[138] where to retain the explanatory power of fiction, the narrower meaning of fiction is required. I take, however, a different approach, despite making use of Teller's distinctions.

For this analysis, I will distinguish a theory (instead of a model) as not fictional (because of its veridical character) from its fictional or veridical components, such as component models or the fictional strategies of prefixing and prefacing. I will also distinguish between fictional and fictive elements. The pure theory of law in such a framework contains several models and fictions and links them meaningfully and consistently. At the same time, following Giere's distinction between the ontological and functional aspect of fictions, I will assume that even though the pure theory of law can ontologically be considered as a fiction, functionally it is not. This assumption stems from the difference, already mentioned, between the process of generalisation and its potential fictive factor, and the fictionality of the objects of events

[137] Giere (n 122) 248.

[138] Giere points out important considerations; mainly, the label 'fiction' in the era of anti-scientific movements is rather unfortunate. Misunderstood can cause a great deal of harm (Giere (n 122) 257). Even if the 'fiction' label was not used by eg anti-vaxxers to prove that science which lay behind the vaccines is a 'mere fiction' it can still cause the misinterpretation of certain theories.

(eg in thought experiments) which do not have their counterpart in realty. While we can compare Kelsen's pure theory of law with the Austrian legal system, there is no way to do the same with the basic norm, or imputation. What is common for the two latter categories is that both serve one purpose: understanding.

So far, I have argued that fictional framework introduced by the basic norm can be defended in GTN. Now it is time to apply this framework to Kelsen's main methodological assumption: the purity of legal science.

4

Fictionalism, Understanding and the Purity Assumption in the General Theory of Norms

SINCE KELSEN'S THEORY concerns an abstract entity, namely law, it might be full of fictional and fictive components; however, the paramount concern is whether fictionalism can provide a solution for the pure theory of law in its final version. As was demonstrated in chapter three, the basic norm read in the spirit of fictionalism was coherent. I also argued that in such a framework the fictional basic norm is rather the tip of an iceberg, the most visible symptom of a larger fictional framework.

In this chapter I elaborate on this argument, starting from the most general framework addressing whether the pure theory of law can be regarded as a fiction. Then I provide an interpretation of Kelsen's purity of theory law in terms of fictionalism and argue that this framework sustains the purity of Kelsen's theory in its final phase. Finally, I argue that fictionalism indicates that the hermeneutical trend in the GTN is much stronger than previously was the case.

4.1. THE PURITY OF LEGAL SCIENCE AND THE FICTIONAL FRAMEWORK

The description of models seems to match some elements of Kelsen's pure theory of law, particularly his notion of the 'purity' of legal science. A theory of law is pure if it is separated from any alien elements. Hence, Kelsen performs two such separations: the separation of Is from Ought; and the separation of law from morality. In this vision, law is isolated and hence can be examined in its pure form. My claim is that this is an artificial procedure. Law is not separated from our reality and all its dimensions.

My references to 'reality' do not speak of any concept steeped in philosophical contemplation. Such a concept, which constitutes the subject of one of philosophy's most profound inquiries, would necessitate the entanglement of numerous debatable presuppositions. Regrettably, this complexity would not contribute to the clarity of my argument. Moreover, it appears that my approach finds applicability particularly within the realm of fictionalism, as its purpose is to circumvent such intricate investigations in order to propel the exploration of the central inquiry forward. At this juncture, I construe reality as that which is encountered by each individual on a day-to-day basis, particularly in its societal dimension.

We live in a large social melting pot, where different perspectives are blended into one whole, which affects us in an invisible way, all the time. We walk and stop because of a red light, and we go to the market to buy apples. We pay for them, not only because this is a legal requirement, but mostly because we believe that this is the right thing to do. At least most of us do. Whenever such acts are performed – and they are performed all the time – there are different stories to tell, depending on who tells them, be it an economist, a sociologist, a lawyer or an ethicist. Despite being different in character, these stories concern the same reality, the same event. What makes a difference is its interpretation, and an interpretation from a legal standpoint is one of them. Hence, claiming that law is separated from these other phenomena is counterfactual, because law is a large part of our social reality; moreover, law only makes sense in social reality. In the context of this study, I will describe such an understanding of reality as 'a child's perspective'.

On the other hand, Kelsen is not wrong when he notes that Ought is separated from Is. Law is not a fact; it is a system of norms. Norms and facts are different modes; in Kelsen's view, they are not reducible one to another. Hence, the claim that law is separated from facts must be understood properly. The question is whether such a separation involves some sort of fiction.

Moreover, Kelsen has important reasons to separate law from morality. On the one hand, legal positivists had a point in treating law as separated from morality, and Hart articulated this aptly in his well-known article 'Positivism and the Separation of Law and Morals'.[1] On the other hand, it is not easy to dismiss Radbruch's formula or contemporary debates on whether law is only grounded in facts, as the legal positivists would have it, or whether such determination also involves some kind of moral component.[2] Certainly, there are relations between law and morality. Again, there is a clear distinction between them, and it can be convincingly argued that one concept cannot be reduced to the other. Hence, this section aims to investigate whether we are dealing with a fiction here, and, if so, of what kind; I argue that these separations can be understood in the framework characteristic for scientific models. For this reason, I first discuss the Is–Ought separation as a model, then move to the separation between law and morality, indicating in which ways and aspects these models work. Finally, I discuss the possibility that there is a fictional component that concerns the purity of legal science, rather than the separations themselves.[3]

[1] HLA Hart, 'Positivism and the Separation of Law and Morals' (1958) 71 *Harvard Law Journal* 593.

[2] See eg: M Greenberg, 'How Facts Make Law' (2004) 10 *Legal Theory* 225, doi.org/10.1017/S1352325204040212.

[3] I would like to thank Carsten Heidemann for our discussions on this matter, which enabled me to clarify this problem.

4.2. THE SEPARATION OF IS AND OUGHT AND THE FICTIONAL FRAMEWORK

As it was noted in chapter two, the Is–Ought separation is not radical. It is rather dependent on the answer to the questions concerning how the Ought is separated from the Is, and what connections are between Is and Ought. In this section, I address the first question, while in the following chapters I explore the possibility of any links between Is and Ought and their potential character.

In order to address the first inquiry, one must start from the more general question of what Kelsen intended by insisting on such a separation. Hence, the first question to be addressed is why Kelsen needed the separation of Is and Ought. The answer is rather well-known: Kelsen was convinced that the foundation of legal science is its purity. Law can be cognised as it is only if it is purified from any alien elements. For this reason, he introduced two kinds of separation which are typical for legal positivism – the separation of law from morals, and his original idea – the separation of Is and Ought. Hence, both separations serve a purpose and should be regarded in this context.

Kelsen's observation that there is a difference between a norm and a fact, ie that normativity cannot be reduced to facts, seems correct. Hume's guillotine guarantees that the Ought is a category distinct from any Is. On the other hand, there is a good reason why many legal positivists consider law a social fact. As was mentioned before, law is in a melting pot with other social facts, which constitute the social layer of the reality we live in, and law can be examined as 'one of such' social phenomena. The key point here is that Kelsen's project was different, however: he aimed to examine law 'as such' rather than 'as something else'.

Such a procedure has a great advantage over any alternative approaches. If norms are in a big social melting pot, yet distinct at the same time, then, to cognise them, they must be separated from other phenomena in the melting pot and examined carefully in the next step. Finally, when law has been isolated and examined, it can be integrated into the social melting pot and re-examined as a social phenomenon. If one examines law as a distinct system first, one avoids the danger of confusing one phenomenon with another, which ultimately facilitates the understanding of social interactions as a whole.

Kelsen's strategy can be compared to work done in a laboratory. Kelsen acts in the same manner as a scientist who examines bacteria under a microscope, and who needs to isolate them from their natural environment (for instance, water from a river) in order to obtain a pure sample. Both an empirical scientist and Kelsen want to cognise the object's structure, and for this reason, they need to isolate it, either by the physical operation of creating a sample or by the mental operation of separating law from facts (and law from morality).

For example, imagine a microbiologist. In order to learn about certain bacteria, she isolates them from their natural environment and then observes their structure and variations under a microscope in the laboratory. She makes sure that the sample she observes is pure. Now she can acquire an adequate and pure model of the bacteria. All of this happens in the framework of the laboratory, which creates artificial (fictional) conditions. This analogy goes further. In the next step, she restores the bacteria to their natural environment; being aware of their distinct features, she can better understand their interactions with the environment. The isolation of the bacteria from their natural environment contains a fiction: the microbiologist, in order to cognise the bacteria 'as such', acts as if they existed outside their natural environment, while the opposite is the case. Bacteria can only exist while interacting with a specific environment. However, bacteria cannot be properly described as long as they interact with their natural environment.

The same can be said about the law. A law outside social reality does not make any sense. Only if there are social interactions can the existence of law, which is about social interactions, be justified. Law has distinct features in this social reality, compared to other social facts. Precisely for this reason – that one cannot derive Ought from Is – the law needs to be separated 'in the laboratory' from Is in order to examine its normativity, ie its distinctive features. This brings us to the question of whether Kelsen's procedure is comparable to the so-called 'laboratory fiction' described by Rouse.[4]

Apart from idealised models, the most canonical cases of fictions in science are simulations, thought experiments, counterfactual reasoning and laboratory fictions, which Rouse defines in terms of experimental systems. Laboratory fictions are 'microworlds', which as

> systems of objects construed under known circumstances and isolated from other influences so that they can be manipulated and kept track of, … [allow scientists to] circumvent the complexity [with which the world more typically confronts us] by constructing artificially simplified worlds.[5]

Rouse argues that such fictions vary: they can be pictorial, verbal or mathematical representations of the world and are distinct from physical models. Such microworlds are characterised as 'novel and reproducible arrangements of some aspect of the world'.[6] The isolation of relevant interactions separates them from confounding influences. It rests on the assumption that the feature in question is already out there in the world waiting for its revelation. Such an approach enables us to find concepts that can describe or help us understand the world adequately, in contrast to the application of traditional well-known ideas. This, in turn, extends the understanding of the phenomenon in question.[7] Rouse sums up: 'the creation of laboratory microworlds is often indispensable to opening

[4] J Rouse, 'Laboratory Fictions' in M Suárez (ed), *Fictions in Science: Philosophical Essays on Modeling and Idealization* (Routledge, 2010) 38.
[5] ibid.
[6] ibid.
[7] ibid 41–42.

domains in which scientific research can proceed to articulate and understand circumscribed aspects of the world'.[8]

So far, so good: at first glance, the fiction of a laboratory fits very well with Kelsen's approach. In the pure theory of law we can find the element of isolation, which separates it from confounding influences in order to reveal the feature in question. Also, the idea of microworlds resonates well with what Kelsen constructed. After all, his idea of the Ought can be perceived as an artificially created microworld. In this manner, the Ought would be separated from the confounding influences of Is facts, in order to reveal aspects of normativity in an evident way.

However, Rouse regards laboratory fiction in terms of an experiment. Typically, experiments belong rather to a context of justification than to one of discovery, and he regards the laboratory fiction in terms of experimental systems, when he notes that 'experimental systems are novel rearrangements of the world that allow some aspects that are not originally manifest and intelligible to *show* themselves clearly and evidently'.[9] If the laboratory fiction is necessarily associated with experimenting, this perspective is absent from Kelsen's theory, unless one considers the separation between Is and Ought as a thought experiment. Such an interpretation, however, would depart too far from Kelsen's original intention by attributing to him the performance of a thought experiment in which he pretended that the Ought is separated from any Is element.

Hence, the possibility that Kelsen performed a thought experiment here must be ruled out. Rather, Kelsen was aware of two premises: (1) law is a normative phenomenon distinct from facts; and (2) law exists in social reality among social facts and is often mistakenly taken as such. These premises led him to the conclusion that, for legal science, we should act 'as if' law was separated from social facts and disregard the latter while constructing the pure theory of law. An experiment understood as a procedure which aims at discovering something unknown or testing a hypothesis does not fit with what Kelsen did. For this reason, the qualification of the fictions he uses as thought experiments is not feasible, and hence his methodological assumptions do not match the laboratory fiction constructed by Rouse. Only the first step, concerning isolating certain phenomena from external conditions, fits well with Kelsen's conduct. I believe this is enough to apply the laboratory fiction to Kelsen's project, particularly his separation of Is and Ought, because the fictional component lies in the act of isolation, not in the procedures which are later performed under 'sterile' conditions. Rouse focused on experiments, but they are not the only activities performed in a laboratory; one can also observe and discover.

One more question needs to be addressed: how to describe the law as separated from facts. In the first step, it has to be observed that as an outcome of

[8] ibid 43.
[9] ibid 41.

purity, some sort of model of law is obtained. Next, it must be noted that each model is representative of something. In this case, the law separated from facts is a representation of law normally blended with other social phenomena. The next step is determining whether we are dealing with a fictional or a fictive component here. As was mentioned before, a fictional component of a model contradicts reality, because no such entity exists. A fictive component concerns the inaccuracy of a model.

At first glance, the separation of Is and Ought does not imply any fictional entities. Still, it is rather a matter of inaccuracy, by abstracting from the fact that law could not meaningfully exist without its social context. However, this separation demands artificial conditions which do not exist in reality. Hence, Rouse was correct in regarding the laboratory as a fiction. The fictional component with regard to the purity of a theory of law in the aspect of the Is–Ought separation consists of the artificial, non-existent conditions under which law is regarded, because law can exist only in a society that is sufficiently organised, in the realm of facts, blended with them. Law is an indicator of an organised society, and only an organised society can produce a legal order. This claim can be supported by, eg, Hart's account of secondary rules or Merkl's account on Stufenbau.[10] Secondary rules, characteristic of law, can show up only in a sufficiently advanced social structure, and this notion stems from the nature of secondary rules or Stufenbau's structure.

The paradox of such purity lies in the fact that, if these conditions were given – if law were isolated from social reality, law could not exist meaningfully, although it is conceivable. Law in its pure form, outside of society, is meaningless, because it is not able to regulate any behaviour, as there is no behaviour to regulate. Even in Kelsen's framework, such a law is not valid, as it is not efficacious; hence, it is self-contradictory and thus meaningless.

In this context, there is one more issue to clarify. This chapter started by explaining the reality with which the fiction of a radical separation of Ought is contrasted. Now it is time to close this circle and ask about the relation between law in its pure form and reality perceived from the child's perspective. It seems that the answer to this question must be analogical to a similar question existing in the philosophy of mind, which explores the relation between the mental and the physical. Here categories can to some extent refer to the mental domain, which would be 'law as such' as a result of the mental operation of separating Is from Ought and the physical domain previously described as the child's perspective. I will explore this relation in more detail in the following chapter; for now it is suffice to say that in Kelsen's case, the potential link between these two domains could be supervenience.

[10] AJ Merkl, 'Prolegomena Einer Theorie Des Rechtlichen Stufenbaues' in H Klecatsky, R Marcic and R Schambeck (eds), *Die Wiener Rechtstheoretische Schule: Schriften von Hans Kelsen, Adolf Merkl Alfred Verdross* (Franz Steiner Verlag, 2010) 1311–61; HLA Hart, *The Concept of Law* (Oxford University Press, 2012) 79–100.

4.3. THE FUNDAMENTALITY OF OUGHT

The conclusion that the radical separation of Is and Ought is paradoxical – because if such a separation existed, law would be unthinkable – leads to the inquiry concerning one more potentially fictional element associated with this separation: the fundamentality of Ought. Fundamentality is understood here in terms of independence 'whereby for any notion of dependence D, an entity is D-fundamental if and only if it does not depend on anything else (or anything else that does not depend on it)'.[11]

This is a general definition of fundamentality, which I will use in the version presented by David Chalmers; the introduction of his definition here sets the stage for the next chapter, where in order to solve puzzles concerning borderline situations in GTN, I use more philosophical tools developed through discussions concerning consciousness and the correctness of physicalism. The notion of the fundamentality of Ought is crucial in the next chapter, for my argument that the link which can explain relations between Is and Ought, which occur in such relations as these between a norm and an act of will, or validity and efficacy, is supervenience.

Chalmers understands the fundamental features in terms of the impossibility of explaining more basic features, while the fundamental laws are primary, and cannot be explained by more basic laws. According to Chalmers, applying fundamental features and laws to a certain domain 'sets everything in place'.[12] Kelsen maintained that in his pure theory of law project, Ought is fundamental in this way. In the Neo-Kantian period, Ought was considered a relative category a priori; one which is undefinable and enables cognition.[13] In GTN, Ought is presupposed; it is a starting point in the process of cognising the norm. The question is whether it can be defended that Ought is fundamental, as Kelsen maintained in the pure theory of law, or perhaps in GTN the fundamental character of Ought also has a fictional character.

At first glance, the second option seems to be a consequence of the fictional paradigm applied here. Possibly even such a reading could be justified. This kind of reading would go as follows: the fictional character of the fundamentality of Ought stems from the fact that it is an artificial assumption. Facts are more fundamental than the mental constructs of the human mind, such as law, since the latter depends on the former in some way. In order to understand law 'as such' one must take a different perspective that makes the relations between law

[11] TE Tahko, 'Fundamentality' in EN Zalta (ed), *The Stanford Encyclopedia of Philosophy*, Fall 2018 (Metaphysics Research Lab, Stanford University, 2018), plato.stanford.edu/archives/fall2018/entries/fundamentality/.

[12] DJ Chalmers, *The Conscious Mind: In Search of a Fundamental Theory* (Oxford University Press, 1996) 126.

[13] See: R Alexy, 'Hans Kelsen's Begriff Des Relativen Apriori' in R Alexy, L Meyer and SL Paulson (eds), *Neukantianismus Und Rechtphilosophie*, *Nomos Verlagsgesellschaft* (Nomos Verlagsgesellschaft, 2002).

and facts irrelevant. This way the fiction of Is–Ought separation is established, which assumes the fundamentality of Ought. The separation of Is and Ought is fictional and made to understand a law's normative aspect. When fiction is discarded, law is perceived in positivistic terms as a social fact.

Such a reading would have the potential to reconcile legal positivism and the pure theory of law by weakening the latter. If this was the only possible interpretation of the Is–Ought separation in GTN, the application of fictionalism would certainly not be very beneficial for Kelsen. It would not be much of an improvement when compared to the original reading where the rejection of the basic norm by attributing it fictional character led to the end of the pure theory of law. Here purity would be sustained, but in a very limited framework.

However, if we look closer, in the light of how fictionalism was applied to the notion of purity in GTN, there is a way to maintain the strong character of fundamentality, known from the pure theory of law, and I would like to advocate for this interpretation. Namely, the fictional framework applied to GTN does not deny the fundamentality of Ought known from the *Pure Theory of Law*. It extracts law from the social reality in which it is blended with other phenomena. In Chapter three, I noted that fictions have negative and positive aspects, and most misunderstandings stem from focusing on the negative aspect only: 'if it is fictional then it is untrue'. The overlooked, positive aspect of fictions lies in the fact that they shed some light on a relevant but hidden aspect of certain phenomena, allowing us to understand it. The fiction of the radical separation between Is and Ought does not deny that Ought is a phenomenon distinct from facts, and as we learned now – a fundamental one. This fiction lies in the fact that law without social context could not exist meaningfully. Hence, the mode of Ought is fundamental and the fiction of separation concerns something else than the fundamentality of Ought, which exists alongside the fundamentality of Is.

4.4. THE SEPARATION BETWEEN LAW AND MORALITY AND THE FICTIONAL FRAMEWORK

Now it remains to investigate whether the separation between law and morality works in the same manner. Although this separation is less problematic in the context of GTN, it concerns the fiction of purity. As such, it should be analysed in order to obtain a full picture of the fictional framework of GTN.

At first glance, the statement that the separation between law and morality contains a fiction seems controversial, especially if it is formed from the positivistic point of view. However, the same can be said about the positivistic slogan that law is separated from morality. This vague slogan is the source of many misunderstandings but, fortunately, some of them were untangled by HLA Hart.[14] My apprehension of the dichotomy between law and morality aligns

[14] Hart (n 1).

with the Hartian account of this matter. It is unnecessary to reiterate the well-established arguments within Hart's article. It is sufficient to affirm that Hart, in the tradition of Austin and Bentham, clarified the distinction between law as it is and law as it ought to be. To apprehend law accurately, one must not confuse these two modes in which the concept of law is envisioned. However, this stance should not be misconstrued as a dismissal of inquiries into the normative dimension of law. These inquiries hold significance; nevertheless, they do not provide a suitable resolution to the fundamental query concerning the nature of law.

It seems that fiction, understood in the philosophical manner presented above, might bring some more clarity, by revealing details concerning this separation and addressing the question of how law is separated from morality. In this part, my inquiry is focused on whether it is possible to apply fictionalism to the separation between law and morals, and if the answer is positive, then in which sense. I will address these inquiries in reverse order, for addressing the latter inquiry will provide the answer to the former.

The answer to the question of the sense in which the separation between law and morals can be said to have a fictional component is not obvious, since this separation seems to have a different character to the separation between law and facts. While the former is associated with logical criteria, such as Hume's guillotine and the naturalistic fallacy, the latter only concerns the normative field. In order to reconstruct a potential fiction, first, I will explore the reasons why Kelsen and the legal positivists claimed that such a separation exists. It suffices to reconstruct Kelsen's reasons for separating law and morality so sharply in the *Pure Theory of Law* and in a vaguer manner due to the rejection of the norm's logic in GTN. To address all the relevant issues, I will supplement Kelsen's views with Hart's famous account of the separation between law and morality.

Kelsen is known for his insistence on the thesis that law is separate from morality. Nonetheless, while the core thesis remained consistent, his perspectives underwent certain alterations over time. For the sake of argument, I will contrast two approaches: one based strongly on logical arguments; the other being the approach that Kelsen took in GTN, associated with the claim about rejecting the logic of norms. My reconstruction of the primary view will be based on the text *Philosophische Groundlagen der Naturrechtslhere und des Rechtspositivismus* from 1928, which was later translated into English and incorporated into the General Theory of Law and State in 1945.[15] Although not the exclusive interpretation of Kelsen's account of the separation thesis, it seems that due to its appearance in the English version so many years later, it can be regarded as representative of a long period, covering both the strong and weak Neo-Kantian accounts.

In these writings, Kelsen supported the thesis on the separation of law and morality with two main arguments. The first one, typical for legal positivists of

[15] H Kelsen, *General Theory of Law and State*, trans A Wedberg (Harward University Press, 1945) 389–447.

his time, referred to the rule of contradiction: two different normative systems cannot be valid (exist) simultaneously, especially when they contradict each other; only one can be valid, and this is law. The second argument explored by Kelsen concerned the unscientific character of morality. He believed that moral absolutism, stemming from metaphysical dualism, is subjective, and hence unscientific. According to Kelsen, moral absolutism has its roots in beliefs in some higher, divine, perfect order, which can provide definite answers to moral inquiries.

For Kelsen, such convictions have no scientific basis and relativism is the only possible standpoint for science. Kelsen's thesis is empirical: we all have our morality and beliefs, therefore there are no objective criteria to determine which morality is better. The solution offered by positivists and Kelsen is that legal science can examine the law as it is, in its form. At the same time, legal science cannot evaluate the content of law, where moral norms can be incorporated, for the abovementioned reasons.

As can be seen, the first argument indicates some supposedly objective reasons – referring to logic – why law and morality are to be separated, while the second one is limited to the scientific account and can be reconstructed as follows: in order to understand what law is scientifically, one must separate law from morality.

In GTN, the first argument became problematic due to the rejection of the norm's logic. It seems that the opposite is the case: two normative systems can exist (be valid) at the same time. But the second argument remains: if one is involved in a scientific project concerning law, one should act as if law were separated from morality. Hence, a fictional component can be detected in such reasoning: two systems can be valid at the same time, and in these circumstances, it cannot be *excluded* that in some cases they overlap in some way. Hence, for legal science, in order to properly distinguish law from morality, one should act as if they were radically separated.

The question remains: what kind of separation between law and morality occurs here, and how should it be defined? In GTN Kelsen does not elaborate much on this matter, however, the answer to this inquiry can be found in Hart's famous 'Positivism and the Separation of Law and Morals', especially in his first argument referring to the clarity of the concept of law. Hart focuses on legal positivism, making references to Austin and Bentham, but many of his remarks are also valid in reference to Kelsen. The division that enables the separation is the division between 'law as it is' and law 'as it ought to be'. Hart defines this division in a narrow sense, as two claims:

> [F]irst, in the absence of an expressed constitutional or legal provision, it could not follow from the mere fact that a rule violated standards of morality that it was not a rule of law; and conversely, it could not follow from the mere fact that a rule was morally desirable that it was a rule of law.[16]

[16] Hart (n 1) 599.

Hence, the separation thesis in this form distinguishes between the existence of law and its merits, as Hart puts it. This in turn enables us to 'attain a new clarity'. According to these claims, in order to attain the clarity of what law is, one assumes that, firstly, even legal norms which violate moral standards are valid, hence they exist, and as a result they are law. Undeniably, the observation that even an extremely unjust legal system – for instance, a totalitarian one – is considered as law is correct. There are enough empirical examples of such thinking about law. Secondly, one assumes that the sole fact that the norm is morally desirable does not make such a norm a legal norm. Certainly, such assumptions also underlie Kelsen's project.

There are, however, strong arguments which are inconvenient for legal positivists. For instance, Radbruch's formula poses a challenge to positivistic convictions.[17] Considerable discourse has been dedicated to Radbruch's formula and its intricate challenges to legal positivism, rendering an exhaustive reiteration of these arguments unnecessary. It suffices to say that the positivistic definition of law sets the limits for legal interpretation, which might lead to extremely unjust judicial decisions if this doctrine is not treated with caution when the law is applied. This most famous example illustrates that this issue is much more complicated than some positivists wish it to be. I do not claim that they falsify positivistic claims; my point is that this debate is far from being settled. One can inquire whether a system which deliberately does not fulfil the justice requirement might be troublesome for legal positivists, and conclude that their answer might not be satisfactory for all. Adding this to Kelsen's revised thesis that two normative systems can exist at the same time poses a threat to the purity of Kelsen's theory.

I claim that fictionalism could restore Kelsen's separation thesis's internal and external strength. As was argued before, fictions always function in a particular context, and Radbruch's argument exists outside the pure theory of law context. For this reason, awareness of the limits of the pure theory of law, and some fictional assumptions should defend the theory from the arguments that concern matters beyond the limitations applied to the pure theory of law.

Hence, what remains now is to define whether fiction occurs here, and if so what kind. It could be argued that the separation of law and morality is one of the most debated issues in jurisprudence. Despite that, this matter is treated as settled in a scientific – that is to say, positivistic – framework. Hence, the fictive (rather than fictional) element might lie in the fact that we act as if there was a consensus in the doctrine on this matter, which is far from the case. Fictionalism can avoid this discussion and state that for a scientific project, which ought to be *objective*, one is supposed to proceed as if a radical separation of law and morals was given.

However, such an approach might be considered as avoiding the real problem. Instead of defining what is fictional and what is gained by this approach, this

[17] Radbruch's formula is the most famous example, however, contemporary debates concerning the issue whether law can be only grounded in facts pose similar challenge. See eg: Greenberg (n 2).

solution only describes the scientific practice, which is rather common. It is not wrong to conclude a fictive element from the lack of scientific consensus, but such a strategy does not address the main inquiry about the nature of such a fiction.

To define the mechanism underlying the fictional account, one should start with the notion of the utility of a fiction. In order to consider a fiction useful, there must be some correctness stemming from it. In case of the separation of law and morality, fiction highlights some aspects of reality by negating some complex occurrences, such as some kind of dependency between law and morality. Even though these dependencies occur, they do not negate the fact that law is a phenomenon that is distinct from morality, with its structure (Stufenbau) and institutions, and it should first be examined as such. This means that the fictive component can be found again in the framework of laboratory fiction in the form of a pretence. Law is isolated from morality in order to examine it 'as it is'. At the same time, law in its pure form, abstracting from morality, probably could not exist in Kelsen's terms, as it would be inefficacious and hence invalid.

Comparing the separation of law and morality with the separation of Is and Ought, it seems that although there is some natural possibility of the existence of law devoid of morality, in the case of the Is–Ought separation such a possibility exists only in the logical sphere when law separated from facts is conceivable but impossible in natural terms, since it is a product of social reality. I elaborate on the aspects in which Is and Ought are separated in chapter six. For now, it suffices to note that in the case of the Is–Ought separation, the fictional component occurs, while in the case of the separation of law and morality, this component only has a fictive character.

Additionally, in the case of the separation of law and morality, the second strategy associated with fictionalism, which is a construction of the model of law, can come into play. Here the focus lies on a law in its pure form, which means that abstraction from the content of law takes place. This division between form and content is characteristic for legal positivism, where examination of the form of law takes place, leaving inquiries about the content aside. What matters here is that the potential links between law and morality exist in the content of law, at least according to the positivists. In Kelsen's case this conduct enables an objective, scientific, ideology-free concept of law based on its form. From the perspective of methodological fictionalism, this procedure resembles a construction of the model of law. By constructing such a model, law can be separated from factors which might disturb its cognition 'as such'. The fictional component here is analogical to the one found in the Is–Ought separation. An empty law – law without any content – does not make sense.

Morality was to be eliminated from the *Pure Theory of Law* as not scientific due to the denied possibility of reducing law to morality, not because of denying any relations between law and morality. This strategy is reminiscent of the approach taken by Kelsen in the case of the Is–Ought separation. In that case, the core issue was also a rejection of the thesis that the reduction of Is to Ought occurs without denying some relations between Is and Ought.

The question remains whether purity thus understood is identical to scientific objectivity. This issue can be formulated as follows: Kelsen argued that only if we eliminate subjective elements and see law as it is can we attain a scientific ideal. Although purity and objectivity seem related, they are not the same. However, eliminating morality from this equation eliminates an evaluative factor in moral judgements and the problem of 'law as it should be'. Due to such an operation, law can be examined 'as it is' and not 'as it ought to be'. As such law can be perceived through an objective lens.

Finally, it is worth investigating whether such an approach removes the vagueness in the slogan that law is separated from morality. Although the answer is positive, the claim that the separation of law and morality is fictional sounds misleading and vague. Although fictionalism provides methodological tools that clarify what it means to say that law is separated from morality, it creates new misunderstandings at the opposite extreme. While the slogan 'law is separated from morality' gives the impression of a radical separation of these two domains, the fictionality claim might lead to the unfortunate conclusion that such a separation is non-existent. Fictionalism only claims that: (1) it is true that law is a distinct phenomenon; and (2) it is false that law is radically separated from morality. Unfortunately, further clarification along these lines would not be beneficial for removing vagueness. Hence, even though in the positivistic model of law, the fictional component can be identified, from a practical point of view, the most proper and precise way of talking about the separation of law and morality is in terms of a model containing fiction.

4.5. THE FICTIONAL CHARACTER OF PURITY

Finally, the question of establishing the relations between the two separations discussed above remains. Returning to Hart, the Is–Ought distinction underlies the separation of law and morality, and draws a line between 'law as it is' and 'law as it ought to be'. Translated into Kelsen's terms, legal science, which examines the law as it is, should be separated from deliberations about 'law as it should be'. Interestingly, in this aspect, Kelsen stands on the ground of Is; however, one should not assume the identity of 'the law as it is' with 'the law as such', which I mentioned in the section above.

'Law as it is' refers to the method of investigation of legal phenomena in which law will be investigated objectively. 'Objectively' means that no evaluation of legal phenomenon will be involved in this investigation. According to Hart, this enables 'men to see steadily the precise issues posed by the existence of morally bad laws, and to understand the specific character of the authority of a legal order'.[18] Otherwise, there is 'the danger that law and its authority may be

[18] Hart (n 1) 597.

dissolved in man's conceptions of what law ought to be and the danger that the existing law may supplant as a final test of conduct and so escape criticism'.[19]

On the other hand, the examination of 'law as such' delves into its normative essence, setting it apart from any other facts or social phenomena and separating it from morality. 'Law as such' is linked to institutions engaged in the processes of law-making and law application (Stufenbau and empowerment). While the former is tied to the pursuit of scientific objectivity and theoretical analysis, the latter, 'law as such', demands the exploration of law in its pure form. One is intrinsically connected to the other, but 'law as such' imposes additional requirements. While 'law as it is' can be understood as a general postulate of the legal positivists, 'law as such' is specific to the pure theory of law due to the additional requirement of the separation of Is and Ought. 'Law as it is' can examine law as something else, such as a sociological phenomenon, and attain scientific objectivity. 'Law as such' requires examining law in its pure form.

Hence, in the framework of the method defined in terms of the separation of law and morality, law can be objectively cognised in more than one aspect. The law can be cognised 'as such' or, for example, 'as social phenomena'. Kelsen's genius lies in the purity method, which guarantees the examination of 'law as it is' and 'law as such'. The reason for the universality of this method lies in its radicality. The concept of law, which is supposed to be the subject of investigation, is purified from *all* alien elements. This method (of purity) contains a fictional element called the 'laboratory fiction'. It is based on the assumption that law is distinguished as a phenomenon which cannot be reduced to facts, due to its normative nature, or to morality, due to (in general terms) institutions which govern law-making and law-applying processes. On the other hand, as was indicated above, law exists in social and moral contexts, and only such contexts make law meaningful. This leads to examining law first in its objective dimension – 'law as it is' – and to the notion of laboratory fiction, which allows the examination of 'law as such'. In terms of methods, purity comes first; this is the main method of Kelsen's procedure. The investigation of 'law as it is' seems to exist on the level of postulates, and this postulate is fulfilled by purity. As a result, one obtains a model of law which is characterised by the fiction of purity.

At this point one might ask: what does 'law as such' mean? The simplest answer would be the model of law envisioned in the pure theory of law. But this answer is too vague and vulnerable to many interpretations. Here I would like to propose a definition provided by Christoph Kletzer, who notes that the pure theory of law concerns the investigation of how 'positive law, … which is fully human and does not rely on theological or otherwise metaphysical presuppositions, could be possible at all.[20]

[19] ibid 598.

[20] Ch Kletzer, *The Idea of a Pure Theory of Law: An Interpretation and Defence* (Hart Publishing, 2018) 18.

It can be noted at this point that the law 'as such' is a relative concept. What is meant here is law as fully human, positive law and not law in general. Moreover, Keltzer notes that the pure theory of law assumes the normative character of law.[21] From this, one can derive in the GTN spirit that this human law is possible thanks to the implicit fictionalism of purity. The assumption of the normative character of law leads to the Is–Ought separation, while law which is human leads to the separation of law and morality, and produces a theory which is pure.

Kletzer develops his inquiry further, addressing the question 'how do we have to conceptualise the nature of positive law so that it is possible as secular or truly human law?'[22] In the framework of fictionalism, this inquiry could be answered in the following way: explicit fictionalism raises awareness of the cognitive processes involved when one thinks about human law and sheds light on how human law is implicitly understood.

However, the question remains whether in the case of the idea of 'law as such' we are dealing with one more particular fiction, and if yes, what kind of practice such a fiction involves. In order to address this inquiry, it is necessary to determine what kind of cognitive processes lead to constructing such a model of law. Two such processes are potential candidates: idealisation and abstraction. Of help here could be a distinction made by Morrison, who notes: 'where idealization distorts or omits properties that are often not necessary for the problem at hand, abstraction … *introduces* a specific type of representation that is not amendable to correction and is necessary for explanation/prediction of the target system'.[23] It seems that the idealisation might be closer to Kelsen's intention, especially in the context of Weberian ideal type, which has been applied by several thinkers to Kelsen's pure theory of law.[24]

[21] ibid 11.

[22] ibid 18.

[23] M Morrison, 'Fictions, Representations, and Reality' in *Fictions in Science: Philosophical Essays on Modeling and Idealization*, by M Suárez (Routledge, 2008) 110, https://doi.org/10.4324/9780203890103-11.

[24] M Weber, *Methodology of Social Sciences*, trans E Shils and F Heary (New Brunswick, NJ, Transaction Publishers, 1949) 49–90; Dhananjai Shivakumar, 'The Pure Theory as Ideal Type: Defending Kelsen on the Basis of Weberian Methodology' (1996) 105 *The Yale Law Journal*. See also: H Ross, 'The Pure Theory of Law and Interpretive Sociology – A Basis for Interdisciplinarity?' in M Freeman (ed), *Law and Sociology* (Oxford University Press, 2006), 69–89, It seems that the Weberian ideal type nicely combines the elements discussed here. It analyses similar concepts to those analysed by Vaihinger, seems closely related to the category of models, and introduces the notion of understanding. Finally, Kelsen was inspired by Weber's writing in his Neo-Kantian phase. However, I prefer to analyse these phenomena separately with regard to different domains and authors, instead of Weber, because his concept, by being specific, has limitations and boundaries, which would lead my interpretation in a direction which might be interesting, but more one-sided. That would be an interpretation of Kelsen's pure theory of law in the Weberian spirit, rather than a more contemporary and analytical account. It seems that the latter interpretation is a better fit, as some sort of supplement of the Neo-Kantian phase, rather than the general theory of norms, and the most beneficial reading should have a chronologically progressive rather than regressive character. By progressive reading, I mean a reading which considers modern concepts, while regressive reading considers concepts already explored by Kelsen. In this book, the Vaihingerian idea

In accordance with Weber's perspective, the social sciences are tasked with facilitating the comprehension of social concepts through the utilisation of heuristic mechanisms. Consequently, the methodological approach should concentrate on one facet of the phenomenon, namely one-dimensional concepts, particularly ideal types, which are designed to model specific aspects of social reality. Ideal types possess a fictional nature, as their validity is not contingent upon their manifestation in reality but upon their adequacy. The ideal type serves as a tool that enables the evaluation of specific attributes or processes of interest to the social scientist in a given case. In this context, they resemble models, as defined in Dąmbska's terminology, in terms of patterns.[25] Dhananjjai Shivakumar even argues that Kelsen's pure theory of law can be perceived as an ideal type, which would replace the doctrine's broadly criticised Neo-Kantian paradigm. He perceives applying an ideal type to validity as particularly successful because such an application can eliminate efficacy from the equation. With this methodology, one does not need to inquire about efficacy because the concept of validity aims to 'emphasize the way officials allocate the authority to establish and apply norms'.[26]

Hence, the practice involved in constructing such a model is abstraction: one acts as if law was devoid of content, while law always has content. Law without content does not make sense, just as in the case of law which is abstracted from its social context. Therefore, the methodological tool used in order to obtain such purity is mostly abstraction. Purification means that the model abstracts from any elements alien to law.

This leads to the final question: what is gained by this approach? Several benefits have previously been mentioned, but they can be described here in terms of clarity. Such a model of law brings clarity about what law is and helps to place the pure theory of law in the larger framework of legal positivism. On the other hand, understanding the processes underlying the purity assumption allows us to define the relations between legal positivism and the pure theory of law, probably in a less confrontational manner than was traditionally done. Namely, it can be assumed that the pure theory of law has a different object than legal positivism. While the former examines law as such, the latter investigates law as a social fact. In the following chapters, this difference will become even more apparent. For now, it is worth noting that with such an approach it is possible to adopt a more tolerant point of view, from which both accounts can be seen to have value due to their shedding some light on different aspects of law. It does not change the fact that Kelsen's perspective might be considered as superior, at least in some aspects.

is an exception which is supposed to lead to a modernised reading of Kelsen's general theory of norms. In this framework, Weber's ideal type can have a similar function, supporting the notion that purity can be perceived in terms of models, and refers to the mode of understanding rather than the explanation.

[25] I Dąmbska, *Dwa studia z teorii naukowego poznania* (Towarzystwo Naukowe w Toruniu, 1962), 22–23.

[26] Dhananjai Shivakumar, 'The Pure Theory as Ideal Type …', 69–89.

Given that by purifying law from any alien elements Kelsen obtains the concept of law 'as such' successfully, he can claim the superiority of his standpoint. The superiority claim 'does not mean a claim that one's arguments are straightforwardly right and the others are simply wrong', as Kletzer notes, offering an understanding of superiority, in which

> all one needs to show is that the other standpoint is encompassed by the standpoint presented as superior, but not the other way around ... one needs to demonstrate, that by taking this standpoint, one can see everything that can be seen from the other standpoint, but not vice versa.[27]

The explanatory primacy is characterised by the relation between the superior to inferior standpoints, wherein 'the higher standpoint gives a better explanation than the lower because it explains everything the lower standpoint does and also explains things the lower standpoint cannot explain'. This leads to the conclusion that the lower standpoint is superfluous.[28] This strong definition of superiority, along with Kletzer's clarification, successfully argues that the pure theory of law, which conceptualises law in terms of a monopolisation of force and coercion, is superior to approaches which focus on law understood in terms of obligation.[29] The model of law as such seems to strengthen this notion, indicating the fundamentality imprinted in this perspective.

The fictional framework applied to the pure theory of law supports another feature of the theory – its fundamentality. This feature does not refer to the competing theories of the same level, but rather to the theories on different levels. The fundamental character of the pure theory of law for constructing other standpoints means that it is impossible to properly build the theory on a higher level, disregarding the more fundamental standpoint. On the other hand, many higher-level standpoints are possible, which are equal to each other and regard the fundamental standpoint. This corresponds to the relation between 'law as such' and 'law as some other phenomena'. The fictional assumptions led us to the notion of law 'as such', which is fundamental to comprehending law 'as something else'. In this framework, one needs to understand what law 'as such' is to move to higher-level standpoints, such as social reality, psychology, or a moral account. In this methodological framework, this step is necessary; however, it does not provide the knowledge obtained at higher levels. For instance, from the concept of law 'as such' one cannot derive a complete sociological account, although the specific understanding of law will determine some elements of the theory.

This relation can be understood in terms of supervenience. This is covered in more detail in the next chapter, but here it suffices to say that supervenience is defined by the slogan 'there is no A difference without B difference', where B is more fundamental than A. The supervenience formula in this case is as

[27] Kletzer (n 20) 13.
[28] ibid.
[29] See eg: ibid 21.

follows: 'A properly constructed higher-level theory will always assume properly defined concept of "law as such"'. Imagine two properly constructed theories. They have the same property of being correctly constructed. According to supervenience, to retain this property both must necessarily assume the concept of properly defined law 'as such'. On the other hand, the supervenience rule requires that two different law 'as such' concepts would bring different results in the correctness of the theory. One theory will be defined appropriately while the other not. Hence, obtaining a properly defined concept of law 'as such' leads to a standpoint which is superior to other standpoints in a weak way, characterised by its fundamentality in terms of supervenience.

To sum up, fictionalism revealed another feature of the pure theory of law. Not only is the theory superior to competing standpoints, but it is also fundamental in relation to other theories of law, and its fundamental character is associated with its superiority in the manner defined by Kletzer. This means that fictionalism is a framework for the purity of Kelsen's theory in GTN.

Another benefit of applying fictionalism can be seen when comparing the vision of law before and after the fictionalisation process. The child's perspective lacks awareness of differences between 'law as such', 'law as something else' and 'law as it ought to be', as it encompasses all these perspectives without reflecting on their differences. Therefore, there is a danger of unintentionally mixing all these perspectives, which might provide a false picture of law. The awareness of the thought processes that lead to fictionalisation allows the use of several models of law (law as such, law as something else, law as it ought to be) with consciousness, and in a way most appropriate to the concrete purpose in mind. This precision guarantees more accuracy in understanding law in its social context in a broad sense.

Finally, the basic norm as a fiction was the tip of a (fictional) iceberg, because the Kelsenist acts as-if law were separated from other phenomena; and the Ought domain was separated from the Is domain. In such a framework, the fictional basic norm results from primary prefacing at the level of the Is–Ought separation. The origin of the basic norm stems from the dilemma brought about by the separation of the normative sphere from facts, for in reality the origin of legal validity is created in law-making processes taking place in factual, concrete and historical circumstances. The fictional character of the basic norm is a consequence of the definition of a norm, which produces self-contradictoriness, while its existence as a fictional entity, in the sense that the basic norm 'does not agree with reality', is a consequence of a purity. It seems that the self-contradictory character of the basic norm stems from the fact that it does not agree with reality because it emerged as a consequence of the purity of Kelsen's theory of law, which has a fictional character. What matters here is that this character of the basic norm does not discard this conception. The basic norm has its utility: it enables the normative dimension of law to be understood in the manner I explained at the beginning of chapter three. In this case, the fictional character of the basic norm is not a threat to the pure theory of law, because it is a consequence of methodological assumptions rather than an independent foundation of the whole structure. This way the essence of the basic norm is weakened in GTN, bu its function remains almost intact – it still serves as a chain in the cognitive process in reference to validity and law recognition.

However, one more function of the basic norm emerges from its fictional character: understanding. Like every fiction, the basic norm enables understanding legal processes and law itself.[30] Hence, in the final section of this chapter I focus on the category of *understanding*. This phrase has been used in this book on many occasions, and now it is time to explain what it means.

4.6. FICTIONALISM AND UNDERSTANDING

The fictionality on which Kelsen's late theory is founded aims at the broader purpose of fictions, namely enabling certain phenomena to be understood. Understanding is referred to a great deal above, and this is no coincidence. Fictions and the hermeneutic mode of understanding are strongly related. Related to fiction, understanding is a significantly more permissive concept regarding truth, as opposed to the realm of scientific explanation. It is worthwhile to briefly analyse these two modes.

In philosophy of science, one of the primary debates focuses on the issue of whether social science phenomena can be explained – just like the phenomena in empirical science – or rather understood. Explanation and understanding are two modes of dealing with scientific problems. What distinguishes empirical science from social science is epistemological representation.[31] In empirical science the procedure revolves around modelling the behaviour of an external object and thus validating it. This allows the object's behaviour to be explained and predicted based on causal relations. On the other hand, some argue that the explanatory mode does not apply to social science models, due to the free will of human beings, which does not conform with the causal chain of events. Hence, the mode used in social science is understanding or comprehension.[32] This hermeneutical approach, notably exemplified in Max Weber's writings, inspired Kelsen during the development of his pure theory of law, particularly within the domain of 'verstehende Soziologie' (interpretive sociology). There were also several attempts to interpret Kelsen's pure theory of law in terms of the sociology represented in Max Weber's work.[33] According to Weber, positivistic

[30] A similar approach to the basic norm as a fiction and discussed in terms of so-called Positive Legal Fictionalism is taken by: M Kiener, 'Fictionalising Kelsen's Pure Theory of Law' in M Jestaedt, R Poscher and J Kammerhofer (eds), *Die Reine Rechtslehre Auf Dem Prufstand*, Archiv Fur Rechts- Und Sozialphilosophie 163 (Franz Steiner Verlag, 2020) 99–124.

[31] G Samuel, M Del Mar, and W Twining, 'Is Law a Fiction?' in M Del Mar and W Twining (eds), *Legal Fictions in Theory and Practice* (Springer International Publishing, 2015) 34.

[32] ibid 34–35.

[33] D Shivakumar, 'The Pure Theory as Ideal Type: Defending Kelsen on the Basis of Weberian Methodology' (1996) 105 *The Yale Law Journal* 1383. See also: H Ross, 'The Pure Theory of Law

science can describe behaviour while disregarding inner motives and formulate certain laws pertaining to it. However, a complete understanding can only be achieved by ascribing meaning to actions, a domain specific to social science. This interpretative process inherently involves a subjective element.

The concept of limited objectivity is achieved when subjective elements are explicated in a causal and teleological manner, where actions are analysed in terms of means and ends. Imputing an end to a particular action is essentially a fictional operation, carried out by the researcher based on their subjective values. Consequently, this means that an action attains objective validity only in the realm of means. Therefore, objectivity in the social sciences can only be regarded as an ideal rather than an attainable reality.[34]

More recently, GH von Wright has advanced a concept of understanding rooted in the same differentiation between explanation and understanding. The choice of this author is dictated by his commonly known proximity to Kelsen. When formulating his final version of the pure theory or law, Kelsen was familiar with von Wright's writing and vice versa – von Wright engaged in some polemics with Kelsen, especially in the problematic issue of the possibility of the norm's logic. He also discussed the problem of the separation of Is and Ought – to name a few of the many links between Kelsen and von Wright.[35]

As a point of departure, von Wright asks how the sciences of nature are related to the study of man'.[36] The attempts to answer this question have proceeded according to two traditions of thought: Galilean and Aristotelian. While the former favours a causal (mechanistic) explanation, the latter is restricted to a teleological (finalistic) explanation. Whereas the causal explanation serves as a prediction, the Aristotelian tradition focuses on 'making facts teleologically or finalistically understandable'.[37]

At the same time, in the nineteenth century, great efforts were made to establish a relationship between empirical science and the humanities. On one hand, positivism, stemming from the Galilean tradition, is characterised by methodological monism, with mathematics and physics as a methodological ideal, and scientific explanation as a causal approach, with the subsumption of individual cases under general laws of nature. This way of thinking considers finalistic explanation as unscientific.[38]

and Interpretive Sociology – A Basis for Interdisciplinarity?' in M Freeman (ed), *Law and Sociology* (Oxford University Press, 2006) 69–89.

[34] Sung Ho Kim, 'Max Weber' in EN Zalta and U Nodelman (eds), *The Stanford Encyclopedia of Philosophy*, Winter 2022 (Metaphysics Research Lab, Stanford University, 2022), plato.stanford.edu/archives/win2022/entries/weber.

[35] GH von Wright, 'Is and Ought' in MC Doeser and JN Kraay (eds), *Facts and Values: Philosophical Reflections from Western and Non-Western Perspectives*, Martinus Nijhoff Philosophy Library (Springer Netherlands, 1986) 31–48; GH von Wright, 'Is There a Logic of Norms? (1991) 4 *Ratio Juris* 265.

[36] GH von Wright, *Explanation and Understanding* (Cornell University Press, 1971) vii.

[37] ibid 3.

[38] ibid 4.

On the other hand, Hermeneutics, as an antipositivistic philosophy of science, rejects methodological monism and the natural science operational model as a methodological ideal, together with other forms of generalisation. The humanities and social science (*Geistwissenschaften*) attempt to identify objects' unique and individual features; they do not explain, like natural science does, but rather enable understanding.

Contrary to explanation, understanding also contains a psychological element, for instance, 'recreation in the mind of the scholar of the mental atmosphere, the thoughts and feelings and motivations of the object of his study'.[39] As well as its psychological element, understanding is also bound up with intentionality and a semantic dimension. As examples of intentionality, von Wright mentions an agent's understanding of aims, the symbol's meaning or the significance of the social institutions.[40] Hence, teleological orientation can be divided into two sub-provinces: one refers to function, purpose and organic wholes, and is useful in biological science; the second, intentionality, is characteristic of behavioural science, social studies and historiography.[41]

Von Wright concludes that this concept is reminiscent of the function of empathy in the process of understanding: 'Empathic understanding is not a "feeling"; it is an ability to participate in a "form of life"'.[42] This approach indicates the existence of specific phenomena that cannot be accounted for by explanation, be it causal or teleological.

Teleological explanation in particular requires understanding of intention, which is not manifested externally. Any teleological explanation (eg he rang a bell because he wanted to open the door) regarding completely alien behaviour is impossible.[43] This fact is specifically essential in the case of the social sciences. Von Wright provides an example of crowds on a street moving in the same direction, shouting and waving flags. Some elements of this event can be explained, for instance that the group is moving toward city hall, or that it is not on a platform or being swept away by the wind, or that the specific sound issuing from the participants' throats is shouting. However, a complete understanding of the whole event requires more than this teleological explanation or an explanation of the movement of each member of the procession.

Hence, von Wright raises the question of recognising whether this is a street demonstration, folk festival, or religious procession. A second-order act of understanding is essential to fully recognise what is happening on the street. As von Wright notes, 'it is a question of interpretation, of understanding the meaning of what is going on'.[44] While an explanation may satisfy an inquiry into why something occurs, understanding is needed to comprehend its nature.[45]

[39] ibid 6.
[40] ibid.
[41] ibid 16.
[42] ibid 28–19.
[43] ibid 114.
[44] ibid 132–33.
[45] ibid 134.

Such a position is compatible with Vaihinger's account, which claims that the human mind is adjusted to fictions and poses the question of how it is possible that false ideas can lead to a true outcome. Despite being untrue, fictions have not only the potential to explain phenomena, but also to predict their behaviour.[46] Fiction is one of the devices which enables us to *understand* a particular phenomenon, while commonly in the doctrine their explanatory power is rejected due to their inability to fulfil truth criteria or their belonging to the chain of causality, they do not fit with either Hempel's deductive-nomological account or Solomon's causal-mechanical account.[47] Also, models associated with fiction require interpretation, which strictly relates to understanding.

Now that the mode of understanding has been clarified, it is time to return to the General Theory of Norms and address the question of its fitness in this context. In empirical science understanding is relevant when an explanation is out of reach. In the social sciences and the humanities, the mode of understanding is rather the rule. But how can this be reconciled with Kelsen's positivistic point of view?

Firstly, although Kelsen belonged to the legal positivism camp, and his aim was a scientific project – a legal science project – the hermeneutical approach was nevertheless directly present in his writings. Secondly, Kelsen was influenced by Weber and his *verstehende Soziologie*. The pure theory of law ensures the proper interpretation (interpretation scheme) of certain phenomena so that one understands them as law. When Kelsen inquiries how to recognise that a man in a robe is a judge issuing a ruling and not an actor, this question is analogical to von Wright's example concerning demonstration. Third, as mentioned in chapter one, on the occasion of the expressive conception of the norm, there are overlaps between the pragmatic approach, which is associated with this conception of a norm, and the hermeneutic approach. It seems that the change in the conception of a norm, from hyletic to expressive entailed that the hermeneutic approach grew in significance in GTN. Finally, fictionalism, which emerged as one of the main paradigms in the last phase of Kelsen's theory made this trend even more apparent and is just one of the pieces of these puzzles.

Let us now analyse how the hermeneutic approach in GTN can be interpreted in von Wright's terms. Kelsen's primary aim in GTN was to provide the answer to the inquiry 'what is law?' This claim can be supported by the first lines of the *Pure Theory of Law*, where Kelsen writes:

[46] Samuel, Del Mar and Twining (n 31) 35.

[47] However, some scholars, for instance, Bokulich, distinguish the category of explanatory fictions and argue that this type of fiction has an explanatory power. She provides three conditions the fictions need to fulfil in order to be explanatory: (1) 'the explanans must make essential reference to a scientific model and this model … involves some idealization and/or fictionalization of the system it represents'; (2) 'that model is taken to explain the explanandum by showing that the pattern of counterfactual dependence in the model mirrors in the relevant respects the pattern of counterfactual dependence in the target system' (3) further justificatory step exists (Bokulich, 'Explanatory Fictions' in M Suárez (ed), *Fictions in Science: Philosophical Essays on Modeling and Idealization* (Routledge, 2010) 104–05).

> The Pure Theory of Law is a theory of positive law. It is a theory of positive law in general, not of a specific legal order. It is a general theory of law, not an interpretation of specific national or international legal norms ... As a theory, its exclusive purpose is to know and describe its object. The theory attempts to answer the question what and how the law *is*, not how it ought to be. It is a science of law (jurisprudence) not legal politics.[48]

In order to achieve this purpose, he created a specific methodology based on the separation of Is and Ought as a division between facts and law. Von Wright's example seems to be very similar to the problem described by Kelsen in the following passage:

> [L]aw – or what is customarily so called – seems at least partly rooted in nature and to have a 'natural' existence. For if you analyze any body of facts interpreted as 'legal' or somehow tied up with law, such as a parliamentary decision, an administrative act, a judgement, a contract, a crime, two elements are distinguishable: one, an act or series of acts -a happening occurring at a certain time and in certain place, perceived by our senses: an external manifestation of human conduct; two, the legal meaning of this act, that is, the meaning conferred upon the act by the law. For example: People assemble in a large room, make speeches, some raise their hands, others do not – this is the external happening. Its meaning is that a statute being passed, that law is created. ... To give other illustrations: A man in a robe and speaking from a dais says some words to a man standing before him; legally this external happening means: a judicial decision was passed. A merchant writes a letter of a certain content to another merchant, who answers with a letter; this means they concluded a legally binding contract. Somebody causes the death of somebody else; legally this means murder.[49]

From this passage, it can be inferred that Kelsen had a similar vision of the relationship between the external manifestation of social facts and their interpretation. Kelsen's claim that a norm should be treated as an interpretation scheme paves the way for the hermeneutic approach. Namely, a lawyer interprets/understands specific facts as law because of a norm, which is an interpretation scheme. This interpretation scheme works because the norm is valid. Its validity stems from the higher norm, and so on. In the end, what grants validity is the basic norm of a fictional character. As such, it enables us to understand and interpret specific social facts as law. Paraphrasing von Wright, the basic norm allows the mental atmosphere of the object of his study – the lawyer – to be recreated in the scholar's mind. The fiction of the basic norm enables the phenomena of law to be understood, thus demonstrating its value.

What Kelsen grasped intuitively, von Wright codified in the broader context of two modes: explanation and understanding. The external manifestation of social facts can be explained in the Is sphere. *Understanding* enables these facts

[48] H Kelsen, *Pure Theory of Law* (The Lawbook Exchange, Ltd, 1967) 1.
[49] ibid 2.

to be perceived through the filter of law. These facts can be interpreted as law through the basic norm of fictional character, which allows transcendence from the factual to the normative, legal sphere. If the concept of the basic norm were not described as fictional but as a real, concrete cognitive process in the brain, it would be rather portrayed as an element in explaining how the brain works in grasping the phenomena of law.

Due to the self-contradictory fictional nature of the concept of the basic norm, it cannot serve as a scientific explanation. Instead, the idea of the basic norm helps us understand law's normative aspect. In fact, the basic norm, as a device which allows specific facts to be interpreted as the law in terms of von Wright's theory, is understanding itself. The same can be said about the fictional aspect of the purity of Kelsen's theory. The aim of establishing purity was not to provide a complete explanation of every aspect of law, but rather to understand one of these aspects, namely law 'as such'. In this framework, normativity is presupposed and fundamental, and law is regarded as free from any alien elements that typically influence law and the perception of law.

To round off the problem of the basic norm as fiction and what it means for the pure theory of law, with regard to the question of whether the basic norm can, as a self-contradictory fiction, still be a part of the legal science project, the answer is positive. As a social science, legal science is mainly ruled by the mode of understanding (or interpretation) and not by the mode of explanation, which is characteristic of empirical science. As such, the basic norm represents a specific way of interpreting certain facts as law. With purity, which contains a fiction, the basic norm provides a coherent vision of what law is, and how it is understood and recognised by jurists. The concern that the existence of the whole object of the theory, namely law, depends on a fictional foundation, vanishes when the basic norm is treated as a consequence or – metaphorically speaking – as a visible 'symptom' of the broader fictional framework, rather than as a real foundation of Kelsen's theory. In this context, it is also worth noting that, referring to the *Münchhausen* Trilemma described by Hans Albert, most theories face the problems of *regressum ad infinitum* – the vicious circle – or dogmatic assertions that end searching. Fiction can be a remedy to that trilemma.[50] It represents an honest approach to this problem, pointing out that each solution from the trilemma contains some sort of fiction.

So far so good. However, one could argue that this 'mental atmosphere' grasped by hermeneutics might sound like some sort of variant of psychologism, which Kelsen rejected in his pure theory of law.[51] This point can be refuted by the argument that the 'mental atmosphere' does not have much in common with the psychologism targeted by Kelsen. Kelsen criticised the psychological approach he was familiar with, which existed at that time. Most probably he

[50] H Albert, *Treatise on Critical Reason* (Princeton University Press, 2016), press.princeton.edu/books/hardcover/9780691639772/treatise-on-critical-reason.

[51] I would like to thank the reviewer for indicating that.

meant Freudian themes, but perhaps he was also criticising Leon Petrażycki's psychological theory of law. The mental processes in question are rather rooted in the analytical tradition, which Kelsen tried to adopt in GTN. Furthermore, Kelsen's critique of psychologism mainly concerns the problem that such theories of law are not pure. They find their explanation in facts. What I argue is intended to have the opposite result: it is supposed to sustain the purity of Kelsen's theory. Overall, Kelsen's pure theory of law is about mental processes, or as Kelsen puts it himself in reference to the basic norm: 'how lawyers think'.

Another consequence of fictionalism paired with hermeneutic model is the liberal approach to investigations in the field of philosophy. For this reason, I did not engage earlier in discussions of the 'truth' or 'reality' from which each fiction deviates. Fictionalism goes along with the mode of understanding and is not compatible with the requirements of scientific explanation. This means it is enough to identify which component is fictional rather than establish the truth. The same goes for reality: it suffices to determine how fiction deviates from reality without the necessity of making some strong ontological commitments to what that reality is. This way, fictionalism does not engender strong statements about truth or the structure of the world, and has no ambitions to scientifically explain the world. It enables understanding it and sometimes can be of assistance when typical scientific tools do not assist in moving a specific enterprise forward.

This means that the framework of fictionalism, if considered one of the paradigms in GTN, restores some coherence to Kelsen's final version of his legal science project. However, it is not sufficient to restore the same level of coherence as was met in the pure theory of law, at least not yet. There is still the puzzle of the strong, explicit links between Is and Ought to solve, especially the definition of a norm as the meaning of an empirically understood act of will, as well as other 'borderline' situations, such as validity and efficacy, or imputation in an individual norm. Only if there is a way to explain how the separation between Is and Ought can be sustained despite these apparent links between them will it be possible to declare success in maintaining the spirit of pure theory of law in GTN. This will be the task of the next chapter.

5

The Problem of the Explanatory Gap and the Pure Theory of Law

5.1. THE SEPARATION OF IS AND OUGHT IN GTN

IN CHAPTERS THREE and four I provided a solution to the first problem which arose in GTN. Namely, I argued that Kelsen's idea that the basic norm is a self-contradictory fiction, if read in a Vaihingerian spirit, can be consistent with the pure theory of law project. This notion emerged from the observation that fictionalism might be a much broader framework in GTN than it seemed at first glance, and it is not limited to the basic norm. Such an interpretation means that one of the two threats to the pure theory of law project can be eliminated by providing an interpretation which transforms it into a new paradigm of fictionalism.

However, there needs to be more to declare victory in this matter. There are still more puzzles to solve, such as the problem of the weakened normativity thesis. This problem is embedded in the definition of a norm and the relations between validity and efficacy. In chapter two I described the impact of these changes on the pure theory of law. Here I would only like to recall that the Is–Ought separation and the thesis about the separation of law from morality determines the purity of legal science. The Is–Ought separation profoundly distinguishes Kelsen's *Reine Rechtslehre* from the positivistic doctrine. Without this thesis, the richness and originality of Kelsen's thought mostly evaporate.

For this reason, the updated definition of a norm, as the meaning of an empirically understood act of will, is cause for concern. It adds to the puzzles regarding efficacy and validity, requiring a new interpretation of these relations. In earlier writings, validity–efficacy relations could be considered as some exception, possibly to be eliminated by proper interpretation or an error made by Kelsen, but one which does not change the understanding of pure theory of law. However, in GTN, when the second piece of the puzzle is added in the form of the definition of a norm, and the Is–Ought separation is broken again, this allows us to assume that this is not an error or coincidence. It seems justified to claim that the Is–Ought separation is substantially weakened in the best-case scenario.

However, this is still a matter of interpretation. When read in a static way, along with the postulation of the radical separation of Is and Ought in PTL, one can even argue that this means the end of the pure theory of law. This interpretation is possible, mainly when this shift is considered in conjunction with a conception of the basic norm as a fiction in its negative aspect, indicating a rejection of the concept of the basic norm. On the other hand, if the interpretation of Is–Ought separation in PTL is perceived not as radical but only as occurring in some specific context, with possible exceptions, this approach creates opportunities for a dynamic interpretation to sustain the pure theory of law project.

The key to solving this problem is to define the character of the relation between Is and Ought in borderline cases, where the sphere of facts is somehow connected with Ought. I distinguish the three most substantial borderline cases, which pertain to the three main domains of law. The norm and the act of will concern the creation of norms, efficacy and validity concern the existence of norms, and imputation concerns the application of norms. The definition of a link between facts and norms in these domains might restore the coherence of the pure theory of law in the last period when Kelsen was constructing his theory. Such a link needs to consider two seemingly conflicting assumptions:

(1) on the one hand, there is a gap of some kind between them;
(2) on the other, however, there is a link of some sort between them.

The question is: what type of link is required in order to sustain the separation between Is and Ought? Initially, it could be argued that it does not seem that Kelsen meant some metaphysical separation between Is and Ought. It instead seems that Kelsen noted some sort of epistemic gap between Is and Ought; that it is not clear how Ought can be inferred from Is.[1]

Similar problems associated with the epistemic and explanatory gap have already been discussed in the doctrine, first in philosophy of mind, and recently in jurisprudence. It seems that analysing the problem of the explanatory gap might help find a solution to Kelsen's dilemma. The issue of the explanatory gap appears to be a reversal of the problem tackled by Kelsen; namely, it involves the following assumptions:

(1) there is some link between social facts and law;
(2) however, there is a gap between these social facts and the law.

In this case, the question is how to define the link in a way that would bridge the explanatory gap between social facts and law. Due to the similarity of these two problems, it is worthwhile to trace the discussion surrounding the explanatory gap problem and apply relevant conclusions to Kelsen's case. The main question here is whether there is a difference between these two approaches – and if so, where – since one apparently aims to 'eliminate' the link and the other seeks to 'eliminate' the gap.

[1] I would like to thank George Pavlakos for the tremendous feedback he gave me in reference to this chapter and his help in giving it the final form.

In this chapter, the problem of the explanatory gap and its relation to Kelsen's theory is a starting point for my argument that supervenience is the link between Is and Ought in GTN. Hence, my approach will be dominated by the attempt to situate Kelsen's normativity thesis in the broader context of contemporary discussions concerning it. This approach aims to shed more light on Kelsen's normativity thesis, mainly to explain Kelsen's strategy in the broader context of the explanatory gap. Hence, I aim to describe the explanatory gap problem, especially in jurisprudence and the broader context of earlier discussion in the philosophy of mind. Then, I will focus on possible strategies for solving the problem. I will argue that one of the strategies used by David Chalmers can be of assistance when interpreting what Kelsen meant by the Is–Ought separation in GTN in the framework proposed in this book.

5.2. THE EXPLANATORY GAP PROBLEM

The first question that needs to be addressed now is what the problem of the explanatory gap is, and why it is related to Kelsen's normativity thesis that Is and Ought are somehow separated. This requires a consideration of the debate concerning the hard problem of consciousness from the philosophy of mind. Initially, the explanatory gap was defined in terms of the impossibility of deriving facts about conscious states a priori from physical facts in the same way that facts about, eg temperature, are derived from physical facts.[2]

According to some, this impossibility stems from the fact that concepts associated with consciousness, such as red or pain are not descriptive, in contrast to physical ones, such as C-fibres. Descriptive concepts can be inferred from other concepts or facts. On the other hand, one thinks of pain or red in a *direct* way only if one has experienced these phenomenal concepts at least once.[3] This means that all we have in such cases is our own experience and we have no access to the experience of others. This observation about the explanatory gap is at the core of the argument against physicalism because the impossibility of full explanation or the reduction of conscious processes to physical processes implied the existence of the explanatory gap.

The problem of the explanatory gap was illustrated with several iconic examples in the field of analytic philosophy. For instance, Jackson's famous thought experiment describes Mary, locked in a black-and-white room. Mary is very knowledgeable about microphysical facts; however, this knowledge does not help her understand what red is.[4] Chalmers, on the other hand, provides several examples, the most famous of which is that of the philosophical zombie. Such a

[2] D Papineau, 'What Exactly Is the Explanatory Gap?' (2011) 39 *Philosophia* 5, 7.
[3] ibid.
[4] F Jackson, 'What Mary Didn't Know' (1986) 83 *The Journal of Philosophy* 291, 291–95.

zombie is identical in terms of physical matter to a human being; however, it is not conscious. Chalmers argues that from the fact that such a zombie is conceivable, it can be derived that the explanatory gap exists. Conceivability means that the truth or possibility of the cases described above cannot be ruled out a priori, as it is possible to imagine that such a situation is the case.[5] Conceivability constitutes an epistemic gap followed by an explanatory gap.

Some identify the source of the epistemic gap by recalling the paradox formulated in Kripke's account of Wittgenstein's concept of rule-following, called Kripkestein. Kripke provides the following example. Imagine an intelligence tester supposing that only one continuation of the sequence 2, 4, 6, 8 exists. Such a test would be poorly constructed because there is an indefinite number of alternative rules to continue this sequence. Hence, no unique appropriate following number for the sequence exists.[6] This means that the source of the epistemic gap, as Pavlakos defines it:

> [L]ies in the epistemic possibility of having multiple mappings from the same sets of descriptive facts of past practice to different meanings for any single collection of such facts is logically compatible with different interpretations of the target concept that is at stake.[7]

The epistemic gap means that explanatory power is also weakened, which leads to the explanatory gap. The inability to transition between two epistemic states fails to deliver a successful explanation due to the lack of transparency between these two epistemic states.[8]

The explanatory gap is associated with 'the why?' inquiry, namely 'Why, given that P is the case, is Q the case?', and takes place when Q cannot be entirely deduced from P. In other words, it is *opaque* why, given P, Q is the case because the truth of Q is not wholly explicable by the truth of P. This means that something more needs to be added to P in order to explain Q fully; otherwise, P can generate different outcomes (mappings), like the world with or without zombies.[9] As Jonathan Schaffer defines it:

> There is an explanatory gap between source and result if and only if it is opaque why the obtaining of this particular source is linked to the obtaining of that particular result (as opposed to some other result or no result at all).[10]

[5] DJ Chalmers, 'Phenomenal Concepts and the Explanatory Gap' in T Alter and S Walter (eds), *Phenomenal Concepts and Phenomenal Knowledge: New Essays on Consciousness and Physicalism* (Oxford University Press, 2007) 168–69.

[6] S Kripke, *Wittgenstein on Rules and Private Language: An Elementary Exposition*, vol 2 (Harvard University Press, 1982) 18.

[7] G Pavlakos, 'A Non-Naturalist Account of Law's Place in Reality' in B Brożek, J Hage and N Vincent (eds), *Law and Mind: A Survey of Law and the Cognitive Sciences* (Cambridge University Press, 2021) 479.

[8] ibid 478.

[9] Chalmers (n 9) 169.

[10] J Schaffer, 'The Ground Between the Gaps' (2017) 17 *Philosopher's Imprint* 1, hdl.handle.net/2027/spo.3521354.0017.011.

An epistemic gap can also imply an ontological gap, but this is not always the case. For instance, in the field of philosophy of mind, some infer from the existence of an epistemic gap with regard to consciousness that if there is an explanatory gap between physical processes and consciousness, then consciousness is not a physical process.[11] However, others who argue in favour of physicalism present strategies that attempt to avoid an ontological gap.

For my argument, there is no need to present these strategies. What matters here in reference to Kelsen's claim concerning the Is–Ought separation is the distinction between the epistemic, explanatory and ontological levels. Secondly, suppose the explanatory gap framework can be applied to his Is–Ought separation, an issue discussed below. In that case, there is still the matter of determining whether an ontological gap follows the epistemic gap. In any case, it seems that the problem of the explanatory gap has the potential to model the Is–Ought separation in the pure theory of law. Before I move to whether and how the issue of the explanatory gap applies to Kelsen, I will briefly present the problem of metaphysical explanation, which is one of the sources of the explanatory gap in jurisprudence.

5.3. METAPHYSICAL EXPLANATION IN JURISPRUDENCE

In the field of jurisprudence, the discussion revolves around the problem of explanation, how legal facts obtain, which type of facts contribute to this explanation, and how to define the relation between legal facts and their grounds. At some point in this exploration, both positivists and non-positivists encounter the problem of the explanatory gap. Its emergence is associated with metaphysical explanation, which deals with different levels of fundamentality. A metaphysical explanation, roughly speaking, is a type of non-causal explanation, hence diachronic. One example of such explanation is: 'Socrates' cloak has a colour because it is green'[12] and is explored in the field of philosophy of mind and jurisprudence.

Let us unfold this. In jurisprudence, the problem of such explanation is regarded in the context of the relation between law and other parts of social or normative reality, which are assumed to be on different levels of fundamentality. The discussion started from the challenge posed in the legal positivistic camp. Legal positivists have the following problem to solve: if, as they claim, the law does not have a fundamental character and depends on and is explained by more fundamental entities, then how exactly are they supposed to define the relation between legal facts and social facts (legal facts and its determinants)?[13]

[11] Chalmers (n 9) 169.

[12] A Brenner et al, 'Metaphysical Explanation' in EN Zalta (ed), *The Stanford Encyclopedia of Philosophy*, Winter 2021 (Metaphysics Research Lab, Stanford University, 2021), plato.stanford.edu/archives/win2021/entries/metaphysical-explanation/.

[13] See: S Chilovi and G Pavlakos, 'Law-Determination as Grounding: A Common Grounding Framework for Jurisprudence' (2019) 25 *Legal Theory* 53.

Since legal positivists and non-positivists agree that legal facts are obtained by virtue of more fundamental facts, both camps need to identify the type of this relation and show how the relation in question provides a full explanation. Pavlakos developed this inquiry into two sub-questions. Firstly, 'what is the relevant relation of dependency between law and its determinants'; and secondly, 'which determinants does the relation pick out?'[14] Since this determination is not empirical, it must be metaphysical. Hence, jurisprudence has explored the idea that metaphysical grounding was proposed as a solution to this problem.[15]

Although grounding is not the centre of attention from the point of view of this book due to its relation to supervenience, for the sake of argument and transparency it is necessary to explain this concept. The discussion concerning grounding is lively and complex; hence, I aim to give a basic explanation of grounding without diving into a detailed reconstruction of these arguments. Instead, I will limit the explanation of grounding to the most essential points.

There are many definitions of grounding. It can be defined as 'something which somehow (…, non-causally and synchronically) determines or makes the second thing exist and be the way it is'.[16] As such, grounding indicates a specific relation designated by intuition, embodied in the words 'by virtue of'; for instance, somebody is right by virtue of his own empirical perception. What is also important is that the priority link has a non-causal character.[17] In this context, Kit Fine aptly notes, 'Ground if you like, stands to philosophy as cause stands to science'.[18] Being distinct from causation, it is described by some as 'metaphysical causation'. Hence, grounding is based on the idea that apart from causal and scientific explanation there is also a distinct kind of it, of a metaphysical character, based on the 'constitutive form of determination'.[19] While causation links its elements across time, grounding does it across levels and with explanatory power.

There are some typical examples of grounding: 'Mental facts obtain because of neurophysiological facts'; 'Meaning is due to non-semantic facts'; 'A set of things is less fundamental than its members'; 'That "snow is white" is true

[14] Pavlakos (n 7) 473.

[15] Gizbert-Studnicki, 'The Social Sources Thesis. Metaphysic Sand Metaphilosophy' in P Banas, A Dyrda and T Gizbert-Studnicki (eds), *Metaphilosophy of Law* (Bloomsbury, 2016) 124. I will not go into details here regarding the relation between metaphysical explanation and grounding. For the purposes of this chapter it suffices to assume with that grounding is a metaphysical explanation of some sort and note that not all authors use the notion of grounding. Instead, for instance Greenberg, writes about 'rational determination', which is interpreted by some as grounding. See: M Greenberg, 'How Facts Make Law' (2004) 10 *Legal Theory* 225, doi.org/10.1017/S1352325204040212.

[16] A-S Maurin, 'Grounding and Metaphysical Explanation: It's Complicated' (2019) 176 *Philosophical Studies* 1573, 1574.

[17] F Correia and B Schnieder, 'Grounding: An Opinionated Introduction' in F Correia and B Schnieder (eds), *Metaphysical Grounding, Understanding the Structure of Reality* (Cambridge University Press, 2012) 1.

[18] K Fine, 'Guide to Ground' in Correia and Schnieder (ibid) 40.

[19] ibid 37.

because snow is white'; and finally 'Legal facts are grounded in non-legal, eg social, facts' and 'Normative facts are based on natural facts'.[20]

All these examples reveal the explanatory function of grounding, which in these examples is apparent. For this reason, grounding is often called 'an explanatory notion',[21] which means that if X counts as ground Y, X must explain Y. Hence, grounding's function is explanatory. In this context, explanation is construed broadly, encompassing the elucidation of the question concerning the question, 'why does a certain fact hold?'. Such an explanation is based on a determination or dependency.[22] Most philosophers who use this expression have in mind a rather vague sense of explanation, but some use 'explanation' in an epistemically and philosophically loaded sense.[23] For the sake of clarity, I will not use 'explanation' in the sense described in chapter four; however, I believe these two meanings are strongly related.

Another notable aspect in these examples is the intuition of one feature's priority and fundamentality over another. In the most general terms, the grounding idea is strictly connected with preference and its converse: dependence.[24] The question 'what is prior to what?' can be substituted with 'what grounds what?'. Such an approach can be specified, thus revealing more substantial features of grounding. Apart from the simple situation that one fact (F1) is grounded by another (F2), F1 might be grounded by F2 … Fn facts, which taken together constitute the full ground. In such case F2 … Fn are partial grounds of F1.[25] This relation is antisymmetric, antireflexive and transitive.

Hence, due to its features, namely its non-causal character, and different levels of fundamentality, the potential explanatory power of grounding is a very interesting candidate for a link between legal and non-legal facts. However, it also generates the problem of the explanatory gap. Now it is time to look closer at this problem in the field of jurisprudence.

5.4. THE EXPLANATORY GAP IN THE FIELD OF JURISPRUDENCE

The notion 'Legal facts are grounded in non-legal facts' is explored by both legal positivists and non-positivists. The disagreement between positivists and non-positivists concerns the role of value facts in this relation.[26] While positivists opt for the social sources thesis, excluding the possibility that legal facts obtain also by virtue of value facts, non-positivists claim otherwise and demonstrate their point with the problem of the explanatory gap generated by the metaphysical

[20] Correia and Schnieder (n 17) 1.
[21] ibid 24.
[22] Gizbert-Studnicki (n 15) 132–34.
[23] Correia and Schnieder (n 17) 24.
[24] ibid.
[25] Gizbert-Studnicki (n 15) 190.
[26] Chilovi and Pavlakos (n 13) 74. See also: Gizbert-Studnicki (n 15).

relation, including grounding. As will be shown later, non-positivists are also unable to avoid this problem. It seems that Pavlakos is correct in observing in the context of the explanatory gap that 'there is nothing to suggest that one must opt for the positivist exclusion of normative truths from the grounds of law or for the non-positivist inclusion of moral truth into the grounds of propositions of law'.[27]

Let us unfold this. The initial assumption underlying the positivistic notion that legal facts are grounded in social facts is that such a collection of facts must be able to explain legal facts *fully*. The challenge formulated by Mark Greenberg emerged from this notion. He distinguishes three features which need to be fulfilled in order to obtain a full explanation as to why legal facts obtain: (1) the determinants of legal facts must make the latter intelligible; (2) the grounds should make it transparent how legal facts obtain, which is followed by the demand that the relation between them cannot be opaque; and (3) the reasons why it is the case that legal facts obtain from certain legal determinants must be provided from the latter.[28] This means that someone who acquired knowledge of all possible determinants is able to derive knowledge of legal facts from such knowledge.[29] Taking into consideration the conditions formulated by Greenberg, it turns out that the challenge of legal positivists is associated with the explanatory gap, which in the field of jurisprudence was conceptualised by Chilovi and Pavlakos as follows:

> The basic idea is that no matter how many descriptive facts about agents' actions, dispositions and mental states one takes into consideration, there'll always be multiple sets of (putative) legal facts compatible with them. Equivalently, the idea is that for any given set of descriptive social facts one starts with, there will be multiple possible mappings from that set to different sets of (putative) legal facts – different models of the contribution of the social facts to the content of law, as Greenberg puts it.[30]

This means that in the framework of legal positivism, even ultimate knowledge of the social facts which determine legal facts would be associated with different mappings, that is, different sets of legal facts. Furthermore, only based on such knowledge, it is impossible to distinguish a privileged set of legal facts.[31] Hence, as Pavlakos and Chilovi put it:

> [T]he thought is that the fact that one can always "cook up" positivistically acceptable legal output for any social source input is meant to show that positivism lacks

[27] Pavlakos 'The Metaphysics of Law: From Supervenience to Rational Justification' in B Brożek, A Rotolo and J Stelmach (eds), *Supervenience and Normativity*, Law and Philosophy Library (Springer International Publishing, 2017) 240.

[28] Greenberg (n 15); S Chilovi and G Pavlakos, 'The Explanatory Demands of Grounding in Law' (2021) 103/4 *Pacific Philosophical Quarterly* 900, 905; Pavlakos (n 7) 477.

[29] Chilovi and Pavlakos (ibid) 905.

[30] ibid 907.

[31] ibid 908.

> the resources to discriminate deviant from non-deviant mappings, to tell real from merely putative law.[32]

Hence, the core issue associated with the positivistic answer to the question 'how do legal facts obtain?' is related to the explanatory gap, based on the observation that the deduction of legal facts from the knowledge of descriptive facts concerning social practice is impossible due to the epistemic possibility of producing multiple mappings from the same set of descriptive facts to legal content.[33] Put more simply, the explanatory gap concerns the identification of the determination type between social facts and legal facts, which would be able to establish one privileged mapping from the same sets of social facts. The claim is that the interpreter cannot distinguish the existing law from deviant interpretations solely on the basis of social facts.

Addressing this inquiry, Greenberg sets the stage for a possible solution, which at the same time, he claims, proves that legal positivism is false. While he captures the relation between law and some kinds of facts as 'rational determination' (which some later regarded as grounding), he adds value facts to the grounding base which, according to positivists, contains social facts only.[34] In Greenberg's intention this is supposed to solve the dilemma that positivists dealt with in a way that was unfavourable for them, but instead, as Chilovi and Pavlakos aptly argue, when investigated more closely, it turns out that the epistemic gap thus formulated also concerns non-positivists.

To illustrate this point, let us assume that a certain model of law is supported by a particular value, for instance fairness. Hence fairness is part of a grounding base, and this grounding base should fully explain the obtained legal facts. However, what if a different value supporting an alternative model of law cannot be ruled out? We must consider that two models of law supported by different values can determine legal facts. As Chilovi and Pavlakos put it:

> [E]ven granting knowledge that the relevant value(s) support(s) a certain model over all the other models, knowing this and the relevant law practices isn't enough to rule out that the law is in fact determined according to the model supported by another value.[35]

This example illustrates that we do not know which value should be added to the grounding base without additional rules clarifying this. The non-positivists claim that a certain value supports a certain model of law. However, they did not notice that even though we assume that one authoritative value, without alternatives, supports a certain model of law, the problem remains that alternative false models supported by alternative values could be conceivable. Furthermore, it might turn out that values do not support an alternative model, but by social

[32] ibid.
[33] Pavlakos (n 7) 479.
[34] Greenberg (n 15).
[35] Chilovi and Pavlakos (n 28) 914.

conventions and legal practice. There is also a danger that such a strategy might lead to the result that enriching the grounding base could turn out to be an infinite process, in which something new is continually added to the grounding base since there are no strict rules when this process should end.[36]

All in all, Greenberg's strategy, although promising and posing a challenge to the positivistic camp, did not manage to solve the explanatory gap problem. Fortunately, there is a remedy for this problem. This remedy, in the form of bridging principles, works for both positivists and non-positivists; as Chilovi and Pavlakos suggest:

> Without further information that, in addition to specifying the legal determinants, also specifies the *way* these combine together to determine legal content, the gap remains open … that facing explanatory gap problem both legal positivists and non-positivists need grounding principles.[37]

Hence, the strategy of bridging the gap is based on creating a so-called bridge between legal facts and their grounds.

The starting point of this strategy is the argument that even though knowledge about the grounds of law might be necessary for legal knowledge to be possible, more is needed due to the problem of the explanatory gap, as described above. What is additionally needed are grounding principles, which can distinguish privileged mapping from others, and as such offer a transparent explanation as to how legal facts obtain.[38]

Interestingly, this strategy could work in the context of the pure theory of law. To present this strategy in that context, first I will address the issue of how the problem of the explanatory gap applies to Kelsen, especially since by claiming the separation of Is and Ought he seems to consider the explanatory gap as good news rather than as a problem. After identifying the explanatory gap question in the pure theory of law, it will be possible to demonstrate the strategy that Kelsen suggested could bridge this gap, which was successfully employed by Pavlakos.[39]

5.5. THE STRATEGY FOR BRIDGING THE GAP AND THE PURE THEORY OF LAW

The most direct way to demonstrate that Kelsen had some hunch concerning the problem of the explanatory gap is to consider his investigation into how we may recognise law among other similar phenomena. In other words, Kelsen asks how it is possible that on seeing raised hands in a large room we know that a statute

[36] ibid 913–14.
[37] ibid 914.
[38] ibid 913.
[39] Pavlakos (n 7) 473–89.

has been passed, and how can we distinguish this situation from a secret organisation voting on their anti-state declaration? This inquiry can be perceived as a type of inquiry into how legal facts obtain from social facts.

Kelsen notes that the legal meaning is not 'immediately perceptible', in the same way that the perception of colours or texture is. Legal meaning is to be obtained by someone who, acting rationally in the first step, 'connects his act with a definite meaning that expresses itself in some way and is understood by others'.[40] This, interestingly, is reminiscent of a distinction made by Papineau in the field of philosophy of mind, namely that phenomenal concepts are obtained in a direct way. In contrast, descriptive concepts can be derived from facts. A similar argument to Kelsen's version is also employed by Greenberg in order to justify rational determination and the falseness of legal positivism.[41]

When looked at more closely, it can be seen that each author used this argument in the context of some sort of a gap; for Papineau, it was to reconstruct the argument about the explanatory gap of his opponents, while Greenberg used this argument in order to demonstrate that legal positivism is false. Still, as a result, it turned out that the problem of the explanatory gap concerns positivists as well as non-positivists. Finally, Kelsen used this argument to demonstrate the gap between legal meaning and the immediate perception of physical phenomena, which reflects his assumption that Is and Ought are to be separated. Hence it can be assumed that the explanatory gap problem concerns the question 'how do we know when a man in a robe is a judge and when is a leader of a secret organisation?'. Now, let us see how Kelsen was able to bridge this gap, according to Pavlakos.[42]

Kelsen formulated the Is–Ought separation thesis and by means of it, along with the thesis on the separation of law from morality, established the autonomy of legal science by declaring its purity. However, as Pavlakos notes, Kelsen encountered two explanatory challenges.[43] Firstly, if there is an abyss between Is and Ought then the question arises of how any knowledge of Ought can be obtained from Is. The second challenge concerns the explanation of the knowledge of the normative sphere without referring to values or facts. These challenges stem from the assumption of the non-fundamental nature of legal facts. In order to support this assumption Pavlakos cites the passage in which Kelsen notes that 'at least part of the essence of law appears to occupy the realm of nature'.[44]

For these purposes, the vocabulary changed. Pavlakos decodes Kelsen's legal propositions as legal facts, while facts are understood by Kelsen as naturalistic

[40] H Kelsen, *Pure Theory of Law* (The Lawbook Exchange, Ltd, 1967) 3.

[41] I would like to thank George Pavlakos for noting the similarities between Kelsen's and Greenberg's arguments.

[42] Pavlakos (n 7) 481.

[43] ibid 482.

[44] ibid.

facts, arising in the context of an intentional action, such as an act of will, as well as facts of social practice. Pavlakos decode the contribution of more fundamental facts as 'meaning' or 'content' in Kelsen's vocabulary. He notes that the same set of facts can be potentially interpreted as the objective or subjective meaning of an act of will. Only the contribution of fundamental facts interpreted in an objective way corresponds with the content of a legal norm. In the final step of setting the stage, Pavlakos explains that 'facts about "the objective meaning of the law" can be readily understood as facts "about the content of the law"'.[45]

Pavlakos starts his argument by observing that since particular facts can be interpreted subjectively or objectively, the objective meaning of relevant non-normative facts is the key to understanding the relation between legal facts (facts about the content of the law) and its grounds. The objective meaning of the norm means that such a norm exists as a legal one, and hence is valid. In the next step, Pavlakos observes that Kelsen explains the structure of legal facts (facts about the content of law) by introducing the category of imputation which occurs in hypothetical judgement, whose content has the structure: if A is, then B ought to be.[46] According to Pavlakos, imputation brings 'additional clarity about the explanatory task that is involved in law determination', which is a crucial advantage of the Kelsenian approach.[47] By this Pavlakos means that the vague category of legal facts gains clarity by acquiring the concrete structure of a hypothetical judgement characteristic for legal norms, at least in *Pure Theory of Law*. Imputation has the capacity to guide a thinker from a knowledge of determinants of legal facts to the recognition of legal facts.

At this point, what remains is to establish a bridge between legal facts and their grounds. This step is necessary due to the impossibility of establishing whether subjective or objective meaning occurs only on behalf of more fundamental determinants (social facts). In other words, a certain social fact, such as an act of will, can be interpreted subjectively or objectively. Without the bridging principle, there is no way to distinguish this. Furthermore, as in the case of the Kripkestein paradox, it is possible that the same set of facts subjected to multiple interpretations can produce multiple mappings of different subjective meanings. This in turn leads to the explanatory gap.

Namely, when Kelsen asks why a certain gathering of people is considered a parliament, it is the problem of how descriptive facts are turned into legal facts in a way that would limit different mappings (possible subjective meanings) and lead to objective meaning.[48] One of the strategies to cope with the problem of the explanatory gap is the introduction of bridging principles, which can restore the clarity of the link between descriptive facts and legal facts and objective

[45] ibid.
[46] ibid 484.
[47] ibid.
[48] ibid 487.

meaning, specifically regarding how descriptive facts determine legal facts. Such a bridging principle is, according to Pavlakos, the basic norm.[49] The structure of his argument is as follows.

In the first step, Pavlakos notes that the legal norm serves as a scheme (model) of interpretation:

> And that's exactly what he does: he suggests that the norm that can function as the model (scheme) of interpretation be understood as the abstract of 'objective meaning' that authorizes transition from more fundamental sources (non-normative facts) to less fundamental results (objective 'meaning-facts' or norms).[50]

Such a norm needs to be valid and hence authorized by some official source designated in a higher norm (*Stufenbau*).

However, the hierarchical structure has limits because Kelsen needs a norm at the top of the hierarchy independent of the higher norm. According to Pavlakos, in this way Kelsen combines imputation, which is an 'abstract formulation of objective meaning (i.e. the norm)', with the norm as the scheme of interpretation. Without the context of any concrete legal system, the norm 'becomes a free-floating, pure instance of imputation', which requires objectivity to be granted. This objectivity is presupposed by means of the basic norm. As such, the basic norm 'postulates the application of imputation concerning any actual, functioning legal order' and eliminates any subjective meanings (deviant mappings).[51] In such a case, imputation and the basic norm bridge the law with its grounds.

Pavlakos made a compelling and innovative attempt to interpret Kelsen's thought regarding grounding. However, this attempt stems from a different assumption of Ought's fundamentality. The question is whether his account can be compatible with the account that postulates Ought's fundamentality and whether the Is–Ought separation is sustained. This thesis seems to be in its weakest version, ruling out the logical entailment between Is and Ought. The most important epistemic dimension cannot be sustained, due to the explanatory power of grounding combined with the bridging principle. If the strategy is to be successful, it must be the case that social facts fully and transparently explain how legal facts obtain.

Another challenge might be interpreting the basic norm in this new framework. If Ought is not fundamental, then do we need a basic norm? In other words, if grounding, along with its principles, offers a solution as to why legal facts obtain, and the answer is that it happens on behalf of social facts, then the basic norm seems superfluous, at least in the sphere of cognition.

This interpretation can still be defended, if the basic norm justifies its existence in the sphere of validity, hence the question is whether in this framework it

[49] ibid 484–86.
[50] ibid 487.
[51] ibid 487–88.

is possible to explain the validity of the first constitution without recalling the basic norm. Such an explanation would proceed as follows: the first constitution is valid because we know that a parliament created it. But how do we know this was a parliament and not some illegal gathering?

The coherent way to avoid the notion of the basic norm is to state that it happens due to the efficacy of the first constitution. This is possible especially since validity and efficacy are connected even when a stronger separation between Is and Ought is sustained. If there is no other separation between Is and Ought than that of a logical character, then efficacy can suffice to explain the validity of the first constitution. In this case, the basic norm is superfluous, and the law is reduced to efficacious norms. In this case, the bridging principle would be efficacy, for there is no justification for the basic norm which falls under Ockham's razor.[52]

This is the price of such an approach, but the great gain is that Kelsen's question of how we can distinguish a parliamentary act from an unlawful one finds a very plausible and elegant solution. Likewise, eliminating the basic norm from the picture can be beneficial. Although the concept of the basic norm is a very interesting solution, from an intellectual perspective it is also seen as controversial and counterintuitive at first glance. Furthermore, Kelsen's claims indicating that he had some hunch regarding the problem of the explanatory gap also seem to support this solution. Finally, such an interpretation is possible in accordance with GTN read in a static way. This means the end of the pure theory of law, the rejection of Normativism, and a turn to the positivistic or even realistic paradigm. Instead, an extremely interesting interpretation is obtained – one full of potential ready for further exploration. Undoubtedly this interpretation demonstrates that the open texture of GTN is good news. With a closer look, the pure theory of law can be reinterpreted in many equally interesting directions.

This book, however, has a different aim– sustaining the spirit of the pure theory of law. It seems that this enterprise is possible if the fundamentality of Ought is assumed. From this point of view, it is clear that Kelsen's answer differs from the investigation concerning the social sources thesis. Instead of the orientation towards facts, he is oriented inwards, towards law. The fiction of the radical separation between Is and Ought sheds light on the fundamental character of Ought and enables normativity to be understood without reference to facts. At the same time, the separation of law and morality enables legal normativity to be comprehended without referring to values. In this case, the basic norm closes the normative system and protects it from interferences from the Is realm. Hence, this perspective tackles the issue of how to preserve the epistemic gap between Is and Ought, despite some connections between these two domains.

[52] The problem of the possibility of applying grounding to the basic norm and *Stufenbau*, which also includes a critique of Pavlakos' argument, was discussed by Carsten Heidemann and myself in the forthcoming chapter 'Grundnorm y Fundamentación' in F Alberto et al, *Hans Kelsen Ante el Siglo XXI. Un Dialogo Critico* (Universidad Nacional Autónoma Mexico, 2023) 199–223.

5.6. CHALMERS' STRATEGY

If this is correct, another strategy is required for the interpretation offered in this book.[53] Fortunately, there is one which might be a good fit, namely the strategy employed by Chalmers, who argues against the physicalism claim, which roughly speaking means that a relation of reduction occurs between phenomenal and physical, as demonstrated in several arguments, of which the most famous is the already mentioned argument of the conceivability of zombies.[54] Now it is time to take a closer look at this argument and Chalmers' argumentation as a whole.

Chalmers claims that it is logically possible for the zombie world to exist. Such a world would be identical to ours, with one difference: there would be no conscious experience. For this reason, this is a world of zombies. If such a zombie – for instance, my zombie-twin, which is exactly the same as me down to the last molecule but differs only in the respect of consciousness and phenomenal feel – is thinkable, therefore it means that logical supervenience, as a relation between the phenomenal and physical, must be ruled out. As Chalmers argues, the intelligibility of the concept of a zombie is enough for such a conclusion. Empirical possibility is irrelevant here.

This means that the reductive explanation of consciousness, which is associated with logical supervenience, cannot be successful. Such explanations might work in terms of structure and function, since structural and functional properties can be a subject of entailment and hence are susceptible to reductive explanation. Consciousness, on the other hand, cannot be explained in terms of structure and function, because structure and function are perfectly coherent with the notion of a philosophical zombie. In order to explain consciousness, something more is required, since consciousness is an additional fact to those explicable by physical facts.[55] Hence, the explanatory gap exists between the physical level and conscious experience, and a physical account is not enough to explain consciousness. Chalmers adds that the occurrence of the explanatory gap does not mean that the physical account is irrelevant when it comes to the explanation of consciousness.[56]

[53] I will avoid detailed consideration of one more potential and interesting solution, namely that of eliminativism, which denies the problem of the explanatory gap, because according to this perspective, the target domain (mental states or law) is illusionary or fictional. Although it might seem that this solution has a great potential due to the occurrence of fiction, this fiction is understood in a common, rather destructive sense. It might potentially fit with the interpretation in which the fictionality of the basic norm is followed by the fictionality of the whole legal system. In ch 3 I rejected this direction of thought, for I believe such a conclusion is possible but not necessary in the light of fictionalism. The consequences of eliminativist approach could be interesting to explore; however, it seems to me that treating the legal domain as fictional would go against the spirit of pure theory of law.

[54] DJ Chalmers, *The Conscious Mind: In Search of a Fundamental Theory* (Oxford University Press, 1996) 94–98.

[55] ibid 106.

[56] ibid 107.

Next, Chalmers turns his argument from his explanatory question, 'Can consciousness be explained by physical theories?' to the ontological question 'Is consciousness physical?'.[57] He notes that some sort of property dualism occurs between physical and phenomenal properties. Not all the properties involved in conscious experience are embedded in physical properties; some properties of conscious experience are ontologically independent of physical properties, which are 'over and above' physical features.[58] The zombie argument demonstrates that consciousness is an extra fact that physical facts cannot guarantee. This, in turn, proves that materialism is false.[59]

Based on Chalmers' argument, consciousness may arise from the physical despite not being embedded in it. He notes that 'arises' is the key feature here. It indicates some gap between the physical and consciousness, which does not occur regarding brain processes. For instance, in reference to reduction, one states that 'learning is a process of a brain' rather than 'learning arises from a brain'.[60] This indicates that consciousness is something over and above physical facts and is another *fundamental* feature, among many already postulated by physics, such as space-time, mass-energy, charge, spin, etc. Fundamental features are understood in terms of the impossibility of explanation through reference to more basic features, while fundamental laws are primitive, and inexplicable by more basic laws. Applying fundamental features and laws to a particular domain 'sets everything in place'.[61]

What remains is to define the link between consciousness and the physical. After rejecting logical supervenience, Chalmers argues that natural supervenience is a good fit here; it does not imply reduction, but rather some systematic dependence of conscious experience on physical structure.[62] This link prevents a fall into some sort of radical dualism, such as that of Descartes. It also might have the potential to resolve the puzzles of GTN.

Now we have a link which does not contradict the fundamentality of Ought, but which at the same time prevents the pure theory of law from falling into some radical version of the normativity thesis. But before I move to this issue, first the issue must be addressed of how this strategy applies to Kelsen.

5.7. THE APPLICATION OF CHALMERS' STRATEGY TO THE PURE THEORY OF LAW

It is time to set the stage. First, when Kelsen makes the following argument, his words can be interpreted as a thesis about the fundamentality of Is and Ought:

[57] ibid 123.
[58] ibid 125.
[59] ibid 123.
[60] ibid 126.
[61] ibid.
[62] Chalmers, 124.

> An Ought cannot be reduced to an Is or an Is to an Ought; and so an Is cannot be inferred from an Ought, or an Ought from an Is. Ought and Is are two wholly different meaning, or – since the plural of meaning is not idiomatic – two wholly different meanings-contents.[63]

Second, his concept of pure Ought is reminiscent of the idea of the philosophical zombie in reverse. While as a side effect of his methodological assumption, Kelsen makes the case that law thought in terms of pure Ought is thinkable, even without an explanation from the Is domain, Chalmers argues that the philosophical zombie is thinkable to demonstrate that consciousness is not reducible to the physical.

Furthermore, both of these concepts can be grasped in the fictionalist framework. Chapter four explained how the Is–Ought separation can be understood in terms of fictionalism. It can be suggested that the philosophical zombie is an excellent example of fiction. It does not agree with reality, and is empirically impossible. However, this example assists in the understanding of some hidden problem in a successful and fruitful way.

Finally, in both cases some sort of dualism occurs. These dualisms lead to conclusions regarding the fundamentality of a feature in question. In Chalmers' case it is consciousness; for Kelsen it is Ought, which is supported by the fictionalist framework.

Now, it is worthwhile to investigate how Chalmers' strategy works in reference to the explanatory gap issue revealed by Pavlakos in the pure theory of law. In order to do that, let us look closer at Kelsen's arguments where he investigates how we can distinguish an act of parliament from the unlawful act of some informal gathering. Kelsen explores this in his famous passage from *Pure Theory of Law* from 1960:

> Besides, law – or what is customarily so called – seems at least partly to be rooted in nature and to have a "natural" existence. For if you analyse any body of facts interpreted as 'legal' or somehow tied up with law, such as a parliamentary decision, an administrative act, a judgement, a contract, or a crime, two elements are distinguishable: an act or series of acts – a happening occurring at a certain time and in a certain place, perceived by our senses: an external manifestation of human conduct; two the legal meaning of this act, that is the meaning conferred upon the act by the law. For example: people assemble in a large room, make speeches, some raise their hands, others do not – this is the external happening. Its meaning is that a statute is being passed, that law is created. We are faced here with the distinction (familiar to jurists) between the process of legislation and its product, the statute.[64]

This quote is associated with the subjective meaning of an act which can turn into an objective meaning, that is, the meaning assigned to the act by law. For instance, if a secret organisation decides to assassinate somebody, for them the

[63] Kelsen (n 40) 58.
[64] ibid 2.

subjective meaning of this act is a 'death penalty', while the objective meaning, according to the law, is a murder. In the case of law, the objective meaning can be obtained by means of a norm, which Kelsen perceives as an interpretation scheme. This means that law governs its own interpretation, 'legal self-interpretation' by including 'a statement which indicates its legal meaning'. Hence, such self-interpretation is included in legal norms, which are interpretation schemes.

As Kelsen notes 'Therein lies the peculiarity of the objects of legal cognition', because plants, for instance, cannot tell a botanist anything about themselves.[65] In such a vision, facts are external and perceived by the senses. They are natural phenomena subjected to the rule of causality. What matters here is that such acts are not an object of legal cognition. This means that the issuance of a statute by parliament or a ruling by a judge is not included in the legal sphere in Kelsen's scope of interest. The catalyst which turns these events into legal or illegal acts is their interpretation, which assigns objective meaning to a particular act. Such an interpretation is carried out according to an interpretation scheme, in other words, a legal norm. 'A legal norm confers legal meaning to the act'.[66]

Kelsen notes and sums up as follows: 'The judgement that an act of human behaviour, performed in time and space, is "legal" (or "illegal") is the result of a specific, namely normative, interpretation'.[67] The key word here is *normative*; it indicates that legal normativity, the legal Ought, is acquired and presupposed in the interpretative process. Such a process is normative because its source is a legal norm. Kelsen notes: 'The norm which confers upon an act the meaning of legality or illegality is itself created by an act, which in turn receives its legal character from yet another norm'.[68] Such a view might lead to a vicious circle, for how can one cognise that a particular norm is of a legal character? Obviously only by means of a higher norm. This *regressum ad inifinitum* is broken by the basic norm, which in GTN is a fictional presupposition and, as was demonstrated before, only makes sense when Ought is regarded as fundamental. Otherwise, it is superfluous.

If Ought is assumed as fundamental, then for Kelsen the starting point and central point is law, while the legal positivists put more emphasis on social *facts* and perceive law in this context. Hence, Kelsen's investigation of 'how law is cognised' cannot be reduced to the inquiry into 'how legal facts are obtained'. While the first can be elaborated into 'assuming normativity as given, how law can be cognised?', the latter holds normativity as unknown, yet to be reconstructed from social facts. Hence, what constitutes the difference is the fundamentality of Ought. If Ought is considered fundamental, the question of 'how legal facts obtain from social facts' lies beyond the scope of consideration because Ought is the starting point of the deliberations.

[65] ibid 3.
[66] ibid 4.
[67] ibid.
[68] ibid.

The parallels between Kelsen and Chalmers are clear. The assumption of fundamentality leads both of them to employ similar strategies. Hence, what is left to explore is the issue of whether the parallels between Chalmers' and Kelsen's strategies also encompass the notion of supervenience. If this turns out to be true, then supervenience can be a potential solution for a second problem of GTN: the weakened Is–Ought separation. As a result, Chalmers' strategy can be used when defining links in 'borderline' situations: the Is domain is fundamental, and so is the Ought domain. Natural supervenience has the potential to reveal links between them in a way which leaves their fundamentality intact.

5.8. TWO PERSPECTIVES

Finally, it is time to compare Kelsen's perspective with the positivistic one. First, it can be noted that grounding does not seem to be a good fit for Kelsen in such a framework, because he does not look for an explanation of how Y, by virtue of X, obtains. This is due to the assumption that any X is a part of the nature of any Y, as Pavlakos puts it. The relation between X and Y occurs when the law is investigated 'as something else', in this case as some kind of social phenomenon. This perspective can be only peripheral for Kelsen, who examines 'law as such'.

If Ought is not fundamental, then the starting point is fact. This positivistic approach seems to be more natural; after all we all live in the realm of facts, so this perspective is the closest to us. But the brilliance of Kelsen's thought is that, despite natural intuitions, he turned the perspective around by arguing that the starting point for the investigation of law is law itself, which governs its own interpretation. This way, the starting point is the sphere of the legal Ought.

One could argue against such an approach by suggesting that perhaps Kelsen was also analysing 'law as X'; in this case, it was law analysed as a normative phenomenon. Such a tactic is possible but would not change much in the whole argumentation. Perhaps law could be reduced to something even more basic than normativity; this more basic category would envision law as such. However, compared with the positivistic vision of law, Kelsen offers a more basic account of law, which can be regarded as 'law as such' in relation to the positivistic view of 'law as something else'.

In short, the perception of law 'as such' does not envision the explanatory gap as a problem to solve, while 'law as something else' does. Therefore, Kelsen's and the legal positivists' approaches cannot be equalised. More importantly, while it seems to be rather impossible to eliminate the normative perspective from the concept of law, it is possible to construct a meaningful theory of law while eliminating all the facts (and values) from it, as Kelsen did. It seems that the only way to defend the objection against the law 'as such' would be to make a radical reduction of a normative phenomenon into a fact that deducts normativity from it.

At first glance, these interpretations could not be compatible in any way. It seems that it is an 'either–or' situation. Should one solution be correct, and the other is wrong. Unless these two are regarded from different perspectives. Kelsen's normative approach is adopted from an internal perspective, which is possible only when adopted from an Ought point of view. In this case, Ought has to be fundamental. This is a perspective which grasps normativity and provides a pure model of law.

The second perspective is external and is more compatible with a direct reading of GTN which challenges the axioms of *Pure Theory of Law*. Instead of focusing on the mind of lawyers and how they cognise law from the inside, a social, broader perspective becomes available, which examines law 'from the outside'. This perspective occupies the Is point of view, in which Ought is no longer fundamental. The conviction regarding the fundamental character of Ought is rejected here and substituted with the grounding relation between legal facts and social facts, which assumes that one level is more fundamental than the other. The inquiry tackled here is different to the one discussed in the case of the fundamentality of Ought, being as follows: how to bridge the gap despite some separation between Is and Ought. Bridging the gap has a side effect: the artificial construct of the basic norm is no longer necessary.

All in all, the legal positivists pose a different question than Kelsen's. These questions are hardly reducible to one another. Kelsen offered the answer to his inquiry by arguing that law is an Ought of a special kind. Assuming the fundamentality of Ought, all law remains in the normative sphere, 'closing' it through the basic norm. The issue he needs to address is: 'given that law is separated from fact, how to explain these few links between Is and Ought which already occur in pure theory of law.

In contrast, legal positivists tackle the opposite problem: 'given that law is a social fact of some kind, how to explain this relation without falling into the naturalistic fallacy'. Hence, there are two distinct inquiries stemming from different assumptions concerning fundamentality: (1) what kind of links are there between Is and Ought, when law is examined as 'law as such'; and (2) what kind of links are there between Is and Ought when law is examined as 'law as a social fact'? The answer to the latter inquiry is provided in discussions among legal positivists.

If Pavlakos' enterprise is successful, legal facts are supposed to be fully explained by social facts. Hence, such an interpretation, instead of being incompatible, can be perceived as constituting a step forward, and by using Kelsen's categories the perspective addresses a significant issue which was not central for *Pure Theory of Law*. Categories from *Pure Theory of Law* have the potential to shed more light on the relationship between law and facts in terms of grounding, offering a sophisticated potential solution to the problem. Pavlakos' solution demonstrates that there are many more angles of scientific investigation. 'How do legal facts obtain?', 'What kind of elements does such a relation require?' – these inquiries are important, but they are not at the centre of attention when the inquiry about law 'as such' is examined.

I do not think one approach is better than the other; I do not even think they compete. They are tackling different issues; as such, both have value by revealing some aspects and elements of the legal domain. Both of these perspectives enable a more profound understanding of legal phenomena, from different angles. The only moment in which one of them needs to be discarded is when a researcher needs to commit to one of them. When one perspective is already chosen, the other one needs to be set aside for coherence in research. My aim in the dynamic interpretation framework is to answer the first inquiry: what kind of links occur between Is and Ought when the law is examined 'as such'?

Hence, the explanatory gap problem is related to Kelsen's assumption that Is and Ought are to be separated. Depending on our stance on Ought's fundamentality, the explanatory gap's problem plays a different function. If Ought is not understood as fundamental, following Pavlakos, Kelsen's pure theory of law provides an excellent example of a strategy of bridging the gap. Or, if Ought is taken to be fundamental, the explanatory gap sheds some light on Kelsen's strategy concerning Is and Ought, by directing attention to Chalmers and how he used the explanatory gap argument to define the relations between consciousness and the physical in the form of natural supervenience.

At this point, I assume the fundamentality of Ought, which potentially allows me to establish relations of supervenience as occurring between elements standing in borderline situations by exploiting the strategy of Chalmers, who demonstrated that phenomenal facts are fundamental and their relation to physical facts is that of natural supervenience. This allows me to formulate the hypothesis that this kind of supervenience has the potential to solve the puzzles concerning the weakening relations between Is and Ought. It seems that supervenience is able to sustain the fundamentality of Ought. The question is whether the application of supervenience to Kelsen's pure theory of law brings some fruitful and coherent results.

6

Natural Supervenience and the Fundamentality of Ought

6.1. THE IDEA OF SUPERVENIENCE

IN THE PREVIOUS chapter, I analysed the explanatory gap problem, tackled in philosophy of mind and jurisprudence. Although it sheds some light on Is–Ought puzzles, it turned out that this perspective differs from the one Kelsen adopted. Instead, he 'follows' Chalmers' strategy, in which the categories in question are fundamental. Hence, none of these categories explains how another is obtained. The core of the problem is moved to the potential link that might shed some light on the relations between Is and Ought, that is, natural supervenience. In this chapter, I will demonstrate why and how supervenience can fulfil the task of being a link between Is and Ought in the framework of pure theory of law. First, I will provide some explanation of the concept of supervenience. Next, I will analyse why this relation was rejected as a solution to the explanatory gap problem. These reasons might shed some light on the usefulness of this link for borderline situations. Finally, regarding Kelsen's normativity thesis, I will address whether this link could work in borderline situations. I will discuss the general framework for applying supervenience in GTN by distinguishing Is and Ought's ontological and epistemological dimensions.

The discussion on supervenience is vast, and this notion is also applied in many philosophical domains, with the two most prominent being philosophy of mind and ethics. For this reason, I will limit my explanation of supervenience to the most substantial knowledge relevant to this book's aim.

Supervenience is often envisioned by the slogan 'there cannot be an A difference without a B difference'.[1] The most useful conceptualisation of this problem from the point of view of this book was put forward by RM Hare, who noted:

> First let us take that characteristic of 'good' which has been called its supervenience. Suppose that we say 'St. Francis was a good man.' It is logically impossible to say thus and to maintain at the same time that there might have been another man

[1] B McLaughlin and K Bennett, 'Supervenience' in EN Zalta (ed), *The Stanford Encyclopedia of Philosophy*, (Metaphysics Research Lab, Stanford University, 2018), plato.stanford.edu/archives/spr2018/entries/supervenience.

> placed exactly in the same circumstances as St. Francis and who behaved in exactly the same way but who differed from St. Francis in this respect only that he was not a good man.[2]

Hence, Hare indicated that if two people share the same sets of moral properties, then it is logically impossible for them to differ regarding their goodness.

This example was later very aptly explained by Jaegwon Kim. Thus, in Hare's example, set A contains the property of being a good man, so it contains two properties (G and -G), and set B contains such properties as being courageous, benevolent and honest. If A weakly supervenes on B, it means that if two men share only two of the same properties from the B set, eg being honest and benevolent, then both of them are either good or not good. Hence, they share the same property in A. In other words, if they have a different property in A, it means that there are some properties in B through which they differ (for instance, x is courageous and y is not). As Kim puts it: 'base properties must determine supervenient properties in the sense that once the former is fixed on the object, there is no freedom to vary the latter for that object'.[3]

For my argument, the starting point will be the so-called 'core idea of supervenience', the simplest and most intuitive version of this concept. Such supervenience is of a purely modal sort, which implies that it has no explanatory power. It states that 'Variation in A-respects depends on variation in B-respects in that A-respects *cannot* vary without variation in B-respects. Variation in the *supervenient* A-respects *requires* variation in the *subvenient* B-respects', as Laughlin defines this kind of supervenience.[4] Supervenience, thus defined, can be developed in several types, from which the most important is the distinction between weak, strong and global supervenience. For the sake of argument, I will focus on the two first kinds of supervenience, since these types are used in arguments concerning the relations between law and facts.[5] Weak supervenience is defined by Jaegwon Kim as follows:

> A weakly supervenes on B if and only if necessarily for any x and y if x and y share all properties in B then x and y share all properties in A – that is, indiscernibility with respect to B entails indiscernibility with respect to A.[6]

Kim explains this definition: A and B are sets of properties, where A is the supervenient family and B is the supervenient base. Kim calls this type of supervenience weak because it works only within one particular and possible world.

[2] RM Hare, *The Language of Morals*, reprint (Oxford University Press, 1991) 137–50. See also J Kim, *Supervenience and Mind: Selected Philosophical Essays*, 1st edition (Cambridge University Press, 1993) 55.

[3] Kim (ibid) 60.

[4] BP McLaughlin, 'Varieties of Supervenience' in E Savellos and O Yalchin (eds), *Supervenience* (Cambridge University Press, 1994) 18.

[5] See eg: B Brożek, 'Law, Normativity, and Supervenience' in B Brożek, A Rotolo and J Stelmach (eds), *Supervenience and Normativity* (Springer International Publishing, 2017) 123–38.

[6] Kim (n 2) 58.

The same properties could produce a random, even contradictory result in other possible worlds.[7]

Kim also introduces strong supervenience,[8] which ensures that the connection between two sets of properties is more than a 'coincidence that varies from world to world'.[9] According to Kim, only the strong type of supervenience allows us to say 'although Charles is not a good man, he would be if he was courageous'.[10] This sentence concerns two possible worlds: the actual one, where Charles is not a good man, and another where, being courageous, Charles is a good man. One could not make such an assumption based on weak supervenience, since in other possible worlds, the property of courage could be irrelevant to being good or bad.

The concept of supervenience was also explored in jurisprudence in the context of the explanatory gap. However, it was rejected as too weak to serve this purpose. In order to gain more clarity as to how Kelsen could use this concept, it will be worthwhile to analyse some arguments concerning the rejection of supervenience due to its lack of explanatory power.

6.2. SUPERVENIENCE IN JURISPRUDENCE

Despite having some potential, supervenience is too weak to fulfil the role of the explanatory link between social and legal facts unless legal facts are understood as non-normative.[11] However, the difficulties met when attempting to solve the problem of the explanatory gap by means of supervenience might be interesting when contrasted with Kelsen's approach. I will focus on the legal positivistic approach because the explanatory gap problem is the most apparent in this case. Also, the proximity of positivistic views to Kelsen's account makes such a limitation justified, and they provide a good starting point for introducing supervenience into GTN by setting the stage in the jurisprudential field.

The main argument against this approach, in the context of the explanatory gap, is that supervenience does not have explanatory power. For instance, Greenberg, throwing down a challenge to the positivistic camp, notes that supervenience seems too weak for positivist needs. He argues that supervenience is insufficient due to lack of explanatory power, and in his elaborated argument he promotes a more demanding relation of rational determination.[12] The theme

[7] ibid 60.
[8] ibid 64.
[9] ibid 60.
[10] ibid.
[11] G Pavlakos, 'The Metaphysics of Law: From Supervenience to Rational Justification' in Brożek, Rotolo and Stelmach (n 5) 270 fn 1.
[12] M Greenberg, 'How Facts Make Law' (2004) 10 *Legal Theory* 225, doi.org/10.1017/S1352325204040212.

of the insufficient character of supervenience is continued by Pavlakos, who elaborates on Greenberg's thought in more detail. According to Pavlakos, supervenience is a surface relation that does not explain how this relation is obtained, as it can be understood in terms of 'mapping from the outside'. As Pavlakos puts it

> [S]upervenience maps the relation between two levels of sets of facts (or other items) as if it were from 'the outside', without explaining its obtaining: it captures the pattern in which the two levels of fact interact with one another, but fails to explain why the supervenience base stands in the relation it does to the supervening level.[13]

Although stronger kinds of supervenience are associated with reduction or grounding, in general, supervenience indicates only some pattern which is not necessarily constitutive of dependency. For example, the ball is red *by virtue of* the laws of physics and not because it is 'red and round'. The latter relation can fall under supervenience, but only the former is a relation defined by grounding. As such, supervenience does not have explanatory power.[14]

A much more detailed argument is provided by Brożek, who analyses the thesis that law supervenes on facts. In the first step, he provides a general definition of supervenience in this context. He defines supervenience as consisting of two conditions:[15]

1. For any possible worlds w_i and w_j, if w_i and w_j are factually identical, then w_i and w_j are legally identical.
2. For any possible worlds w_i and w_j, if w_i and w_j are legally identical, w_i and w_j are not necessarily factually identical.

As can be seen, this definition has a strong character, assuming that supervenience occurs on the level of possible worlds. This character of supervenience is enforced by elements which supervenience is supposed to bind: law and facts.

Just from this definition, it can be seen that Kelsen's task is more modest. Namely, assuming that law is distinct from facts, only borderline cases need to be investigated. Hence, the inquiry in Kelsen's case does not concern the general relation between law and facts, but rather tackles the question: 'what kind of link occurs in borderline cases, such as a norm and the act of will – validity and efficacy and perhaps imputation?'.

But Brożek does not rest here. He elaborates his definition in an interesting direction from Kelsen's perspective. He notes that although supervenience might have the potential to explain the relation between law and facts, it might be unable to provide an entirely satisfactory answer since some facts do not change

[13] G Pavlakos, 'The Metaphysics of Law: From Supervenience to Rational Justification', SSRN Scholarly Paper (Social Science Research Network, 13 December 2014) 243, papers.ssrn.com/abstract=2589845.

[14] K Fine, 'Guide to Ground' in F Correia and B Schnieder, *Metaphysical Grounding, Understanding the Structure of Reality* (Cambridge University Press, 2012) 38.

[15] Brożek (n 5) 164.

the legal world. The question is what kind of properties constitute the identity of w_i and w_j. Thus, Brożek provides a modification of his formula:[16]

1. For any possible worlds w_i and w_j, if w_i and w_j have the same distribution of the natural properties, then w_i and w_j are legally identical.
2. For any possible worlds w_i and w_j, if w_i and w_j are legally identical, w_i and w_j do not necessarily have the same distribution of properties.

Brożek notes that such a formulation requires some external criterion in order to distinguish relevant facts for the subvenient level of legal phenomena because several different conceptions of law (eg law as a social fact or law as a psychological fact) might compete with each other on this level.[17]

The second problem indicated by Brożek is associated with the issue of the identity of legal properties. The supervenience relation implies that properties on a factual level are to be identical in w_i and w_j, in order to constitute legal facts which are also alike in w_i and w_j. The problem is: what if some social facts are identical and, at the same time, legal facts are not. If legal properties are statements such as 'being married to Z', it can easily be imagined that two identical worlds exist, except for one fact: John is married to Jane in w_1 and is not in w_2.[18]

This is an important objection, which will be a challenge for some borderline situations. In other words, the same social facts can produce different results in the normative sphere. Hence, I will discuss this in more detail in the following chapter, where I analyse particular cases of supervenience. For now, it suffices to say that in the dynamic framework of pure theory of law there is a way to avoid this difficulty if these relations are considered as scientific models of legal thinking. As will be shown in the next chapter, the aim of supervenience is not to 'explain' how legal facts obtain from social facts, but rather to reconstruct the patterns of legal thinking which occur in borderline situations. What supervenience does is provide a scientific model of legal thinking, which means it leaves aside other less privileged mappings that might occur in reality.

Next, Brożek argues that although on the level of legal properties supervenience would not work, supervenience would still be possible on the level of legal rules, and he operates on the following example of legal rules:[19]

If a person x caused damage to a person y, then x ought to pay compensation to y.

If a person x killed a person y with cruelty, then x should be sentenced to life imprisonment.

What is interesting is that Brożek's example has some resemblance to imputation, especially since he mentions such natural properties as 'killed with

[16] ibid 164.
[17] ibid 165–66.
[18] ibid 168–169.
[19] ibid 169.

cruelty', and 'caused damage to', which are paired with such legal properties as: 'ought to pay compensation', 'being sentenced to life imprisonment'. Eventually, Brożek derives from these properties the above legal rules, reminiscent of Kelsen's imputation, understood in terms of a condition and a consequence linked by an ought operator.

However, as much as I am convinced that imputation is strongly associated with supervenience, or is even some type of supervenience, in Kelsen's case, this conception of imputation does not come without difficulties. I will discuss them in the next chapter. In any case, even if it turned out that imputation in the version known from *Pure Theory of Law* is not a case of a borderline situation between Is and Ought, it is worthwhile exploring it in this context as well, due to its close relation to supervenience. As such, initially, I will add imputation to borderline situations and discuss whether such an interpretation of imputation as a link between facts and norms is possible in terms of the pure theory of law. This, in turn, might shed more light on the criterion for the legal properties mentioned by Brożek.

The level change, from legal properties to legal rules, brings another problem: how legal rules fit into the already drawn framework. There might be two ways of tackling this issue, depending on whether legal rules are derivative or constitutive. Legal rules are derivative of legal properties if they describe the supervenience pattern. They reflect the pattern between natural properties (caused damage; killed with cruelty) and legal properties (ought to pay compensation; sentenced to life imprisonment), which is supervenience. Hence, rules are recognised by identifying some patterns and regularities in legal properties. In such a case, which properties are legal must already be known. Hence supervenience depends on the definition of 'legal'.[20]

In the case of derivative rules, the requirement of an external normative criterion for legal properties seems to fit more with Pavlakos's solution to the problem of the explanatory gap in the pure theory of law. This additional criterion is missing to distinguish legal properties from less privileged mappings, that is, properties that are not legal but could be derived from natural properties. In the framework of this solution, the basic norm combined with imputation provides such a criterion, and they bridge the explanatory gap between social facts and legal facts.

This means that the fundamental character of Ought is associated with the constitutive character of rules. If legal rules are of a constitutive character and are at the centre of legal ontology, then they themselves determine the legal character of certain properties, and as Brożek puts it, generate a relation of supervenience. As such, they are normative prior to supervenience being put in motion.[21] In this framework, we know that a certain gathering is a parliament

[20] ibid 168.
[21] ibid 170.

issuing a legal norm, because the constitution grants parliament the authority to issue such a norm, and the validity of the constitution stems from the assumption of the basic norm.

Brożek concludes that legal rules are not supervenient entities in each case because this function is ascribed to legal properties. Hence, in each case, an external criterion is necessary to determine facts constituting a subvenient level of legal phenomena or to establish the criterion that underlies the normativity of legal rules. This means that supervenience fails to provide a full account of the existence of the normative sphere, and in each case, a normative sphere remains which does not fall under the relation of supervenience.[22]

While supervenience is insufficient in the context of the discussion surrounding the problem of the explanatory gap, for the dynamic interpretation of GTN, such conclusions are good news. The constitutive character of legal rules is aligned with the assumption of the fundamentality of Ought. The rejection of supervenience might be interesting from Kelsen's point of view since he denied the possibility that law can be explained in terms of social facts – at least for legal science. Hence, Brożek's argument concerning the insufficiency of supervenience supports my hypothesis that supervenience can be the link between Is and Ought when their fundamentality is assumed.

To sum up, the approach focused on the relation between law and facts is natural for legal positivists, and indeed, from the point of view of legal positivism, supervenience cannot fulfil the expectation of fully explaining the link between legal and social facts. Supervenience indicates some dependency, but a dependency that is weak and has no explanatory power. Supervenience cannot turn factual into normative; it always requires additional assumptions or rules that make normativity happen. In the best-case scenario, supervenience can be the mechanism which explains how these two spheres – the factual and the normative – work together. As such, it cannot fulfil the hopes of the legal positivists, but it might be very promising for Kelsen.

Furthermore, to round off the explanatory gap issue, treating this gap as a problem to be solved is not Kelsen's perspective. For the same reasons that the legal positivists and non-positivists had to reject supervenience in the framework of this discussion, it might be precisely the link needed for Kelsen's legal science. By being weak, supervenience respects this distinct character of law, which is normative and 'as such' cannot be regarded as some sort of fact. At the same time, supervenience offers a potential mechanism by virtue of which law and facts co-exist and influence each other in borderline situations. Supervenience's weak character might be an answer to this riddle because its task is to provide the link that would not reduce Ought to Is and that would sustain the separation rather than provide an explanation of how a natural fact becomes a legal fact.

[22] ibid.

At this stage, I have demonstrated the general claim that in GTN supervenience has the potential to be the relation which links law with facts. This claim is supported by Brożek's observation that the notion of supervenience makes sense if legal rules are at the centre of legal ontology and are of a constitutive character.[23] The assumption of the fundamentality of Ought solves this problem. In addition, in the case of imputation, Brożek provided a useful framework and tools to interpret it as supervenience. Now, it is time to provide a framework for applying supervenience to Kelsen's GTN.

6.3. THE ONTOLOGICAL AND EPISTEMOLOGICAL DIMENSIONS OF IS AND OUGHT

If the idea of pure theory of law is to be sustained in the final phase of Kelsen's investigations, the most crucial problem is determining whether supervenience impairs Kelsen's separation of Is and Ought and how it can be reconciled with the fictional paradigm. This is a middle ground between the radicality of the separation between Is and Ought, and the overly strong connection in the form of grounding. As such, it is compatible with two theses I defend: (1) Kelsen claimed some separation between Is and Ought (law and facts); and (2) Kelsen was aware that these two realms are somehow related to each other. The task right now is to reconcile these two theses, namely, how Is and Ought can be separated and linked simultaneously. In other words, in which aspect or meaning are Is and Ought separated, and in which aspect or sense are they linked? I will argue that the solution lies in the distinction between Is and Ought's ontological and epistemological aspects, which is analogical to Chalmers' argument.

In the first step, it is necessary to establish how the ontological and epistemological levels are conceptualised in the GTN framework. Many scholars mentioned these levels. For instance, following Jerzy Wróblewski, three levels of the Is–Ought duality can be distinguished: the logical level, the epistemic level and the ontological level.[24] In the same manner, Heidemann, concerning GTN distinguishes the field of cognition (*Erkenntnisebene*) and the field of given objects (*gegebene Gegenstande*). The legal norm as an object is understood in terms of the empirical dimension and realism; the norm as an entity belonging to the ideal sphere can be cognised scientifically as long as the cognition is empirically verifiable. In this case, this means that either it is dependent on

[23] ibid 166.

[24] J Wróblewski, *Krytyka normatywistycznej teorii prawa i państwa Hansa Kelsena* (PWN, 1955) 34–57. On logical level the question is whether supervenience would impair Hume's guillotine. According to Gizbert-Studnicki, this is not the case since in supervenience Ought is not derived from Is. A similar answer is provided by Brożek, who pointed out that supervenience is a much weaker relation than material implication. Hence, also in the field of logic this separation remains weakened.

facts or it is the meaning of a particular fact.[25] Hence, these two dimensions – ontological and epistemological – are the most relevant for solving the problem.

The Neo-Kantian thesis influenced the epistemological dimension that the method of cognition determines the object of cognition. This approach is reminiscent of Kelsen's classical tactic and the methodological aspect is primary here. In order to answer the question of whether supervenience weakens the Is–Ought duality on this level, it is worth explaining why Kelsen needed this separation. The answer is commonly known, since it is outlined in the title of his best-known book: *Pure Theory of Law*. Here Kelsen was inquiring about the conditions of legal science and argued that legal science is possible only if it is pure, in other words, if it is not ideological. This means that such a theory has no factual (sociological or psychological) or moral elements. Hence, Kelsen needed the separability thesis to examine law 'as such'. In practice, this approach meant the prohibition of explaining any legal phenomena by social facts or morality for the needs of legal science. And to this extent, there should indeed be no relations between Is and Ought. For this reason, the fiction of purity is employed in GTN.

At the same time, this solution corresponds with the epistemic gap, although it is not identical to it. The epistemic gap indicates a lack of transparency when one enquires about how legal facts are obtained from social facts. Kelsen goes further here. He claims that it is impossible to explain Ought by referring to the Is domain if one is engaged in a legal science project that is cognising law as such. The observation that the epistemic gap exists between law and facts supports his claim. Still, Kelsen's claim is stronger, since the epistemic gap argument does not exclude the possibility of explaining legal facts by social facts. Rather, it poses a challenge to those who want to explain one by the other.

If that is the case, we can go back to the problem of whether supervenience weakens the separation of Is and Ought in Kelsen's terms. I believe this is not the case, since supervenience only states some relations and patterns between law and facts without attributing a constitutive character to them. Moreover, the supervenience claim concerns the ontological level rather than the epistemic one. On the ontological level, the world of Is influences the world of Ought in a visible way, especially in borderline situations. On the epistemological level, the separation becomes radical due to the fiction of purity. Still, borderline situations do not belong to the process of cognition, but rather are an emanation of two surfaces linked to each other: one concerns norms, the other facts. The question is: how to specify the way in which they are linked, and how exactly could supervenience work in such a framework?

Fortunately, we have Chalmers' strategy, which was already described in chapter five and displayed satisfying parallels with Kelsen's train of thought.

[25] C Heidemann, *Die Norm Als Tatsache* (Nomos Verlagsgesellschaft, 1997) 161.

Chalmers also distinguishes between the epistemic and ontological dimensions on which he bases his argument. The problem of the epistemic gap concerns the epistemic level, from which he derives the notion of the fundamentality of consciousness on the ontological level. For him, the gap between the physical and consciousness cannot be bridged; that is, consciousness cannot find its full explanation in the physical because of the fundamental character of these two domains. Fundamentality refers to the ontological level. Chalmers does not deny that there are links between consciousness and the physical; he just denies that consciousness can be reduced to the physical and explained by it. Consequently, as a link between the physical and consciousness, he proposes natural supervenience, which is weaker than the logical type of supervenience. The latter is associated with reduction.

It seems that this strategy could work in Kelsen's case: Is and Ought occur on the ontological level, both are fundamental in nature, and there are links between them in the form of supervenience. Hence, supervenience occurs on the ontological level. The epistemic level is dominated by fictionalism. What remains from this analogy is to specify what Chalmers meant by logical and natural supervenience and how it applies to Kelsen. Following Chalmers, I assume that metaphysical necessity has the same strength as logical necessity. Hence, I will limit my argument to the latter form.

6.4. NATURAL SUPERVENIENCE AS A LINK BETWEEN IS AND OUGHT

Supervenience appears in different modal strengths.[26] Logical supervenience is defined by Chalmers as follows: 'B-properties supervene *logically* on A-properties if no two *logically possible* situations are identical concerning their A-properties but distinct concerning their B-properties'.[27] This type of supervenience is connected to logical possibility understood in the broadest sense. Such possibility does not exclude that pigs can fly; it only excludes logical contradictions; for instance, a married bachelor is excluded as a logically impossible concept.[28]

It seems that, due to its strength, logical supervenience cannot even be reconciled with Pavlakos's interpretation of the explanatory gap, which can be extrapolated from Kelsen, because his solution assumed a very weak separation of Is and Ought, which excluded only the possibility that Is entails Ought. By contrast, logical supervenience is associated with A-fact entailing B-fact in such a manner that 'it is logically impossible for the first to hold without the second'.[29]

[26] McLaughlin and Bennett (n 1).

[27] DJ Chalmers, *The Conscious Mind: In Search of a Fundamental Theory* (Oxford University Press, 1996) 35.

[28] ibid.

[29] ibid.

In the case of Pavlakos's interpretation, the bridging principle is added to fully explain A-facts, that is, legal facts, which set his interpretation closer to natural supervenience or grounding.

The fundamentality of Ought excludes logical supervenience even more clearly. Legal facts cannot be entailed in social facts, or explained by them. At this point, it is worth recalling that the fundamentality notion in this framework stems from the Zombie argument, and thought about the law in the pure Ought realm, without any reference to facts. Given that both the philosophical zombie and the theory of law in terms of purity are conceivable, logical supervenience is excluded. One thing requires clarification here. As I argued in chapter four, the world of 'pure law' is inconceivable. Law without its social context does not make sense. This means that law is not fundamental, but rather the Ought domain is fundamental. Although this stems directly from Kelsen's *Lehre*, it is important to highlight what is considered fundamental in order to avoid misunderstandings.

At the same time, fundamentality does not mean no relations between the physical and the Is realm. The connection between the domains in question is natural supervenience, which, being weaker than logical supervenience, is compatible with the assumption of fundamentality because it excludes the entailment of A-facts in B-facts. Chalmers defines natural supervenience as follows: 'B-properties supervene naturally on A-properties if any two *naturally possible* situations with the same A-properties have the same B-properties … when the A-facts about situation naturally necessitate B-facts'.[30] This means that the world in which A-facts hold without B-facts is conceivable.[31]

This is followed by lawful correlation, that is, a correlation that is not coincidental, 'when instantiating the A-properties will always bring about the B-properties, wherever, and whenever this happens'. Such co-occurrence must take place in the case of natural supervenience, but not necessarily in the case of logical supervenience.[32] This kind of supervenience additionally requires some bridging principle between A-facts and B-facts, associated with natural possibility. With the example of flying pigs, there is such a logical possibility; for instance, on a different planet with different physical conditions pigs might be able to fly. However, the natural possibility is excluded in this case by virtue of the existing laws of nature. Hence, logical possibility includes the subset of natural possibilities.[33]

The example of zombies provides a clear illustration of this difference. Logically a creature which is physically identical to a conscious individual may have no conscious experience, but this is impossible in nature. This excludes

[30] ibid 36.
[31] ibid 41.
[32] ibid 37.
[33] ibid.

logical supervenience and sustains natural supervenience. Chalmers explains these complex relations in a very compelling and clear way:

> If B-properties supervene logically on A-properties, then once God (hypothetically) creates a world with certain A-facts, the B-facts come along for free as an automatic consequence. If B-properties merely supervene naturally on A-properties, however, then after making sure of the A-facts, God has to do more work in order to make sure of the B-facts. He has to makes sure there is a law relating to A-facts and B-facts .... Once the law is in place, the relevant A-facts will automatically bring along the B-facts.[34]

Hence, natural supervenience binds A-facts and B-facts, provided that some additional laws relate to A-facts and B-facts. They are necessary because in the case of fundamental features supervenience is silent, which is why the pattern in question holds.[35]

A fundamental issue exists concerning the metaphysical character of supervenience within the framework of the pure theory of law, due to a crucial assumption of Kelsen's theory, which involves the categorical rejection of metaphysical considerations. Consequently, a puzzling dilemma emerges: how can the concept of supervenience align harmoniously with Kelsen's original intentions?

Arguably, a viable avenue exists for rationalising the inclusion of supervenience within the pure theory of law, notwithstanding its metaphysical nature. Central to this deliberation is the exploration of why Kelsen rejected metaphysical elements in the first place. The answer to this question hinges on his critical examination of natural law doctrines and their lack of scientific character. Kelsen's arguments were primarily directed towards discrediting such metaphysical dualism.[36] Within this context, it becomes apparent that the metaphysical character of supervenience, a concept extensively employed within analytical philosophy, may not inherently contravene Kelsen's original intentions. It could be argued that this concept serves to reinstate a degree of coherence to his final work and shed light on the complex nature of the dichotomy between 'Is' and 'Ought'.

Summing up, laws of nature of some sort constitute the pattern of natural supervenience in the case of consciousness. On the other hand, the pure theory of law seems to constitute its own principles, according to which natural supervenience in borderline situations can work. In order to identify these principles, each borderline situation needs to be regarded separately, as the laws of nature are established separately for each particular domain. For instance, different laws concern thermodynamics and different ones refer to quantum mechanics, etc. The same might be the case with borderline situations and imputation

[34] ibid 38.
[35] McLaughlin and Bennett (n 1). I would like to thank George Pavlakos for this remark.
[36] H Kelsen, *General Theory of Law and State*, trans A Wedberg (Harward University Press, 1945) 419–44.

In the next chapter, I will apply supervenience to these three cases: imputation, the norm, and the act of will; and efficacy, validity, and the basic norm. Before I analyse particular cases of borderline situations, it will be useful to specify what I mean by them.

6.5. BORDERLINE SITUATIONS

The argument which leads me to the notion of borderline situations is as follows. Borderline situations, especially efficacy in relation to validity, and will in relation to the norm, at first glance constitute a threat to the normativity thesis, which is the core of the pure theory of law. However, Brożek's observation that radical separation does not do any good for Kelsen's approach is good news because it makes perfect sense that there are some links between Is and Ought.[37] This in turn requires looking at the normativity thesis from a different angle than its simplified version, namely with the awareness that there is an irreconcilable abyss between Is and Ought. For this reason, there is a need to identify a link between Is and Ought which would leave the normativity thesis intact. After examining the explanatory gap problem and applying Chalmers' strategy based on the assumption of the fundamentality of the category in question, be it consciousness or Ought, it turned out that supervenience is a fit here. Hence, I argued earlier that natural supervenience has the potential to be a kind of link which occurs in borderline situations in the pure theory of law.

Now I will specify what I mean by the borderline situations in which supervenience occurs. By claiming the distinguished character of law, Kelsen needs a weak link which would not interfere with the elements of his theory. These elements need to be selected in accordance with their link to the sphere of Is. Some of these elements were distinguished by Kelsen himself as bridging principles.[38] However, some bridging principles refer directly to rules of logic. Hence, I took a different approach, searching for 'borderline situations' by following Bulygin's argument described in chapter two.

Borderline situations occur in three essential domains of law: legal application, legal creation, and the problem of validity. Hence, the three domains where supervenience may appear are imputation, the norm, and the act of will, validity, and efficacy. Although when read directly imputation exists only in the sphere of Ought, it seems to be strongly related to supervenience, which can be seen in Brożek's argument mentioned earlier in this chapter. Hence, I will examine the borderline situation in the domain of legal application covered by imputation, which is the link between facts and norms.

[37] Brożek (n 5) 158.

[38] See: T Fitzsche, 'Die Reine Rechtslehre Im Lichte Des Kritischen Rationalismus', *Schriftenreihe Des Hans Kelsen Instituts* (nd).

Table 6.1 below presents pairs of categories which are at the borderline. They constitute dangers and great potential for the final version of pure theory of law.

Table 6.1 Borderline situations

Supervenience	**Ought**	**Is**
Imputation:	Consequence	Condition
	Legal norm	Act of will
	Validity, the basic norm	Efficacy

This is not an exhaustive list of potential 'supervenience pairs'. For instance, supervenience probably occurs in the relation between a legal and natural act, or between a natural person and an individual. However, they are to be distinguished from borderline situations. I aim not to explore all the manifestations of supervenience that might occur in GTN, because they do not substantially challenge the normativity thesis.

I aim to provide a general framework which can explain how the Is–Ought separation is sustained despite links between these two domains. Hence, I will focus only on borderline situations of legal application, which is represented by imputation; on law creation, which is represented by the norm and the act of will; and on the domain of validity, where the relation between validity (and the basic norm) and efficacy occurs. Other relations will most probably belong to one of these domains. For instance, the natural and legal person relation will probably reflect imputation, while the natural and legal act relation reflects the norm and act of will relation.

7

Supervenience as a Relation between Is and Ought

In the previous chapter, I posited an argument concerning the concept of supervenience as the relation between law and facts in Kelsen's GTN. Now it is time to provide examples of how this relation could work in the framework of dynamic interpretation. I have demarcated primary spheres wherein this relation is manifested, designating them as 'borderline situations'. The selection of borderline situations is guided by their significance within the framework of dynamic interpretation. In this context, I shall consider three principal instances of borderline situations: legal norms and acts of will; validity and efficacy; and imputation.[1] Additionally, notwithstanding the intriguing nature of the issue, it appears to provide only minimal novel insights into the dynamic interpretation advanced within the present work.

7.1. THE NORM, AND THE ACT OF WILL

As noted in chapter one, the legal norm in GTN is defined as the meaning of an act of will. Kelsen explains that the act of will, which belongs to the Is sphere, has the meaning of Ought.[2] The act of will in this understanding has an empirical character (Is sphere), and parliamentary enactments can serve as an example, while the legal norm, as the meaning attached to such an act is in the normative (Ought) sphere.

The assignment of such an Ought as the meaning to an act of will generates any norm, not only a legal one, as Kelsen notes:

> Generally: not every Ought which is the meaning of an act of will is a binding *norm*. For instance, I can will 'Everyone is to marry upon reaching a certain age.' That is not

[1] Supervenience might occur between many other less prominent, although essential elements of the pure theory of law, such as the norms and will of the lawmaker, or *Stufenbau*, natural person and individual; natural act and legal act. The exploration of the supervenient connections within the dynamic structure of law will not be undertaken here, as such analysis has already been addressed elsewhere (M Zalewska, 'Empowerment and the Act of Will in Hans Kelsen's General Theory of Norms' in G Villa-Rosas and T Spaak (eds), *Legal Power and Legal Competence*, t 140, Law and Philosophy Library (Springer International Publishing, 2023) 305–16, doi.org/10.1007/978-3-031-28555-4_15).

[2] Kelsen, *General Theory of Norms* (Clarendon Press, 1979) 27.

> a binding norm for there is no norm of a positive moral or legal order which empowers me to posit such norm.'

These require for law that the meaning of the act of will be objective.[3]

Hence, from a legal point of view, what matters while specifying the rules of supervenience is the objective meaning of an act of will and the relation to its meaning. Here, for the sake of clarity, I put emphasis on the meaning of the act, rather than the norm. From these two supervenience rules the following can be derived:

(1) If the meanings of acts of will are different in terms of objectivity, then the *acts* of will are different.
(2) If the *acts* of will are the same, then their meanings in terms of objectivity are the same.

First, it should be noted that this solution can work only if the lawmaker is understood broadly, as any organ which takes part in the law-creation process. Otherwise, if another organ derogated the legal norm, which was the meaning of the act of will of another organ, the supervenience rule would not work.

Secondly, although these rules do not seem a significant accomplishment, they provide more information than meets the eye. For dynamic interpretation, it is enough if they are coherent, and they are. This is important in the context of borderline situations since it does not interfere with the Is–Ought separation – in fact, it constitutes a link between these two domains. Hence, they support the thesis that supervenience can be applied in borderline situations and fulfil its initial task. Anything else that is gained by the application of supervenience is added value.

While supervenience applies to the relations between the norm and the act of will, alone it cannot *fully* explain this relation. This observation is particularly beneficial if one assumes the fundamentality of the Ought dimension. For instance, supervenience does not explain why such a norm obtains from social facts. All we know is that the same acts of will generate the same outcomes in terms of objectivity and subjectivity. However, this in itself is a great deal. What supervenience also does is reveal the rules which set the firm boundaries of law without specifying what these boundaries are. As such it closes the legal system to the influence of other norms.

The application of supervenience in this case reveals that the boundaries of law are determined by specific rules whose content can vary depending on the legal system. Contrary to other normative systems, which grant only the subjective meaning of the act, these rules and boundaries allow us to predict which act of will has the potential to be a legal norm and which does not.

For instance, when observing parliament debating, we know that these debates are to be finalised with the issuance of legal norms, but not all norms

[3] ibid.

which appear during these debates will be legal norms. We know this because we assign a specific meaning to parliament's acts, while we do not assign an objective meaning to some other events, even those that take place in parliament. In some heated discussion, a deputy might say to his opponent 'go to hell'. Despite this happening in parliament, and there was no disclaimer that this rule only has a subjective meaning, we only assign a subjective meaning to it, because it differs from the objective acts of will which require empowerment.

This brings us back to the question: how do we know when a parliament issues a legally binding act and when it is just a wish expressed in a heated discussion? First of all, as was explained in chapter six, natural supervenience requires some additional rules, analogical to some kind of laws of nature in the case of consciousness. In this case, these rules stem from legal norms ordered in the structure of law (*Stufenbau*) and the basic norm. We know that a particular act is legally binding because an empowered organ issued it, and this chain of empowerments leads us to the basic norm.

This solution is similar to Pavlakos's account. The difference between them is that the fundamentality of Ought is assumed in this case and the explanatory motivations are out of the picture. The objective meaning of a norm is only possible in the context of the hierarchical structure of law, which is *Stufenbau*. The norm creation process manifests itself in this structure and the relations between the norm and the act of will can only be fully explained in the context of it. Hence, the connection between the norm and the act of will gains in significance in the dynamic aspect, which is the hierarchical structure of law (*Stufenbau*).[4]

7.2. EFFICACY, VALIDITY AND THE BASIC NORM

I explained Kelsen's concept of validity and efficacy in chapter one. Here I would like to recall that Kelsen defines validity as the existence of the legal norm. There are several conditions for the norm to be valid. The legal norm is valid if: (1) it was issued by the organ empowered in the higher norm in accordance with it; (2) it belongs to an efficacious legal system. At the same time, and most importantly, the validity of the legal system is dependent in some way upon the efficacy of the legal system. The problem is to define in which way validity is dependent on efficacy. Supervenience might potentially shed some light on this problem.

As was mentioned in chapter one, binding validity with efficacy is problematic from the point of view of the separation between Is and Ought. It means that in order to create legal science, which is supposed to be pure, one needs to limit oneself to the normative sphere. No factual and causal explanations are possible if the purity is to be sustained. However, efficacy is a factual criterion

[4] I have elaborated on this matter in 'Empowerment and the Act of Will in Hans Kelsen's General Theory of Norms' in Villa Rosas and Spaak (n 1).

and is crucial for the existence of legal norms. Furthermore, as Bulygin compellingly notes, this is not the end of these puzzles, since the relations between validity and efficacy can be fully understood only if the basic norm is added to this equation. Hence, the problem lies in establishing the character of the link which binds the normative (validity and basic norm) with the factual (efficacy), and in this section I will explore the relations between these three elements.

The rules for validity and efficacy would be as follows:

(1) If there is a difference in the validities of legal systems, then there is a difference in the efficacies of legal systems.
(2) If the efficacies of legal systems are the same, then the validities of legal systems are the same.

From these two rules it can be inferred that according to the first supervenience rule, the change (which is a difference in the aspect of time) in validity is followed by a change in efficacy. Namely, if a legal system at one point was valid, then it was efficacious. When at some other point the legal system ceased to be valid, the legal system also ceased to be efficacious.

The principle positing that an alteration in validity must be accompanied by a corresponding modification in efficacy appears self-evident. In the event that the legal system loses its validity, its efficacy would likewise be compromised. Conversely, initiating a new legal system's validity should be mirrored by its efficacy. However, such a validity and efficacy model operates exclusively within the normative realm. I shall refer to this conceptual framework as the 'normative model of validity'.

One might ask how such dependence was established. After all, a valid system could be paired with an inefficacious one. Supervenience does not explain that. Some other rule is required to ensure this common-sense configuration. Such a rule can be derived from Kelsen's understanding of validity. Namely, he states that the 'validity of a norm consists in the fact that it *ought* to be observed and if not observed, then applied'. Observation or application are two modes in which efficacy can be realized.[5] Hence, the meaning of validity and efficacy ensures that supervenience binds them in the way presented above and not otherwise.

The second problem concerns why a change in efficacy is not necessarily followed by a change in validity. This might sound counterintuitive. Kelsen explains it as follows:

> [T]he effectiveness of a norm – which is a Is – is the condition for the validity of the norm – which is and Ought – in the sense that a norm loses its validity when it loses its effectiveness or the possibility of effectiveness, but not in the sense that norm has to be effective in order to be valid, since a norm becomes valid before it is effective and it can become effective, only once it has become valid.[6]

[5] Kelsen (n 2) 138–39.
[6] ibid 140.

This means that during the law-creation process, there is a moment when the legal norm is already valid without being efficacious. On the level of the legal system's validity, this is the case when a new constitution is established but not yet efficacious.

Finally, the supervenience rule states that the unchanged status of efficacy causes the unchanged validity status. Hence, unchanged efficacy means that the validity status remains the same. This rule indicates that the assumption that there are no changes in efficacy allows one to assume that no changes in validity occurred. This assumption is possible, if, again, one perceives the supervenience rule as the normative model of validity. In other words, in idealised situations, it can be expected that the observed unchanged efficacy of the legal system is followed by the unchanged validity of the legal system. On the other hand, unchanged validity does not imply unchanged efficacy, because the norm becomes valid before being efficacious.

There is one problem with such an interpretation. According to Kelsen efficacy can only derogate; the introduction of supervenience and normative model of validity modifies this assumption. The change in efficacy is not necessarily followed by the change in validity. In this scenario, the constitution, which is inefficacious, can be considered valid as long as there are actors who are in power to consider validity of such constitution.[7] When efficacy determines validity, the second scenario takes place.

This means that these rules are true if they are treated as a model and if the fiction of purity, which constitutes a normative perspective, is applied. In this scenario the basic norm cannot depend on efficacy, but rather on the validity of the legal system and remains unchanged as long as validity of the legal system is unchanged. Such an interpretation is in accordance with the *Pure Theory of Law*, where the validity of basic norm and the validity of the legal system are equiprimordial.

If the basic norm changes, the order seems reversed, and the second scenario comes into play. A change in efficacy is followed by a change in validity. This is however a factual perspective, when something extraordinary happens in reality that causes Is (efficacy) to supervene on Ought (validity), not vice-versa. From a factual perspective, the hypothetical situation can be imagined that the legal system ceased to be valid.

In the factual scenario, the following formula must make sense: if efficacy does not change, the validity of a legal system either changes or does not. In such a case, how can we imagine a system that is, for instance, efficacious but its validity changed from valid to invalid in time? It cannot be ruled out in concrete cases that an abnormal deviation from this model could occur and unchanged

[7] Such a situation took place in Poland, in 2015–23. As a result of the Government's actions, despite lacking the majority to amend the Constitution, certain parts of the Constitution have been rendered ineffective. Nevertheless, the judiciary and the opposition still regard these sections as legally valid. This situation lays the groundwork for the future restoration of the rule of law.

efficacy will not be followed by unchanged validity. The word 'concrete case' is key here. The normative perspective offers an idealised model, while the factual perspective must consider all possible scenarios, including abnormal and rare ones.

Consider, for example, a normative system that was once efficacious and valid but, over time, loses its validity, perhaps due to moral considerations. Conversely, in situations such as revolutions, a newly established efficacious legal system may be initially deemed invalid, only to later gain recognition and validity. Such dissonance between validity and efficacy exists within a nuanced realm that blurs the boundaries between normative and factual scenarios. Simultaneously challenging and intriguing, these scenarios pose particular complexity for the interpretation proposed in this context.

Hence, there are two perspectives to be considered: normative and factual. The normative model of law represents an idealised version of relations between validity and efficacy; in this model, the change in efficacy does not necessarily deprive the legal system of validity.

In a factual scenario, the supervenience rules are reversed. A change in efficacy requires a change in validity and unchanged validity requires unchanged efficacy. Here efficacy has a derogative power. In this framework, unchanged validity indicates that efficacy did not change, which suggests the dependence of validity on efficacy which potentially might be defined in terms of grounding. Since this interpretation is out of the scope of the dynamic approach presented in this book, I will not explore this hypothesis.

This means that the solution employing supervenience can solve the dilemma presented by Bulygin, namely that if the basic norm depends upon efficacy, then validity depends upon efficacy. As a result, the Is–Ought separation cannot be sustained. If the basic norm is strongly connected with efficacy, then Bulygin is right. A strong connection between the basic norm and efficacy can ensure Bulygin's claim. However, such a perspective is factual, and thus probably not endorsed by Kelsen. The dilemma is solved if the basic norm is strongly connected with validity, as Kelsen wanted. Efficacy is bound with validity by the rule of supervenience, which ensures the separation between Is and Ought.

Three conclusions stem from the application of supervenience in the case of validity and efficacy. First, these perspectives adopt a more radical stance compared to the original solution. They either assert a greater independence of validity from efficacy or emphasise a heightened dependence on efficacy. In turn, such interpretations provide enhanced clarity regarding the relations between validity efficacy and basic norm.

Second, only the former perspective is in accordance with the methodological assumption of purity. Although correct before the fiction of purity is applied, the latter perspective is the source of misunderstandings concerning the relations between efficacy and validity in the pure theory of law. The key issue here is that when the fiction of purity is applied, the validity problem cannot have its starting point in facts.

Third, this approach explains what rules govern the occurrence of natural supervenience in the case of efficacy and validity. In this case, the candidate is obvious: it is the basic norm, which indicates validity or, in a factual perspective, is strongly bound with efficacy. This is also in accordance with Pavlakos's findings, which recognised the basic norm as a bridging principle, and my argument that when validity is analysed from the factual perspective, the basic norm becomes (too) strongly bound with efficacy.

Finally, the perspective choice, either normative or factual, can determine the outcome of an unstable legal situation or whether the revolution is successful or not. The normative perspective supports validity which stems from the constitution, by leaving the basic norm unchanged. The factual perspective indicates a successful revolution and the rejection of the old legal order, by changing the basic norm. This means that such a theoretical and abstract problem as the fictional assumption of purity, or the relation between facts and legal norms, might have practical implications for law during turbulent times. The choice of the perspective in such situations can also be political.

7.3. IMPUTATION IN *GENERAL THEORY OF NORMS*

'Imputation' refers to the application of law, a situation which involves contact between Is and Ought. So far, I have assumed that there is a type of imputation, which I will call Type 2, that links facts and norms and stems from a dynamic reading of GTN. This type of imputation does not occur in earlier versions of the pure theory of law. The familiar version of imputation, which I will call Type 1, links two states of affairs in the Ought sphere and does not fall under borderline situations. However, there are two reasons why the new Type 2 imputation should be examined, although it is not a typical version known from earlier versions of the pure theory of law.

First, this new type is a consequence of identifying borderline situations. One of them refers to the application of law. In this area, facts visibly influence law, and imputation is part of this thought process. This happens in a similar manner to that in which efficacy influences validity or will influences norm creation. Since this type of imputation refers to the application of law, it consists of the factual state of affairs of breaking the secondary norm, and its consequence, which is an individual norm containing a sanction. This kind of imputation is conceivable as a thought process when certain behaviour is connected with an individual norm. Second, as will be shown below, the new type of imputation resembles the link of supervenience from Hare's example of St Francis.

Although at first glance it seems that only Type 1 imputation is the proper one, there is reason to think that imputation as a link between a statement about a fact and some normative element yet to be identified, namely Type 2 imputation, could also exist in GTN as a distinct type of imputation. Hence, I will look more closely at this issue in order to determine whether some passages in GTN.7 justify my assumption of the possible existence of this type of imputation.

My main argument is that this type of imputation is possible in GTN because Kelsen extended his theory on individual norms. In this case, the inquiry concerning an analogical link between condition and consequence in the case of individual norms is justified and Type 2 imputation offers a plausible solution. I believe this argument is sufficient to justify the introduction of this element. But there are also other hints in GTN that might indirectly indicate that Kelsen extended the understanding of the imputation category and are worth examining.

Imputation in GTN is rather secondary to the issues concerning the norm's existence. If the norm exists (is valid), then imputation, linking the condition and the consequence, is given. Imputation in legal science can be perceived as the structure of a thought process, eventually leading to a coercive act.[8] On the other hand, a general norm might 'produce' the link between the fact of breaking a norm and the individual norm issued by a judge in a particular case.[9] In this way, imputation can be regarded in the context of the application of law (Type 2), as well as in the context of pure cognition (Type 1), as characteristic for *Pure Theory of Law*.[10] The difference between PTL and GTN is that while the former described only general norms, the latter focused on individual norms, allowing us to assume that imputation Type 2 can be introduced. Hence, it can be concluded that in GTN Kelsen understands imputation as a broad category and just favours one subcategory. Type 1 imputation is the first step in the process in which legal science identifies an appropriate condition and an appropriate consequence in the general norm, and links them with imputation.

[8] See: G Pavlakos, 'A Non-Naturalist Account of Law's Place in Reality' in B Brożek, J Hage and N Vincent (eds), *Law and Mind: A Survey of Law and the Cognitive Sciences* (Cambridge University Press, 2021).

[9] See the definition of imputation in GTN: 'The normative necessity in the relation between condition and consequence is to be found also in the linking produced by a general legal norm which prescribes a coercive act, a so-called sanction, as a consequence in the event that a certain behaviour occurs (a behaviour characterized as illegal' (Kelsen (n 2) 23).

[10] Type 2 imputation can also be deduced from some passages in GTN. For instance, in ch 15, where Kelsen writes about primary and secondary norms, he reconstructs the way a judge thinks by stating two possible ways of dealing with the case depending on whether Schultze stole $1,000 from Maier or not. The first variant is as follows: Schultze was to refrain from stealing $1,000 from Maier. Schultze stole $1,000 from Maier. Schultze is to be imprisoned (Conviction). The second variant is as follows: Schultze was to refrain from stealing $1,000 from Maier. Schultze did not steal $1,000 from Maier. Schultze is not to be imprisoned (Acquittal). Kelsen provides this example to demonstrate that the secondary norm is a defendable construction, but one that is artificial and superfluous. He also rejects the possibility of a normative syllogism, which is in accordance with Kelsen's conviction that there are no logical relations between norms. But what matters in the context of imputation is that while the first premise seems to stem from the secondary general norm applied to the case of Schulze,[10] the second premise and the conclusion seem to be linked by Type 2 imputation and concern the primary norm. The second premise is a statement about a fact, and the conclusion, even though formulated as an assertion, can be perceived as legal proposition about an individual norm to be issued by a judge in order to impose the sanction on Schultze. Furthermore, since the secondary norm vanishes from this equation, the primary norm gains even more importance, along with its imputation, for this norm is all that the judge has to rule on (Kelsen (n 2) 57).

Such a primary norm eventually leads to the coercive act in the individual norm issued by a judge.

Moreover, it seems that Type 1 and Type 2 imputation can be perceived from two perspectives.[11] The first perspective is that of the 'legal scientist' who is reading the legal text. What he sees are the general norms, therefore, the state of affairs expresses only potential behaviour, which might happen at any time in the sphere of facts. The second perspective is that of the judge who needs to deal with a particular case. He is faced with the concrete fact of someone breaking the law, for instance, that Smith has stolen a car which belonged to Jones. In both cases, a lawyer is confronted with the law and applies imputation in his legal thinking.

In the first case, Kelsen does that *in abstracto*, while in the second he does it *in concreto*. Primarily, Kelsen meant the perspective *in abstracto*, however, in GTN both perspectives are possible and imputation occurs in both. This is because legal thinking is neither limited to thinking about law *in abstracto* nor about law *in concreto*. Hence, the state of affairs can be either the potential behaviour expressed in the norm or the concrete illegal behaviour committed by Smith.

This means that each type of imputation refers to a different perspective. Type 1 refers to the legal science perspective, while Type 2 has a narrower scope and is reserved for a judge or another organ who applies the law. The 'trigger' of the judge's action is specific concrete behaviour, which along with the Type 1 imputation produced by a general norm leads to the issuance of an individual norm. In this framework, Type 1 provides an interpretation scheme, which allows Type 2 imputation to be constituted as a connection between the individual norm and behaviour.

Since Type 2 imputation is coherent with GTN, which is focused not only on the general legal norm, but also on individual norms, it is necessary to identify the elements of imputation of interest in terms of borderline situations. While Type 1 imputation does not concern borderline situations, I will focus on Type 2.

7.4. THE ELEMENTS OF TYPE 2 IMPUTATION

As was mentioned in chapter one, imputation is understood as a normative link between two states of affairs (*Tatsache*) in which 'under a certain condition a certain consequence is to occur'.[12] Since supervenience is the relation between two elements, the elements of imputation require some clarification: what

[11] I would like to thank Carsten Heidemann, who, during a discussion concerning the problem of imputation in the grounding context, drew attention to the fact that several perspectives exist and depending on which perspective is considered, the outcome of what the 'state of affairs' is will be different.

[12] Kelsen (n 2) 22.

exactly are the 'states of affairs' which Type 2 imputation links? My initial claim is that this is the link between facts and individual norms. Now it is time to look more closely at this statement.

Kelsen refers to the first state of affairs as the 'condition', and the latter as the 'consequence'. They occur in legal statements. For instance: if X stole a car, then X should be punished. The condition is the theft of the car by X, while the consequence is the punishment of X. Hence, the first state of affairs is certain behaviour characterised as illegal.[13]

However, such a definition sounds like a vicious circle, because if the separation of Is and Ought exists, then the plain fact cannot be illegal. It becomes such only in reference to the legal system. On the level of general norms this paradox can be solved by the introduction of the primary and secondary norm. This distinction already existed in older versions of legal positivism, but Kelsen developed this concept and reversed the meaning of the categories of the primary and secondary norm. In the original version, the primary norm was the norm which prohibited X. For instance: 'one shall not steal'. The secondary norm was the norm which imposed the sanction.

Kelsen takes the primary norm to be the norm which imposes the sanction. For him, only such a norm was typical for law (if X stole a car, X should be punished). Kelsen's secondary norm is typical for any normative system. Its structure fits the behaviour prohibited by law as well as morality or good manners. Furthermore, in reference to law, the secondary norm is superfluous, in a way that law would make perfect sense without secondary norms. Kletzer explains the reason behind this in a very apt way when he writes:

> We could call this person [someone faced with rule], in line with Hart's analysis the *puzzled man*: if I am pondering whether or not to kill B and take into account that ... my killing of B would render anybody else's killing of me lawful, then I would already know that in a legal sense I ought not to kill B. The explicit rule, 'No one ought to kill anybody', would not be invalid or inexistent, it would be superfluous; it would be pointless to explicitly posit this rule.[14]

The primary and secondary norm can explain why Kelsen could speak consistently about 'illegal behaviour'. The behaviour was illegal by virtue of the secondary norm, while the primary norm consists of imputation and authorises the judge to use force. Hence, the primary norm does not indicate whether the behaviour is legal or illegal; it just indicates a situation where the use of force by a legal organ is authorised.[15] With such an interpretation the value judgement (legal/illegal) is detached from the concept of law and the condition in the imputation structure is detached from its normative meaning. It just describes

[13] ibid.

[14] Ch Kletzer, *The Idea of a Pure Theory of Law: An Interpretation and Defence* (Hart Publishing, 2018) 59.

[15] ibid.

a behaviour that triggers an empowerment to impose a sanction. What grants the primary norm its normative meaning, which makes this condition legally relevant, is imputation.

In the case of Type 2 imputation, illegal behaviour is recognised by virtue of the general norm. The consequence – the element which seems to be the most important from the judge's perspective, as the person dealing with a particular case – is the individual norm, containing a sanction which the judge is about to issue. Since the elements of imputation have been identified, it is time to examine the possibility of interpreting Type 2 imputation as supervenience.

7.5. IMPUTATION AS SUPERVENIENCE

With regard to imputation, I argued that I am most interested in Type 2, understood as the link between the condition (factual behaviour) and the individual norm. The question is what the relation of imputation to supervenience is in this case, and my claim is that imputation is a supervenience of some kind. Hare's example of St Francis as a good man might hint at how this is possible, which I described in chapter six. Now I will demonstrate how this is possible.

Hare argued that if St Francis, who possesses certain qualities in certain circumstances, is considered a good man, then another individual would have to be considered a good man if he possesses the same qualities in the same circumstances. The similarity of this example to Type 2 imputation can be demonstrated as follows.

In the case of Type 2 imputation, which concerns a judge's perspective, we are dealing with a link between factual (certain behaviour) and the normative sphere (an individual norm). In such a case, a set of features decides whether certain behaviour amounts to theft. If all the features from this set are present in a certain case, then X is a thief, and hence the sanction should be imposed. Supervenience as the rule 'there is no A difference without B difference' specifies this even more clearly. Given a specific pair of facts (in terms of supervenience vocabulary – belonging to B – B1 and B2) (eg B1: Jones stole a car; B2: Smith stole a car), the individual norm is issued (A1 and A2 respectively) by a judge and contains a specific sanction for B1 and B2 respectively. Hence, the consequence supervenes on the condition, in the following manner:

(1) If the consequences are different (the individual norms: Jones ought to be put in prison; Smith ought to pay a fine), the conditions are different (Jones stole a car; Smith stole a toy).
(2) If the conditions are the same (Jones stole a car; Smith stole a car), the consequences are the same (the individual norms: Jones ought to be put in prison for two years, Smith ought to be put in prison for two years).

Under close examination, the resemblance to Hare's example of the case of St Francis becomes apparent. In both cases the B elements concern behaviour and circumstances. In A, elements of supervenience are connected with the result of the behaviour in both cases. In ethics, the consequence is bound with a positive value judgement, while in the case of law the consequence is bound with the issuance of an individual norm containing a sanction.

As chapter six mentions, natural supervenience requires additional rules by virtue of which such supervenience stands. In the case of Type 2 imputation, such a rule is the legal norm which constitutes the scheme of interpretation when the use of force by a legal organ is authorised. This scheme of interpretation operates in the framework of Type 1 imputation.

One could argue that the law does not work this way. How do we reconcile this with the reality that courts issue different rulings? After all, two different courts can issue two different sanctions for the same deeds in the authorised range. Both courts would thereby rule appropriately.[16] This objection can be dismissed if imputation can be understood as a model, rather than as a description of reality, or even the standard imposed by law.

First, the sanction range exists in the general norm because of the variety of circumstances to be considered; this stems from the nature of the general norm which is supposed to encompass as many potential states of affairs as possible.

Second, even though in reality imposing two different sanctions on perpetrators of exactly the same crime is accepted, it seems that there is some sort of belief that *exactly* the same circumstances require the same sanction. If Jones and Smith, being in *exactly* the same circumstances, committed *exactly* the same crime, *exactly* the same sanction should be imposed, according to the model of imputation understood in terms of supervenience.

Imagine that Jones and Smith met after committing exactly the same crime in exactly the same circumstances. If they found out that one had been sentenced to 10 years in prison and the other to five years, they would probably consider one of the sentences unfair. They would expect that in the same circumstances two persons should be sentenced to *exactly* the same sanctions; however, this condition is impossible to fulfil in reality.

Therefore, supervenience as imputation could be perceived as some sort of model of equality, where the component of a kind of fairness is added. Such a model contains a fictional element, namely the requirement that *exactly* the same treatment is given under *exactly* the same circumstances. This can help understand the difference between idealisations included in models and one's acceptance that such accuracy does not exist in reality.

While the concept of equality is already associated with the general norm, supervenience strengthens it by adding the fairness component.[17] As was shown, the general norm does not prevent different rulings from being issued in the same circumstances. Smith and Jones can be sentenced to five and 10 years

[16] I would like to thank the Reviewer for that remark.

[17] See HLA Hart, 'Positivism and the Separation of Law and Morals' (1958) 71 *Harvard Law Journal* 593. Hart associated the concept of equality with general norm.

respectively, and the law is appropriately applied in both cases. Supervenience provides an additional implicit rule of fairness to the equality rule stemming from the general norm. Nobody requires this condition to be fulfilled perfectly, but it might be beneficial if judges had this directive in mind when ruling.

Such idealisation enforces a distinction between outcomes: on the one hand, the individual norm issued by a judge in a concrete case, and on the other a model of judicial thinking, which can be perceived as an instruction directed to the judge as to what should be taken into consideration when ruling. Supervenience concerns the latter. As such, this type of imputation functions in the form of a regulative idea. The conclusion is that the pure theory of law contains some models, such as the model of *Stufenbau*, or Type 2 imputation. At the same time, the deviation from these models is explained by virtue of their structure based on idealisation and approximation, which was elaborated in chapter three. In the case of Type 2 imputation, these idealisations are useful since they function as guidelines for jurists on properly applying law.

This notion is followed by the question of whether the equality and fairness principles are not against Kelsen's assertion that only the form of law matters, not its content. There are two reasons why equality and fairness thus understood might not be against Kelsen's intention. First of all, Kelsen did not deny that some assumptions about law exist in its content. For instance, in *Pure Theory of Law* such a principle is the principle of contradiction, or the whole construction of the dynamic structure of law. They limit the claim that the law can have any content.

Second, the principles of equality and fairness were derived from Kelsen's methodological assumptions, along with supervenience, in the process of deduction, which resembles these assumptions. There is a difference between building a theory of law in which the starting point or foundation of the concept of law is some value and the situation when the analytical process leads to a new element. In such a framework the paradox of introducing some values to pure theory, such as the values of equality and fairness, vanishes. On the contrary, it adds to the external strength of the pure theory of law. Finally, these values are translated in objective terms into the 'algorithm' of supervenience, which means that the scientific and objective character of pure theory of law is sustained.

When juxtaposing such an understanding of imputation with the standard familiar from the *Pure Theory of Law*, it can be noticed that such imputation is an extension of Kelsen's theory in three dimensions.

Firstly, as the link between act and norm, it passes the boundaries of law as a normative phenomenon and becomes one of the borderline situations. It is not part of legal science as a pure domain, but rather concerns the issue of the relation of law to the factual sphere in situations in which these two spheres are in touch. Type 2 imputation belongs to a more advanced stage of inquiries concerning the law, when – after identifying the boundaries of the law – in the next step, the links between law and other domains, especially the Is-domain, are examined.

Secondly, Type 2 imputation concerns the issue of the legal thinking involved in law application. As was indicated, Kelsen gave some attention to this problem in GTN, but it can hardly be regarded as a solid theory of adjudication. Therefore, legal dynamics was extended to describe the processes in law, contrary to the Neo-Kantian version of imputation which belongs to legal statics.

Finally, although Type 2 imputation can be directly inferred from GTN, supervenience is a new element which Kelsen never introduced and requires further justification. Supervenience as imputation refers to legal thinking in respect to the ideal application of law, which stems from the implicit conviction that law is associated with some kind of equality and fairness, and the belief that in exactly the same circumstances all people should be treated exactly alike.

Closing the imputation problem, it is worthwhile to address one more issue. Since imputation as supervenience is a consequence of the pure theory of law, rather than its inherent part, the issue of whether imputation as supervenience is justified in the context of the pure theory of law should be addressed again. There are several reasons why Type 2 imputation as supervenience can be regarded as a valid and valuable extension of Kelsen's theory.

Firstly, supervenience is consistent with Kelsen's pure theory of law, if it is placed in borderline situations, when the links between norms and facts are established. Kelsen performed such operations himself, for instance, when defining the norm as the meaning of an act of will, or, to some extent, by binding validity to efficacy. Hence, it can be assumed that such an operation is allowed in the framework of his theory. This argument is supported by analogical reasoning in the philosophy of mind, as exemplified by Chalmers, from whence the notion of supervenience stems.

Secondly, supervenience brings added value by enhancing the reflection on imputation, revealing new dimensions of it and its resemblance to imputation in morality. Type 2 imputation reveals implicit convictions concerning the law even in the positivistic paradigm, supporting the thesis that equality is integral to it. This raises interesting questions concerning the normativity of the pure theory. Namely, the pure theory of law seems to include some normativity in its description – how law ought to work. But this is only weak normativity, which also exists in the natural sciences. For instance, health is defined by medicine in a similar manner – by specifying the way an absolutely healthy organism works. In this way, by means of such fiction, science makes it possible to recognise anomalies.

To conclude, it seems that imputation understood as supervenience passed both tests: the test of coherence; and the test of utility. In this interpretation, imputation does not seem to make the pure theory of law less coherent and, at the same time, it goes hand in hand with a better understanding of the relations between norms and facts, revealing some hidden assumptions in the idea of law. The interpretation provides a coherent understanding of the link in borderline situations where the law is applied. At the same time, such an interpretation brought to light more fictional elements and displayed the relation between the category of imputation and a model.

7.6. SUPERVENIENCE AS A LINK BETWEEN THE LAW 'AS SUCH' AND THE REALITY

To sum up, all borderline situations can be explained regarding supervenience. In most cases, it is only possible if they are treated as a model. One could argue that the introduction of supervenience means adding some new elements to Kelsen's theory, such as the equality rule, certainty, or the concept of fairness, which validate the occurrence of supervenience; however, since these concepts are limited to formal components, they are consistent with the pure theory of law. The principle of equality or the fairness thus formulated does not introduce ideology to the concept of legal science. On the contrary, these concepts were inferred from other categories introduced by Kelsen, based on his methodology, which is aligned with the scientific method. It does not seem that introducing these rules would be against Kelsen's intentions, especially since he searched for solutions to ensure the formal rule of law. The most apparent solution he proposed was the model of the constitutional court.

After examining the most significant examples it can be noted that in borderline situations supervenience acts upon an overarching rule, articulated as follows:

(1) if Ought domains are different then Is domains are different; and
(2) if Is domains are the same, the Ought domains are the same.

The operationality of the supervenience rule is contingent upon the conceptualisation of the legal aspect under consideration as a model, idealisation, or regulative idea. This implies that the pure theory of law does not encompass all conceivable manifestations of legal phenomena but delineates an idealised form of law. The law 'as such', is obtained through the application of the purity fiction, a mechanism that alters the perception of legal phenomena when viewed from a child's perspective. Supervenience, in this context, elucidates the interconnections between the realms of 'Is' and 'Ought' when these domains are considered to be fundamentally equivalent. The fiction of purity facilitates the comprehension of law within the 'Ought' domain, which is regarded as fundamental. This also implies that the inquiry of how legal facts are obtained from social facts is beyond the scope of the pure theory of law. Kelsen's project specifically concentrates on elucidating the independence of law and its distinctive nature concerning factual elements. To address this, Kelsen refined certain theses and employed the fiction of purity. Conversely, legal positivism appears to centre its attention on the law as a subset of social facts, emphasising the similarities between the two.

All in all, it seems that natural supervenience is a mechanism that is able to clarify borderline situations without rejecting the assumption of the fundamentality of Ought. Supervenience explains relations between law and facts and reconciles them with the claim of the separation of Is and Ought. At the same time, it does not weaken Hume's guillotine or the separation of Is and Ought on any other level, neither ontological nor epistemic.

8

Conclusions

Fictionalism and Supervenience in the *General Theory of Norms*

8.1. FICTIONALISM AND SUPERVENIENCE

THIS CHAPTER AIMS to put together the findings of this book. Several issues still require consideration. Firstly, there is a need to explore how the fictional framework interacts with the framework derived from the application of supervenience. The second is whether the dynamic approach to the General Theory of Norms turned out to be successful – and if yes, to what extent. Hence, I will begin by addressing the first issue, and in the final section, I will turn to the latter.

The compatibility of the fictional perspective with supervenience might not be apparent at the first glance. However, they are compatible, and the key to understanding this mechanism as a whole is the distinction between the ontological and epistemological dimension of the separation between Is and Ought, which I covered in chapter six. This means that the Is–Ought separation can be considered from two perspectives. The epistemological perspective involves fictionalism, while the ontological one involves supervenience. Let us start from the fictional perspective.

As was noted in chapter four, in the framework of fictionalism the Is–Ought separation is treated in fictional terms, which enables law to be cognised 'as such'. When cognising law 'as such', the lawyer thinks as if there was a strict separation between Is and Ought. Since on the ontological level there are connections between these two spheres, the fiction of purity works only as a general framework on the epistemic level. Connections between Is and Ought can still be examined on the ontological level. It can be done by examining borderline situations, as it was done in chapter seven, or by defining the relation of the law as such to the law blended with other phenomena in reality, as it was done in chapter four.

The fiction of separation allows us to move from the negative thesis 'law is not a social fact' to the positive thesis addressing the question of what law is. Thanks to this fiction, law can be cognised as a normative phenomenon (the 'law is a norm' thesis). After establishing the norm as a distinct, autonomous and normative phenomenon by applying appropriate methodology on the epistemic level, Ought reveals its fundamental nature. The fundamentality of Ought is a key assumption of the pure theory of law in the dynamic framework. In the next step, when the fundamentality of Ought has been established, on the ontological level borderline situations show the links between these two distinct entities – law and facts. These links are defined in terms of natural supervenience.

Here, the analogy with Chalmers' strategy is apparent. To demonstrate the fundamentality of consciousness, Chalmers initiated his inquiry with the zombie argument, a form of fiction. Following the assertion of the fundamentality of consciousness, Chalmers noted that the fundamentality of consciousness does not deny connections with the physical and introduced natural supervenience as a governing relation shaping the interactions between these two fundamentals. I would like to highlight this point: the same train of thought can be reconstructed in the case of the fictional paradigm in the pure theory of law. The fiction of purity sheds light on the fundamental character of Ought without denying that there are connections with Is on the ontological level. The connections manifested in borderline situations are governed by natural supervenience. They serve as a bridge between two foundational categories, thereby preserving the separation between Is and Ought.

8.2. FOUR STAGES OF LAW COGNITION IN POSITIVISTIC TERMS

All in all, the whole process of law cognition in positivistic terms can be presented in four steps. The first step can be called the child's perspective, in which all phenomena – such as law, morality and social facts – are blended together. In natural science, we could imagine a bacterium living in its environment.

In the second step, fiction is employed and the law is separated from any other phenomena, to be cognised as such, in its pure form. This cognitive process aims to shed light on the fundamentality of Ought, which is obscure due to connections on the ontological level to other phenomena. At the same time, by separating law from morality, this process establishes the autonomy of legal science.

In natural science, this stage is represented by examining the sample in the laboratory. The fiction of the radical separation of Is and Ought and the fictional sterile conditions in the laboratory have the exact same origin. The law does not function in separation from the world, nor do bacteria exist outside their environment. This fiction aims to understand the law as an autonomous phenomenon, in the same way that the scientist examines a bacterium in the laboratory, without the danger that a contaminated sample will produce a false result. This stage also results in the boundaries of law being established.

The third phase involves a return to the world and concerns the ontological level. The scientist examines the interaction between bacteria and their environment.

When the legal scientist establishes the boundaries of law and conceives law as an autonomous phenomenon detached from other realms such as factual or moral domains, it becomes feasible to scrutinise it in its distinct and intrinsic 'as such' nature, albeit within the framework of social or moral contexts.

At this stage, possible links with borderline situations can be studied when the law is in touch with facts or values. Natural supervenience is the link between two independent realms rather than an explanation of one in terms of another. As such, it brings coherence to the relations between Is and Ought in *General Theory of Norms* (GTN). It is a connection based on the assumption that law is a normative phenomenon, distinct from facts, but with the acknowledgement that there are links between these spheres. At the same time, it guarantees that the relations between these two worlds is not random.

These two phases in examining legal phenomena underscore the distinctions between Kelsen's methodology and that legal positivists advocate. While legal positivists claim that law is some sort of a social fact, Kelsen seems to maintain the contrary position that law and facts are to be separated in the field of legal science. Both claims seem to be superfluous in their extreme versions. The thesis about the reduction of law to some sort of social facts does not solve the problem of the character of this reduction. The consequences of such an assumption are also problematic. At the same time, if read straightforwardly, Kelsen seems to contradict himself. On the one hand, he maintains that Is and Ought are separated. On the other, he provides a definition of a norm or defines relations between validity and efficacy, which seems to deny his own methodological assumption. Without a sufficient link being provided, the endeavour to fully explain this contradiction might be incomplete in the best-case scenario.

Therefore, unsurprisingly, both sides had to revise their sharp positions. By investigating the problem of the social sources thesis, the legal positivists did this differently from Kelsen, who just directly pointed out some links between Is and Ought. For this reason, a third way is needed in both cases. Legal positivists must find a link strong enough to support the claim that law is a social fact without reducing it to such. The central inquiry within the doctrine of legal positivism revolves around the transformation in quality – why the factual transitions into the normative – and the answer can only be secured through a link which is strong. It seems that legal positivism found its potential 'third-way' solution in grounding. On the other hand, Kelsen needed to avoid such a change in quality, since it would weaken his thesis about the Is–Ought separation and the fundamentality of both spheres. The normativity in Kelsen's case is presupposed, and its source lies in the fundamentality of Ought. This leads Kelsen to the category of the basic norm and imputation.

Consequently, Kelsen's inquiry is different to the positivistic one. Kelsen asks 'What is the link between the normative and the factual spheres – when these are treated as fundamental (the Is–Ought separation) but still influencing each other?' Such a link needs to be weak, due to the independent character of legal science, and should not 'explain' one by another, because this would interfere with Kelsen's sophisticated relations between the categories of the pure theory of law, especially the basic norm and imputation. This link is supposed to maintain the Is–Ought separation, but is also sufficient for borderline cases. In other words, in Kelsen's case, the potential solution should sustain the separation of Is and Ought without denying some links between both spheres. Natural supervenience fulfils this task successfully.

The necessity for this requirement arises from Kelsen's adoption of the normative perspective, which was well illustrated by the relations between validity and efficacy in chapter seven. The result of this interaction, contingent upon establishing the supervenient and subvenient categories, dictates the embrace of either a normative or positivistic understanding of law. As a result, there is no singular, definitive approach to the examination of legal phenomena. The starting point can either lie within the domain of Is or Ought. It is a matter of choice. However, it is essential to maintain internal consistency when this choice is made between the positivistic or normative viewpoints. These perspectives should not be combined within a single theoretical framework without awareness that the starting point for each is different.

Finally, a fourth stage is not covered by the pure theory of law, by default. The fiction of purity has its price, as does every fiction. In this case, it hides in the shadow of the aspects associated with the transformation of the non-normative into the normative on the ontological level. It does not illustrate this process but rather the result of it, when Ought is already established and comes into relations with Is.

In this sense, the fiction of separations also indicates the boundaries of Kelsen's theory. The complete picture of the positivistic theory of law can be ensured by the final stage, which closes the circle inquiring about the origins of law and the origins of normativity. The inquiry into how legal facts are obtained necessitates a return to the first perspective, from the social facts point of view, but on a different level; it is not a 'child's' perspective anymore, because of the awareness of what law is and of its character distinct from facts. Thus the hermeneutical circle is closed.

8.3. ASSESSMENT OF THE DYNAMIC APPROACH TO *GENERAL THEORY OF NORMS*

After analysing potential solutions to the problems generated by the updated definition of a norm in GTN, it is time to form a final conclusion as to whether the dynamic approach to GTN, which found its solutions in fictionalism and supervenience, turns out to be successful. I believe it does because the application of these solutions fulfilled the aim of this book. Namely, this interpretation provides a plausible solution: a final revision of the pure theory of law which retains the normative thesis intact. In this way, the problem of the unfitness of the GTN to Kelsen's pure theory of law is solved.

There is also an added value which stems from the proposed interpretation. The introduction of solutions described in this book shed more light on Kelsen's well-known categories and opened many new fields for potential discussion. I do not think I have exhausted the subject by proposing these solutions. Instead, this marks the commencement of an exploration after the general framework of a distinct approach to Kelsen's pure theory has been shown. This framework can be developed, enriched or criticised. One thing is sure: Kelsen's pure theory of law is still very much alive and has an unlimited potential for further development in its unique spirit.

At the same time, Stanley Paulson is right in stating that GTN means the end of the pure theory of law as we know it. The change of paradigm from Neo-Kantian to fictional, as well as the application of new philosophical tools from the philosophy of mind, entailed that this version of the pure theory of law, which stems from the dynamic approach, is not very reminiscent of the pure theory of law in its classic version. What remained is the main thought and most signature categories and ideas which distinguish Kelsen's project from any others.

Finally, in this way, the dynamic approach demonstrated that the unfinished character of GTN, as well as its incoherence, can be perceived not as a disadvantage, but rather as an opportunity to update Kelsen's pure theory of law over and over again in response to the most up-to-date debates in the field of jurisprudence. It holds symbolic significance that Kelsen left his incomplete manuscript to his students, entrusting them with the decision of its fate. I understand this gesture as opening his pure theory of law for future reinterpretation by the next generations of Kelsenists. This is his testament that the pure theory of law has always been and is a work in progress. Even though it achieved the level of a masterpiece in its classic version, Kelsen's scientific spirit, intellectual curiosity and open-mindedness did not allow him to rest there. He had the courage to depart from the paradigms of his own masterpiece. So I believe subsequent generations can continue this project, adopting new approaches and interpretations.

Bibliography

Albert, H, *Treatise on Critical Reason* (Princeton University Press, 2016), press.princeton.edu/books/hardcover/9780691639772/treatise-on-critical-reason.

Alchourrón, CE and Bulygin, E, 'The Expressive Conception of Norms' in SL Paulson, *Normativity and Norms* (Oxford University Press, 1999).

Alexy, R, 'Hans Kelsen's Begriff Des Relativen Apriori' in R Alexy, L Meyer and SL Paulson (eds), *Neukantianismus Und Rechtphilosophie* (Nomos Verlagsgesellschaft, 2002).

Appiah, KA, *As If: Idealization and Ideals* (Harvard University Press, 2017).

Bokulich, A,'Explanatory Fictions' in M Suárez (ed), *Fictions in Science: Philosophical Essays on Modeling and Idealization* (Routledge, 2010).

Brenner, A et al, 'Metaphysical Explanation' in EN Zalta (ed), *The Stanford Encyclopedia of Philosophy*, Winter 2021 (Metaphysics Research Lab, Stanford University, 2021).

Brożek, B, 'Law, Normativity, and Supervenience' in B Brożek, A Rotolo and J Stelmach (eds), *Supervenience and Normativity* (Springer International Publishing, 2017).

Bulygin, E, 'Norms and Logic. Hans Kelsen and Ota Weinberger on the Ontology of Norms' in C Bernal et al (eds), *Essays in Legal Philosophy* (Oxford University Press, 2015).

—— 'Remarks on Kelsen's "Validity and Efficacy of the Law"' in C Bernal et al (eds), *Essays in Legal Philosophy* (Oxford University Press, 2015).

—— 'An Antinomy in Kelsen's Pure Theory of Law' in SL Paulson, *Normativity and Norms* (Oxford University Press, 1999).

Carnap, R, *Der Logische Aufbau Der Welt* (Ohlenrothsche Buchdruckerei Erfurt, 1928).

Celano, B, 'Norm Conflicts: Kelsen's View in the Late Period and a Rejoinder', SL Paulson and B Litschewski Paulson (eds), trans B Litschewski Paulson and M Sherberg (Clarendon Press, 1998).

Chalmers, DJ, 'Phenomenal Concepts and the Explanatory Gap' in T Alter and S Walter (eds), *Phenomenal Concepts and Phenomenal Knowledge: New Essays on Consciousness and Physicalism* (Oxford University Press, 2007).

—— *The Conscious Mind: In Search of a Fundamental Theory* (Oxford University Press, 1996).

Chilovi, S and Pavlakos, G, 'Law-Determination as Grounding: A Common Grounding Framework for Jurisprudence' (2019) 25 *Legal Theory* 53.

—— 'The Explanatory Demands of Grounding in Law' (2021) 103/4 *Pacific Philosophical Quarterly* 900.

Correia, F and Schnieder, B, 'Grounding: An Opinionated Introduction' in F Correia and B Schnieder (eds), *Metahysical Grounding, Understanding the Structure of Reality* (Cambridge University Press, 2012).

Dąmbska, I, *Dwa studia z teorii naukowego poznania* (Towarzystwo Naukowe w Toruniu, 1962).

Dascal, M, 'Hermeneutic Interpretation and Pragmatic Interpretation' (1989) 22 *Philosophy and Rhetoric* 239.

Duxbury, N, 'Kelsen's Endgame' (2008) 67 *CLJ* 51.

—— 'The Basic Norm: An Unsolved Murder Mystery' (2007) 17 *LSE Law, Society and Economy Working Papers* 2.

Eklund, M, 'Fictionalism' in EN Zalta (ed), *The Stanford Encyclopedia of Philosophy*, Winter 2019 (Metaphysics Research Lab, Stanford University, 2019).

Elgin, C, 'Exemplification, Idealization, and Scientific Understanding' in M Suárez (ed), *Fictions in Science: Philosophical Essays on Modeling and Idealization* (Routledge, 2010).

Fine, A, 'Fictionalism' (1993) 18 *Midwest Studies in Philosophy* 1.

Fine, K, 'Guide to Ground' in F Correia and B Schnieder, *Metaphysical Grounding, Understanding the Structure of Reality* (Cambridge University Press, 2012).

Fitzsche, T, 'Die Reine Rechtslehre Im Lichte Des Kritischen Rationalismus', *Schriftenreihe Des Hans Kelsen Instituts* (nd).
—— *Hans Kelsen Und Kritische Rationalismus* (Schriftenreiche Des Hans Kelsen-Instituts, 2002).
Fraassen, BC van, *The Scientific Image* (Clarendon Press, 1980).
Giere, R, 'Why Scientific Models Should Not Be Regarded as Works of Fiction' in M Suárez (ed), *Fictions in Science: Philosophical Essays on Modeling and Idealization* (Routledge, 2010).
Gizbert-Studnicki, T, 'The Social Sources Thesis. Metaphysic Sand Metaphilosophy' in P Banas, A Dyrda and T Gizbert-Studnicki (eds), *Metaphilosophy of Law* (Bloomsbury, 2016).
Green, MS, 'The Semantic Thesis in Legal Positivism' in T Spaak and P Mindus (eds), *The Cambridge Companion to Legal Positivism*, Cambridge Companions to Law (Cambridge University Press, 2021).
Greenberg, M, 'How Facts Make Law' (2004) 10 *Legal Theory* 225, doi.org/10.1017/S1352325204040212.
Guastini, R, 'Kelsen on Validity (Once More)' (2016) 29 *Ratio Juris* 402.
Gustafsson, H, 'Fiction of Law' (2010) 41 *Rechtstheorie* 319.
Hare, RM, *The Language of Morals*, reprint (Oxford University Press, 1991).
Hart, HLA, 'Positivism and the Separation of Law and Morals' (1958) 71 *Harvard Law Journal* 593.
—— *The Concept of Law* (Oxford University Press, 2012).
Hartney, M, 'Introduction: The Final Form of the Pure Theory of Law' in H Kelsen, *General Theory of Norms*, trans M Hartney (Clarendon Press, 1991).
Heidemann, C, *Die Norm Als Tatsache* (Nomos Verlagsgesellschaft, 1997).
Heidemann, C and Zalewska, M, 'Grundnorm y Fundamentación' in F Alberto et al, *Hans Kelsen Ante el Siglo XXI. Un Dialogo Critico* (Universidad Nacional Autónoma Mexico, 2023) 199–223.
Jabloner, C, 'Kein Imperativ Ohne Imperator. Anmerkungen Zu Einer Theorie Kelsens' in T Olechowski and K Zeleny (eds), *Methodenreinheit und Erkenntinisvielfalt* (Manzlische Verlags – und Universitaetsbuchhandlung 2013).
Jackson, F, 'What Mary Didn't Know' (1986) 83 *The Journal of Philosophy* 291.
Katsuoshi, K, *Introduction to the General Theory of Law*, 4th edn (independently published, 2023).
Kim, J, *Supervenience and Mind: Selected Philosophical Essays*, 1st edn (Cambridge University Press, 1993).
Kelsen, H, *Das Problem Der Souveränität Und Die Theorie Des Völkerrechts* (Mohr Siebeck, nd).
—— *General Theory of Law and State*, trans A Wedberg (Harward University Press, 1945).
—— *General Theory of Norms* (Clarendon Press, 1979).
—— *Hauptprobleme Der Staatsrechtslehre* (Scienta, 1923).
—— 'On the Theory of Juridic Fictions. With Special Consideration of Vaihinger's Philosophy of the As-If' in W Twining and M Del Mar (eds), *Legal Fictions in Theory and Practice*, trans Ch Kletzer (Springer Verlag, 2015).
—— *Pure Theory of Law* (The Lawbook Exchange, Ltd, 1967).
—— 'Zur Theorie Der Juristischen Fiktionen. Mit besonderer Berücksichtigung von Vaihingers Philosophie Des Als Ob' (1919) 1 *Annalen Der Philosophie* 630.
Kiener, M, 'Fictionalising Kelsen's Pure Theory of Law' in M Jestaedt, R Poscher and J Kammerhofer (eds), *Die Reine Rechtslehre Auf Dem Prufstand*, Archiv Fur Rechts- Und Sozialphilosophie 163 (Franz Steiner Verlag, 2020).
Kletzer, Ch, *The Idea of a Pure Theory of Law: An Interpretation and Defence* (Hart Publishing, 2018).
Kripke, S, *Wittgenstein on Rules and Private Language: An Elementary Exposition*, vol 2 (Harvard University Press, 1982).
Kroon, F, McKeown-Green, J and Brock, S, *A Critical Introduction to Fictionalism* (Bloomsbury Publishing, 2018).
Lakoff, G and Johnson, M, *Metaphors We Live By*, 2nd edn (University Of Chicago Press, 2003).
Lind, D, 'The Pragmatic Value of Legal Fiction' in M Del Mar and W Twining (eds), *Legal Fictions in Theory and Practice* (Springer International Publishing, 2015).
Maurin, A-S, 'Grounding and Metaphysical Explanation: It's Complicated' (2019) 176 *Philosophical Studies* 1573.

McLaughlin, B and Bennett, K, 'Supervenience' in EN Zalta (ed), *The Stanford Encyclopedia of Philosophy* (Metaphysics Research Lab, Stanford University, 2018).
McLaughlin, BP, 'Varieties of Supervenience' in E Savellos and O Yalchin (eds), *Supervenience* (Cambridge University Press, 1994).
Merkl, AJ, 'Prolegomena Einer Theorie Des Rechtlichen Stufenbaues' in H Klecatsky, R Marcic and R Schambeck (eds), *Die Wiener Rechtstheoretische Schule: Schriften von Hans Kelsen, Adolf Merkl Alfred Verdross* (Franz Steiner Verlag, 2010).
Morrison, M, 'Fictions, Representations, and Reality' in M Suárez (ed), *Fictions in Science: Philosophical Essays on Modeling and Idealization* (Routledge, 2010), doi.org/10.4324/9780203890103-11.
Opałek, K, *Uberlegungen Zu Hans Kelsens 'Allgemeine Theorie Der Normen'* (Schriftenreihe Des Hans Kelsen Instituts, 1980).
Palafox, FI, et al, *Hans Kelsen Ante el Siglo XXI. Un Dialogo Critico* (Universidad Nacional Autónoma Mexico, 2023).
Papineau, D, 'What Exactly Is the Explanatory Gap?' (2011) 39 *Philosophia* 5.
Pavlakos, G, 'A Non-Naturalist Account of Law's Place in Reality' in B Brożek, J Hage and N Vincent (eds), *Law and Mind: A Survey of Law and the Cognitive Sciences* (Cambridge University Press, 2021).
—— 'The Metaphysics of Law: From Supervenience to Rational Justification' in B Brożek, A Rotolo and J Stelmach (eds), *Supervenience and Normativity*, Law and Philosophy Library (Springer International Publishing, 2017).
—— 'The Metaphysics of Law: From Supervenience to Rational Justification' SSRN Scholarly Paper (Social Science Research Network, 13 December 2014).
Paulson, SL, 'An Empowerment Theory of Legal Norms' (1988) 1 *Ratio Juris* 58.
—— 'Arriving at a Defensible Periodization of Hans Kelsen's Legal Theory' (1999) 19 *Oxford Journal of Legal Studies* 351.
—— 'Die Zurechnung Als Apriorische Kategorie in Der Rechtslehre Hans Kelsens' in M Kaufmann and J Renzikowski (eds), *Zurechnung Als Operationalisierung von Verantwortung* (Peter Lang, 2004).
—— *Hans Kelsen as Outlier The Defence of a Radical Norm Theory, Contemporary Perspectives on Legal Obligation* (Routledge, 2020).
—— 'Metamorphosis in Hans Kelsen's Legal Philosophy' (2017) 80 *MLR* 860.
—— 'On the Origins of Hans Kelsen's Spatlehre' in D Diner and M Stolleis (eds), *Hans Kelsen and Carl Schmitt. A Juxtaposition* (Bleicher Verlag, 1999).
—— 'The Neo-Kantian Dimension of Kelsen's Pure Theory of Law' (1992) 12 *OJLS* 311.
—— 'Toward a Periodization of the Pure Theory of Law' in L Gianformaggio Bastida (ed), *Hans Kelsen' s Legal Theory: A Diachronic Point of View* (Torino, 1990).
Pfersmann, O, 'Die Wiener Schule Und Der Moralische Realismus. Ein Problemskitze' in C Jabloner and F Stadler (eds), *Logischer Empirismus Und Reine Rechtslehre* (Springer Vienna, 2001).
Potacs, M, 'EU-Recht Und Staatlichen Recht Im Lichte Der Stufenbaulehre' in C Jabloner, Th Olechowski and J Kulik (eds), *Hans Kelsen in Der Tschechischenund Internationalen Rechtslehre*, Schriftenreiche Des Hans Kelsen-Instituts 39 (Manz'sche Verlag und Universitaets-buchhandlung, 2018).
Renzikowski, J, 'Der Begriff Der "Zurechnung" in Der Reinen Rechtlehre Hans Kelsens' in R Alexy et al (eds), *Neukantianismus Und Rechtphilosophie* (Nomos Verlagsgesellschaft, 2002).
Rosen, G, 'Metaphysics as a Fiction' in B Armour-Garb and F Kroon (eds), *Fictionalism in Philosophy* (Oxford University Press, 2020).
Ross H, 'The Pure Theory of Law and Interpretive Sociology – A Basis for Interdisciplinarity?' in M Freeman (ed), *Law and Sociology* (Oxford University Press, 2006).
Rouse, J, 'Laboratory Fictions' in M Suárez (ed), *Fictions in Science: Philosophical Essays on Modelling and Idealization* (Routledge, 2010).
Samuel, G, Del Mar, M and Twining, W, 'Is Law a Fiction?' in M Del Mar and W Twining (eds), *Legal Fictions in Theory and Practice* (Springer International Publishing, 2015).

Schaffer, J, 'The Ground Between the Gaps' (2017) 17 *Philosopher's Imprint* 1, hdl.handle.net/2027/spo.3521354.0017.011.
Shivakumar, D, 'The Pure Theory as Ideal Type: Defending Kelsen on the Basis of Weberian Methodology' (1996) 105 *The Yale Law Journal* 1383.
Spaak, T, 'Kelsen's Metaethics' (2022) 35 *Ratio Juris* 158.
Suárez, M, 'Scientific Fictions as Rules of Inference' in M Suárez (ed), *Fictions in Science: Philosophical Essays on Modeling and Idealization* (Routledge, 2010).
Sung Ho, K, 'Max Weber' in EN Zalta and U Nodelman (eds), *The Stanford Encyclopedia of Philosophy*, Winter 2022 (Metaphysics Research Lab, Stanford University, 2022), plato.stanford.edu/archives/win2022/entries/weber/.
Tahko, TE, 'Fundamentality' in EN Zalta (ed), *The Stanford Encyclopedia of Philosophy*, Fall 2018 (Metaphysics Research Lab, Stanford University, 2018).
Vaihinger, H, *Philosophy of As If: A System of the Theoretical, Practical and Religious Fictions of Mankind*, trans CK Ogden, 2nd edn (Routledge & Kegan Paul, 1984).
—— *The Philosophy 'As If'*, trans Ch Ogden (Routledge & Kegan Paul LTD, 1911).
Villa Rosas, G and Spaak, T (eds), *Legal Power and Legal Competence: Meaning, Normativity, Officials and Theories* (Springer, 2023).
Walter, R, 'Das Problem Des Normativen Syllogismus' in W Krawietz and J Wróblewski, *Sprach, Performanz Und Ontologie Des Rechts* (Duncker Humbolt, 1993).
—— 'Wirksamkeit Und Geltung' (1961) IX(3/4) *Österrieches Zeitschrift Für Öffentliches Recht* 531.
Walton, KL, *Mimesis as Make-Believe: On the Foundations of the Representational Arts* (Harvard University Press, 1990).
Weber, M, *Methodology of Social Sciences*, trans E Shils and F Heary (Transaction Publishers, 1949).
Weinberger, O, 'Introduction: Hans Kelsen as Philosopher' in H Kelsen, *Essays in Legal and Moral Philosophy* (D Reidel Publishing Company, 1973).
—— *Normtheorie Als Grundlage Der Jurisprudenz Und Ethik* (Duncker Humbolt, 1981).
Weinberger, O, 'Reine Rechtslehre Zwischen Kritizizsmus Und Analytischer Philosophie' (2000) 55 *Zeitschrift fur offentliches Recht* 367.
Wright, GH von, *Explanation and Understanding* (Cornell University Press, 1971).
—— 'Is and Ought' in MC Doeser and JN Kraay (eds), *Facts and Values: Philosophical Reflections from Western and Non-Western Perspectives*, Martinus Nijhoff Philosophy Library (Springer Netherlands, 1986).
—— 'Is There a Logic of Norms? (1991) 4 *Ratio Juris* 265.
Wróblewski, J, *Krytyka normatywistycznej teorii prawa i państwa Hansa Kelsena* (PWN, 1955).
Yablo, S, 'Does Ontology Rest on a Mistake?' (1998) 72 *Aristotelian Society Supplementary Volume* 229.
Yablo, S, 'A Paradox of Existence' in A Everett and Th Hofweber (eds), *Empty Names, Fiction and the Puzzles of Non-Existence* (CSLI Publications, 2000).
Yoshino, H, 'Zu Anewndbarkeit Der Regeln Der Logic Auf Rechtsnormen' (Schriftenreihe Des Hans Kelsen Instituts, 1982).
Zalewska, M, 'Empowerment and the Act of Will in Hans Kelsen's General Theory of Norms' in G Villa-Rosas and T Spaak (eds), *Legal Power and Legal Competence*, t. 140, Law and Philosophy Library (Springer International Publishing, 2023), doi.org/10.1007/978-3-031-28555-4_15.
—— 'Objectivity and Hans Kelsen's concept of imputation' in AFL De Paula, A Santacoloma and GV Rosas GV (eds), *Truth and objectivity in law and morals* II (Mohr Siebeck, 2016) 147.
Zirk-Sadowski, M, 'Norma prawna jako kategoria pragmatyczna' in M Zirk-Sadowski, *Prawo w kulturze. Eseje wybrane z teorii i filozofii prawa* (Wolters Kluwer, 2023).

Index

www.ingramcontent.com/pod-product-compliance
Ingram Content Group UK Ltd.
Pitfield, Milton Keynes, MK11 3LW, UK
UKHW020820290926
15470UKWH00003B/1267

9 781509 942763